IN THE NAME OF

GUCCI

IN THE NAME OF
GUCCI

A Memoir

PATRICIA GUCCI

WITH WENDY HOLDEN

CROWN
ARCHETYPE
NEW YORK

All rights reserved.
Published in the United States by Crown Archetype,
an imprint of the Crown Publishing Group, a division
of Penguin Random House LLC, New York.
crownpublishing.com

Crown Archetype and colophon is a registered
trademark of Penguin Random House LLC.

Library of Congress Cataloging-in-Publication Data
Names: Gucci, Patricia.
Title: In the name of Gucci : a memoir / Patricia Gucci.
Other titles: Gucci. English
Description: First Edition. | New York : Crown Archetype, 2016.
Identifiers: LCCN 2015037677| ISBN 9780804138932
(hardback) | ISBN 9780804138949 (ebook)
Subjects: LCSH: Gucci (Firm)—History. | Gucci family. | Gucci,
Patrizia. | Fashion designers—Italy—Biography. | Clothing
trade—Italy—History—20th century. | BISAC: BIOGRAPHY
& AUTOBIOGRAPHY / Rich & Famous. | DESIGN / Fashion.
| BIOGRAPHY & AUTOBIOGRAPHY / Personal Memoirs.
Classification: LCC HD9940.I84 G8513 2016
| DDC 338.7/6174692092—dc23 LC record
available at http://lccn.loc.gov/2015037677

ISBN 978-0-8041-3893-2
eBook ISBN 978-0-8041-3894-9

Printed in the United States of America

Jacket design by Christopher Brand
Jacket photograph (front) by Roger Powers_HP/©Houston Chronicle
All photographs are courtesy of the author unless otherwise credited.

1 3 5 7 9 10 8 6 4 2

First Edition

For my mother

*The events portrayed in this book are based
on that which I witnessed and experienced,
or on what my parents and others told me.
Wherever possible, I have tried to verify them
independently but I accept that they may not
be always as others remember them. In a few
instances I have changed names to protect people
or avoid causing offense. Any mistakes are my
own.*

IN THE NAME OF

GUCCI

PROLOGUE

*T*he day of my father's funeral, nothing felt solid beneath my feet. The earth had tilted on its axis and I hadn't yet tilted with it.

Misshapen by grief and pregnancy, I was twenty-six years old and less than a month away from giving birth to my second child when I watched his coffin carried into the church in Rome. His was the first funeral I had ever attended and the concept of his vital presence being contained inside a wooden box robbed me of what little balance I had left.

Gripping my pew, I glanced at my mother, Bruna, sitting motionless beside me, her big brown eyes hidden behind huge sunglasses. She was so lost in her own desolation that she could offer me no solace. I felt like an orphan—and not for the first time.

Truth was that she and Papà had lived in their own special world since long before I pushed my way into it. From the earliest days of their illicit romance in the 1950s, their bond was unfathomably deep. I was the unexpected love child, sent by my father to be born in another country to avoid a scandal.

Aldo Gucci, the creative visionary behind the famous fashion house, was not a man to be argued with. A trailblazing businessman of extraordinary dynamism, he'd transformed his father's small Florentine luggage company into a global phenomenon that came to epitomize Italian chic. Then, in a catastrophic turn of events, I witnessed firsthand his heartbreaking downfall and the destruction of a family legacy he had fought so hard to uphold. During the last five years of his life a series of betrayals that brought to mind the tragedy of King Lear culminated in the sale of his business and ultimately led to his demise.

To me, though, Papà wasn't someone to be judged or pitied. He was just the handsome daddy with the ready smile and distinctive cologne who flew in and out of our lives with a blast of movement and noise like some exotic bird. Lanky, loose-limbed, and perpetually on the move, he'd arrive in a flurry to fill our still, silent spaces with his energy and laughter. A man like no other, he was human, vulnerable, and deeply flawed. Even though we never saw him often enough or for long enough, for Mamma and me he was the glue that bound us together.

Now he was gone and we had his funeral to get through. Not only the hour-long church service but also an onerous three-hour journey to the Gucci mausoleum outside Florence. It would be an interminable day after a long and difficult few weeks. Mamma, Papà, and I had been holed up together at the private Catholic clinic waiting for the end—never quite believing it would come.

As nuns glided silently to and fro, my mother had taken up her position on one side of his bed while I sat on the other. We were the keepers of secrets and the guardians of his truth—the two women who knew the real Aldo Gucci and who loved him anyway.

The moment my married father first set eyes on "La Bella

Bruna" when she went to work as a salesgirl in his Rome store, he lost his head—and his heart. The coy eighteen-year-old was to become my father's true north and the compass by which he would plot the rest of his life. In the three decades when he criss-crossed the globe to build his empire it was to Bruna that "Dottor" Gucci—as he was often known—always secretly returned for succor and sanctuary. And it was she who clasped his hand as he died.

The young beauty, whose looks had been compared to those of some of the most famous Italian movie stars of her era, paid a heavy price for being hidden away for all those years. And so—consequently—did I. A reserved child who'd had to grow up fast, I was mystified by my mother's slow, sorrowful withdrawal from the world and the way she excluded me from their inner sanctum.

Their remarkable history seemed to have been forgotten at the Chiesa di Santa Chiara on the northwestern fringes of Rome on the morning of his funeral in January 1991. My father's chauffeur, Franco, drove us in silence to the modern terracotta-colored church. Joining the throng of mourners, we made our bewildered way up the sweeping stone steps and were ushered into pews alongside members of the staff and business associates who'd flown in from all over the world to pay their respects to the famed Gucci patriarch.

Across the aisle sat my father's first wife, Olwen, propped up by my three half brothers, Giorgio, Paolo, and Roberto, whose existence I'd been unaware of until I was ten years old. Never before had both families been together under the same roof and the atmosphere was chilling. It was also the first time I'd ever set eyes on their mother. If I'd thought about her at all, I suppose I'd imagined her to be an elegant, elderly Englishwoman, ramrod straight in twinset and pearls. Instead, she was a shrunken little old lady in a wheelchair and her physical and mental frailty at eighty-one shocked me. My mother, stiff with sorrow, didn't even appear to notice.

Nor did we register our marked separation from that side of my father's family. This was our default position. On that bitter morning, in that unattractive building, all I could do was fan my fingers over my unborn child and wonder how we'd survive without my father's protection from the family storms. He'd been gone for less than a week and although my mother still saw him every night in her dreams, we both felt utterly adrift.

True to form, Papà had set his affairs in order long before he slipped into his final, fatal coma. He had organized his own funeral before entrusting the arrangements to his most devoted staff. It was to be a simple service with no flowers and few eulogies.

Eager to pay tribute to my mother, he'd penned his own obituary to be issued upon his death. Aldo Gucci, he wrote, left behind his *wife* Bruna Palombo and his *companion* Olwen Price. Some of the Italian newspapers faithfully printed the distinction between the two women just as my father had intended.

The *New York Times*, however, did not. Published two days after he died, its obituary quoted President John F. Kennedy's description of him as "the first Italian ambassador of fashion." The article ended with the sentence "Mr. Gucci is survived by his wife, the former Olwen Price, and three sons, Roberto, Giorgio and Paolo."

There was no mention of my mother, or of me.

It was a glaring omission, probably stage-managed by the other side of the family, but there was nothing we could do about it. Nor were we able to counter any of the other unwelcome things written about my father after his death. Legally, and for a long time, I was obliged to remain as invisible as others would have me and forbidden from divulging anything.

Until now.

Twenty-five years on, this is the untold story—my father's, my mother's, and that of the global empire he created that ultimately shaped all of our lives.

It is now mine to tell.

ONE

*T*he years after my father died weren't easy for my mother and me. Our relationship had always been rocky but we were both consumed by our own problems and his absence only made it worse.

Bereft of the man who'd become a father figure, friend, husband, and son all rolled into one, my mother was overcome by grief and fear. She felt rudderless without the force that had been driving us forward. Whenever I tried to comfort her, she pushed me away, and I became too busy to try again. My marriage was crumbling, I had a new baby, and it fell to me to deal with the lawyers for my father's estate. There was no time to grieve. Unable to guide my mother, I was powerless as she struggled to accept the loss that, for a while, rendered her completely incoherent.

Her helplessness effectively shut down all channels of communication between us at a time when I needed her most. For the next few years we hardly connected at all. By the time I was in my forties I was counting the cost of two failed marriages and the toll they had taken on my three daughters. For reasons I hadn't yet understood, I seemed to attract the wrong kind of man and suffered immensely as a result. True love—the kind my parents shared during their long and complex relationship—had eluded me.

Thankfully, I had some wonderful friends, but they could only support me so much. Prayer and meditation helped, but I realized that part of the problem was that I didn't feel grounded. I had never met my grandparents and I barely knew my brothers. I had only really come to know my father properly in the last phase of his life, and my mother remained a mystery to me. The more I delved into my own psyche, I began to appreciate that my misguided choices seemed to stem from my fractured childhood and dysfunctional family relationships. In order to move forward, I needed to go back to my roots and reconcile with my past.

Eventually, it occurred to me that it might help to write a book about my father. I wanted to chronicle our lives with him as we experienced it—as a record for my family. I hoped to give my children a unique and truthful memento, not one sensationalized by others. Most important, I believed that he deserved his rightful place in history, not only for his role in establishing Gucci but as a pioneer of the iconic "Made in Italy" label throughout the world.

What I didn't expect was that my research would lead me back to my mother. After years of estrangement, I could finally begin to understand their unique bond and give her the credit she deserved.

My epiphany began in 2009 when I visited her in Rome. After a lamentable lapse of six months interspersed only with twice-weekly telephone calls, I sat with her and began to talk. Hoping to learn from her own long journey of self-discovery, I spoke about my experiences of the previous few months, including my travels and visits to spiritual retreats. She understood that I was still trying to find myself.

"I've met many interesting people and a few of them have made me realize just how many blanks there are in my childhood memories," I told her, treading softly. "In fact, there's just one big black hole. I appreciate that I never asked, but I know so little about you and Papà and your life when you were younger and I'd love to know more."

I could tell from my mother's body language that she was uncomfortable with the direction I was going in and would rather not speak about such matters. Every time I'd tried in the past, she'd pushed me away, saying that she didn't remember or—more tellingly—that she didn't want to. Her habit of bottling things up, never explaining anything, and keeping me in the dark was a pattern that had been repeated my entire life, so I feared that nothing much would change.

Sure enough, after looking askance at me she shrugged her shoulders and asked, "What good will it do after all this time?"

"Well, I thought opening up might help you too," I replied. "I know that you've never felt understood."

She looked at me for a moment in silence. When she stood abruptly and went to her bedroom I thought I'd gone too far and that our conversation was over. But something I said that day must have resonated, because she returned with a leather pouch bearing the distinctive Gucci insignia. Handing it to me, she said, "Your father wrote me many letters. I kept them all. Here, I want to give them to you."

Until that moment in that sun-filled apartment, I had no idea that Papà had penned a single note to my mother. He lived his life at a gallop and I couldn't imagine when he'd have had time to write her so many *lettere d'amore*.

Wisely, I held my tongue, unzipped the pouch, and pulled out a bundle of letters, some on blue airmail paper, some on hotel stationery, some typed or written in my father's distinctive hand, all of them in Italian. The treasured archive of their courtship years between 1958 and 1961 was interspersed with telegrams from overseas. Why had she kept these for over fifty years?

Quickly flicking through them, my eyes settled on a sentence—"*My treasure, my love, don't leave me! Do not destroy the very best part of my life . . . do not push me away; this feeling is not just infatuation but a vast and boundless love.*"

I could hardly believe what I was reading. My mother watched me for a moment as I sifted through them and then she rose to make some tea. "They are such beautiful letters," she said softly from the doorway. "Your father had a wonderful way with words. It was one of the things that first attracted me to him."

"Will you read them with me?" I asked, but she raised her hand and shook her head.

"I can't. I remember how they made me feel all those years ago. That is enough."

My eyes filling with tears, I realized she had just handed me a priceless legacy. Two decades after his death, she'd opened a window to their secret life together—my first glimpse into what had been a mystery for so long.

"But these are incredible, Mamma!" I exclaimed.

"Yes," she added. "It was a kind of *fiaba* [fairy tale]—but not necessarily one with a happy ending."

Her gift marked the start of my quest to piece together the jigsaw of my parents' lives, and ultimately of my own. My father's words sparked a thousand questions, many of which she agreed to answer over the next few years. Subsequent research took me on an intriguing journey back to my Florentine and Roman origins, which has enlightened me on many levels.

So much has been written about the "saga" of the House of Gucci, with far too much emphasis given to my father's fall from grace and the bitter family relationships that led to scandal, divorce, and even murder. So little has been said about what a great man he was or how much he loved my mother.

Through the power of his words, I discovered him as a passionate and sensitive person, in sharp contrast with his public reputation as the ruthless chairman who ruled with an iron fist. Mostly, I gained a whole new perspective on the unorthodox love story between my parents in the golden age of *la dolce vita*. This has been a deeply insightful experience for me after a somewhat scattered childhood. I have come to appreciate not only my father's trials and tribulations but also the sacrifices my mother made as a young woman destined to become the mistress and lifelong companion of an unsung hero of modern Italy.

In the course of my pilgrimage, she has finally felt able to open up and show me the unseen Aldo Gucci—glimpses of whom I witnessed for myself only at the end of his life. "There was another side to him," she insists. "A side that only I knew. That was the real Aldo."

And in revealing him to me, she has allowed me to see her through his eyes for the first time.

TWO

As someone who grew up in England and who thinks of herself as mostly British in spite of Italian parentage, it has always seemed fitting to me that the story of Gucci began in London more than a century ago.

My paternal grandfather was christened Guccio Giovanbattista Giacinto Dario Maria Gucci, which I'm sure would have been too much of a mouthful when he arrived at the service entrance of the Savoy Hotel overlooking London's river Thames in 1897. The lithe teenager from Tuscany who'd grown up in a small town twenty-five miles west of Florence had run away to seek his fortune at sixteen. After making his way to the coast, he earned his passage to England stoking coal on a steam freighter. His uncle's straw-hat business in Florence, which employed his father, was in dire straits and would soon be taken over, leaving the family penniless.

Guccio, keen to do whatever he could to help, would have undoubtedly heard tales of riches to be made in the nation ruled over by Queen Victoria in fin de siècle Britain. It was the era known as the "gay" or "naughty nineties"—a period of frivolity, ostentation, and opulence enjoyed by the upper classes especially. Grand tours of Europe had become the fashion as wealthy Americans and those in the colonies, eager to spend the millions they'd made from diamonds, railroads, industry, or gold, flocked to London before embarking on extravagant travels around the Continent.

My grandfather died ten years before I was born, so I was never able to ask him who suggested he seek employment at the capital's premiere deluxe hotel. The Savoy archives reveal that there were several Italians already on the staff and that young olive-skinned boys with cherubic faces were much sought-after as pages. Their starched white gloves, jaunty caps, and smart livery would have been a reassuring sight for the cream of society, who were falling for the novel concept of staying somewhere that offered impeccable service along with newfangled electricity and hot and cold running water in en suite bathrooms. Booking rooms was far preferable to maintaining drafty gas-lit private townhouses with few such luxuries. It even had its own elevators, known as "ascending rooms," which offered two speeds so as not to cause ladies to faint.

The etiquette of travel in the 1890s dictated that guests alight from their horse-drawn carriages and be whisked to reception on the first floor riverside. Their footmen remained in the courtyard to advise the pages which luggage belonged to whom. These beautiful hand-tooled bags, often embossed with initials and family crests, would have been made by a handful of leather goods manufacturers in Europe, most notably perhaps Louis Vuitton of Paris, H. J. Cave & Sons of London, and Asprey of New Bond Street, whose dressing cases, trunks, and traveling bags are still licensed under royal warrant.

Although he would have spoken little English when he arrived, young Guccio was employed as a page for the entire four years that he worked at the Savoy. My grandfather's primary role then would have been to carry those towering stacks of bags from the inner courtyard—in those days accessed via large gates with granite pillars on Savoy Hill—up to the opulent River Suites via stairs or a service elevator. There, he would have been expected to help separate and sort the luggage before leaving it for maids and valets to unpack. It was a job for which servility, stamina, and sign language were all that was required.

To be a page was a lowly job, paying less than two shillings and sixpence a week plus bed and board (approximately $2), but a half-sovereign tip ($5) from a generous guest could transform a lad's fortunes.

After his relatively parochial childhood, my grandfather must have been amazed to find himself in the first hotel of its kind in London, an establishment that had its glitzy champagne opening in 1889. A place I've always had a special affection for, the Savoy is still considered one of the grandest establishments in London. It is easy to imagine how refreshingly stylish it must have been for its day.

The Berkeley, Carlton, and Ritz hotels weren't even built yet and Claridge's—owned by the Savoy's proprietor, the theatrical impresario Richard D'Oyly Carte—was more akin to a comfortable club for the gentry. With César Ritz as general manager and the first celebrity cook, Auguste Escoffier, as *maître chef*, the Savoy promoted the groundbreaking idea that a hotel was a decent place for the aristocracy—even royalty—to be seen. It became a destination venue and not somewhere people simply slept. The likes of Noël Coward and George Gershwin entertained clientele that comprised the new "international set," including show business stars such as Sarah Bernhardt, Dame Nellie Melba, and Lillie Langtry, all of whom had special dishes created for them there.

I often wonder if my grandfather ever met any of these stars. Did Noël Coward throw him a coin? Was Lillie Langtry sweet to him? Whether he encountered them or not, I'm sure he would have been staggered to think that had they lived beyond their time, his surname would have become known to them all.

The hotel's River Restaurant, which I know so well, was one of the first places where it became acceptable for ladies to dine out in public. This, in turn, led to a growing interest in fashion and emerging new trends. All of which meant even more hatboxes, valises, Gladstone bags, and parasol cases for fresh-faced young pages like my grandfather to carry.

By 1901, however, the mood in Britain had changed. On January 22, Queen Victoria died after an almost sixty-four-year reign, sending her people spiraling into shock. The Anglo-Boer War had created further uncertainty and political upheaval, and the Gilded Age no longer seemed quite so golden. It was in this year that the twenty-year-old Guccio decided to turn his back on the city he had come to love and head home to Florence with the half sovereigns he'd carefully saved.

Back in the bosom of his family, he set about looking for a new job but first found himself a wife, a charismatic single mother named Aida Calvelli who worked as a seamstress and whose father was a local tailor. Guccio also adopted Aida's illegitimate child, Ugo, whose father had died before he could marry her. That must have been quite a scandal at the time but Guccio broke with convention by making her his wife and taking on her son. He never fully accepted Ugo as his own, however, and they eventually became estranged.

Within a few years, Guccio and Aida had a daughter, my aunt Grimalda, and four sons, including my father, Aldo, who was born on May 26, 1905. One boy later died in childhood, leaving three brothers whose destinies would become inextricably entwined with mine.

With a reference from the Savoy, my grandfather soon found

work at the Belgian-owned Compagnie Internationale des Wagons-Lits, which operated Europe's most luxurious steam trains, including the Blue Train and the Orient Express. But his hopes of forging a career there were cut short by his conscription into national service. He was thirty-four when Italy entered the First World War in 1915 and he was ordered to report as a driver to the army's transport unit.

All that I have ever known about his time during the brutal trench warfare in the mountains between Italy and the Austro-Hungarian Empire is that he somehow emerged from it unscathed, when more than seven hundred thousand died. After the war he found employment at Franzi, the Milan leather goods manufacturer founded in 1864 by Rocco Franzi and his son Felice, which had cornered the Italian luggage market for sophisticated European travelers. Their stylish trunks and eponymous suitcase made of "Franzi leather" infused with exotic essences had become ubiquitous on almost every transatlantic steamer and first-class train, and would have been a frequent sight at the Savoy. Whether this was a deliberate career move on my grandfather's part or just a chance job offer, history doesn't record.

Within a short time of working there, however, he became quite convinced that there was a future for him in luxury leather goods. Having started as an apprentice learning how to select and treat hides in order to create high-end, durable but supple products, he ended up managing Franzi's Rome tannery. He commuted to the Italian capital to begin with after my grandmother stubbornly refused to uproot her young family and leave her native Florence. In time, the formidable powerhouse that was Aida persuaded her husband to take probably the biggest risk of his life—hand in his notice, return to their home in the Oltrarno district south of the river Arno, and set up his own business.

My grandparents bought a small shop in a cobblestoned street north of the river and not far from the chic fashion and café district dominated by Via de' Tornabuoni. The new premises were cleverly sited within walking distance of the famous Ponte Vecchio, which virtually every visitor to Florence feels compelled to cross. Early reports suggest the modest shop was crammed from floor to ceiling with suitcases, handbags, briefcases, and trunks of every description. It also had its own workshop that Guccio filled with leather from Germany, acquired wholesale at a very affordable price thanks to the favorable postwar exchange rate.

A man of impeccable taste, my grandfather hoped to create the kind of superior leather goods he'd been handling since he was a boy, only using cheaper hides enhanced by skilled dyeing and treating techniques. His own elegant designs based loosely on English tailoring and style were pieced together by Florentine craftsmen with their eye for detail. Each new item carried the first Gucci monogram—a tiny image of a young page in full livery and a cap carrying a suitcase in one hand and a Gladstone bag in the other. It was my grandfather's quiet nod to his formative days.

Guccio Gucci opened for business at 7 Via della Vigna Nuova in 1921. The name of the street translates to "new vineyard," and he surely hoped for a vintage beginning. The silvered name "G. GUCCI & Co." was set in black marble above an Art Deco door. I have been there many times—it now forms part of the bigger Gucci premises whose main entrance is on Via de' Tornabuoni—but it isn't hard to imagine what it looked like almost one hundred years ago.

An early advertisement in the Florentine newspaper *Sassaiola Fiorentina* described the store's specialty as *valigeria Inglese* (English travel cases). It also offered *articoli finissimi per regali* (fine articles for gifts). My grandfather was named as the *direttore comproprietario* (copartner, shared with an unnamed business investor), "previously employed at leather manufacturer Franzi."

The forty-year-old father of three who'd merely carried such bags as a boy must have been nervous but proud as he stood behind the glass-topped counter with his waxed mustache waiting for his first customer.

Cleverly, he focused on durability and was said to have jumped up and down on his suitcases to demonstrate how sturdy they were. Quality was paramount and he knew word of mouth would sell his wares. Business was slow at first but his newspaper advertisements soon brought people in, along with the recommendations from satisfied customers, just as he'd dreamed. In time, he also undertook repairs on luggage damaged during arduous journeys by road, sea, or rail—a problem he knew only too well from his days as a page. Fixing broken straps and polishing out ugly scratches became such a profitable sideline that my grandfather, with his growing appetite for commercial success, was able to open a new workshop.

My father, Aldo, was fourteen the year the family business began—not much younger than his own father had been when he'd stoked coal to earn his passage to England. Although Papà studied botany at college later (sparking a lifelong passion for gardening), any thoughts of higher education were largely forgotten as he and his younger brother—my uncle Vasco—were set to work as delivery boys on bicycles after school and on weekends. Their little brother, Rodolfo, aged nine, was too young to do deliveries, and, besides, he had other dreams.

My aunt Grimalda, their eighteen-year-old sister, operated the cash register along with Grandmother Aida, a veritable force in the business. Dressed in her starched white pinafore, she ruled the impeccably outfitted staff with exacting standards, just as she ran the household. Papà adored her although he did admit she could be *"diabolic"* and described her as a woman without fear. She

certainly took no prisoners and believed she could do anything—
just like he did.

Her husband was an honest man with many good qualities
but also frequently uncompromising and occasionally tyrannical.
With a short temper and little patience, he was a perfectionist—a
trait he passed down to my father and then to me. From household chores to personal grooming, he expected excellence. Puffing on a fat Toscano cigar, he was a "front of house" proprietor in
the old-fashioned sense, checking that everything was immaculate
before the doors were unlocked promptly on the stroke of his gold
fob watch. Once they were open for business, he would wait on
the shop floor in his dapper three-piece suit, ready to turn on the
charm.

He was determined to make his company at least as successful as Franzi and—as with that firm—fully expected his sons to
be as devoted to it as he was. Family and commitment to the business came first, he always insisted. Often pitting one son against
the other, Guccio also instilled an early sense of competition in his
boys. My aunt Grimalda was expected to pitch in too, but being a
woman, she was never part of his business plan.

Regardless of their gender, my grandfather insisted that all
his children maintain the unimpeachable manners, appearance,
and behavior of those working for a high-end, high-achieving firm.
He fully embraced the age-old Italian tradition known as *bella
figura*, which refers to the way people present themselves to the
world with fine clothes, grace, and gentility to make the best possible impression.

Papà didn't disappoint. With his fine-boned features, and as
the only child with piercing blue eyes, the family's eldest son was
without doubt *numero uno*. A born wheeler-dealer who'd inherited
his mother's guile and his father's entrepreneurial spirit, he was

an eager apprentice and stepped up to the challenge of building the family business. Nimble and an early riser, he was usually first out of the door to deliver beautifully wrapped leather goods to customers all over Florence by bicycle, often braving the elements on narrow streets teeming with horse carriages.

By the time he was twenty and working full-time, my father had learned to mimic my grandfather's fastidiousness, carefully examining the window displays and checking each stitch of every item the company made. Both men insisted that the sales staff spend long hours on the shop floor in order to keep in touch with their customers and ensure that the store bearing their name was a gleaming testament to quality and excellence. Behind the scenes, though, things weren't quite so prosperous. Business was patchy to begin with and at one point my grandfather almost had to close shop. He was only saved by a loan offered by the fiancé of my aunt Grimalda. The advance saved the company until trade picked up again, allowing my grandfather to not only pay off his debt but open a second store nearby on Via del Parione.

Before long Papà proved adept enough to be sent out into the field as Gucci's first-ever salesman, a job that appealed to his innate wanderlust and roving eye. Carrying suitcases full of merchandise, he'd boldly fill luggage racks on the train carriage, leaving little room for anyone else. With what some described as *faccia tosta* (chutzpah), he had an innate arrogance about him but was somehow allowed to get away with it. A handsome young bachelor of means, he quickly discovered the unexpected advantages of daily contact with fellow shopkeepers, foreign visitors, wealthy customers, and their staff, especially if they happened to be female.

He traveled widely, but it was in Florence that he was to meet the first woman to make a profound impact on his life.

THREE

When I look at the photograph of my father and his wife taken on their wedding day, I am surprised to see an apprehensive young man. His clenched fists and uncertain expression reveal the burden of responsibility he must have felt at just twenty-two years of age. Interestingly, I can also see myself in him—the shape of his nose, his sloping eyes and elongated face.

His bride, on the other hand, seems far more at ease, with her head tilted toward her husband ever so slightly and her mouth open, almost as if she is about to say something. She has an air of expectation about her, not only because she was pregnant at the time but because of the future that lay ahead.

Olwen Price was a comely strawberry-blond teenager who hailed from Shropshire in the English Midlands, close to the Welsh border. Her Protestant family worked in wood, making furniture, wheels, and coffins. The eldest of six children, she'd trained as a dressmaker but somehow escaped a life of provincial drudgery to go into service as a teenager and become a lady's maid.

One of Olwen's duties while working for a Romanian princess

named Elisabeth, who'd married King George II of Greece, was to collect items for her employer from the exclusive retail establishments she liked to frequent. The little shop of G. Gucci & Co. in Via della Vigna Nuova, Florence, was one of her many stops and the place Olwen first fell under my father's spell.

In the spring of 1927, Princess Elisabeth paid the store an unexpected visit—alone. The arrival of a European royal was always a cause for celebration (a bell used to be rung for such appearances at the Savoy), but there was little joyful clamor this time. The princess hadn't come to buy; she had come to lodge a complaint. Miss Price, her unmarried employee, for whom she bore some level of responsibility, had been secretly having an affair with my father, she told my grandfather curtly. Worse still, Olwen was pregnant with his child.

Guccio was mortified. He knew that his hot-blooded son was incapable of controlling his desires and could seduce virtually any woman within range. His increasingly feckless encounters were becoming the stuff of legend in the workshop and included a claim that he once locked eyes with a nun on a train who allowed him to caress her. Nobody was out of bounds, but getting a girl into trouble was a step too far.

My father must have felt like he could go anywhere or do anything at the time when he discovered that Olwen was pregnant, but his father's lessons about respect for family had made an impression. He also had genuine affection for the pretty young maid as well as a lifelong fascination for all things British, also instilled in him by my grandfather. Without fully considering the consequences, Papà offered to marry the nineteen-year-old and provide for their unborn child.

It was an offer the princess found acceptable, so when Olwen was three months pregnant and not yet showing, she married my father at Our Lady and St. Oswald's Catholic Church, not far from her home in Oswestry, England. The date was August 22, 1927. Olwen, who was much shorter than my father, wore a knee-length white dress, a short veil, and a crescent-shaped headdress studded with pearls. A large bouquet of flowers was gripped firmly in front of her bump. Some might say her expression is one of triumph.

My grandparents didn't cross the English Channel to witness the marriage, as that would have meant closing the store and unnecessary expense. My father described himself in the church register as a leather goods merchant and enlisted the local tobacconist as his best man.

As was the Italian custom then—and to a certain extent again now—the bride came home to live with her groom and his parents in their modest two-story house in Florence. Although Olwen was well traveled, she soon felt like a fish out of water in a country where she barely spoke the language, didn't get on particularly well with her mother-in-law, and wasn't that keen on the food.

With a demanding new baby, Giorgio, who was born on February 2, 1928, she had no time to socialize, so my father increasingly went out on his own, for work and for pleasure. With two more sons in quick succession, Paolo, born in March 1931, and Roberto in November 1932, his wife devoted herself to raising her boys. Needing more space, the couple moved to their own home outside the city, where Olwen became even more isolated from her dynamic husband with the Latin spirit whose appetite for life—and women—never waned.

Italy between the wars was largely in thrall to its prime minister Benito Mussolini, head of the Fascist Party. With the clever use of propaganda and promises of economic growth the man known as Il Duce created a cult following and ruled as a one-party dictator with the help of his feared Blackshirts.

My father was never the slightest bit interested in politics and had little time for the Fascists. He and my grandfather were too busy scheming. Even though their country was in the grip of a depression, they were determined to push ahead with their plans to expand the company using their imported hides. My uncles Vasco and Rodolfo both showed early promise but they never shared quite the same zeal for the future of the business as my father did. In 1935, when Papà had just turned thirty, politics unexpectedly interfered with his plans. Mussolini ordered the invasion of Abyssinia (also known as Ethiopia) over an ongoing border dispute with the Italian colony of Somalia. The seven-month conflict sparked worldwide outrage and the League of Nations, of which both countries were members, imposed a series of sanctions that resulted in a trade blockade on Italy.

In danger of losing access to their vital supplies of German leather, my father and grandfather had to act quickly, little knowing that their decisions would set the tone for Gucci's future. Papà was able to source some calfskin hides from a tannery in the historic Santa Croce quarter of Florence, on the southeastern fringes of the city. Realizing that this high-grade and much more expensive material, known as *cuoio grasso,* would have to be used more frugally, he then found Italian suppliers of jute, rope, linen, and Naples hemp, materials he planned to use in order to supplement the leather.

For what was to become their bestselling suitcase, he chose a tan-colored canvas printed with a distinctive geometric pattern in dark brown that became known as the "*rombi* design." This signature cloth with leather trim is still used on Gucci products and was later personalized with a series of interlocking double G's for the name Guccio Gucci, yet another of my father's clever innovations.

The Italo-Abyssinian War ended the same month as his thirty-first birthday but its effects on the design and feel of Gucci products would be lifelong. The company had not only managed to survive the trade embargo but business was booming. Papà felt invincible despite the distant rumblings of another conflict. My uncle Vasco had settled into his role in charge of the factory and Uncle Rodolfo had followed his dream to become a film actor under the stage name Maurizio D'Ancora.

My father, still the number one son, was itching to expand to Rome and then farther afield but it took him two years and numerous heated battles with my grandfather before he could persuade him that such a risk made financial sense. Guccio had become more cautious in middle age, especially whenever he recalled how his family had once nearly lost everything. The business in Florence was doing better than he expected and that was all he'd hoped for. "Why would we risk all that with an unknown venture in a city we have no connection with? Especially when there are rumors of another war." But beneath my grandfather's gruff exterior was still the adventurous young boy who'd run away to England to seek his fortune, and secretly, he admired my father's courage and indomitable will—what Italians would call his *forza*.

Under relentless pressure, he eventually allowed my father to purchase a new store in Rome at number 21 Via Condotti, a fashionable central location not far from the Spanish Steps. The shop was largely modeled on the first, complete with the same ivory handles carved like olives. No expense was spared on display cases, carpeting, and lighting. The two-story corner premises even had a spacious apartment upstairs for Olwen and their three sons. Rome became their new home.

On September 1, 1938, Papà presided over the opening of the new *bottega*, or store, on Via Condotti. I can only imagine the sense of excitement he must have felt in branching out from Florence for the first time as his ambitious spirit finally found its outlet. He assured his father of guaranteed sales from the growing numbers of American and other tourists flooding into the city, all eager to return home with quality leather goods.

What he hadn't bargained for was the outbreak of the Second World War exactly one year to the day after the shop's official opening. When Mussolini then joined forces with Germany in 1940, the future looked bleak—not only for the business but also for just about every commercial venture across Europe. If it weren't for the fortitude of their friendly bank and a contract to divert their artisans into making boots for the Italian infantry, G. Gucci & Co. would almost certainly have gone under.

My father managed to avoid conscription thanks to Il Duce's insistence that businesses in the Italian capital continue to operate as normal in order to keep up morale. His brothers in Florence weren't so lucky and both saw frontline service. Rome didn't escape the war completely, however, and was bombed by the Allies in 1943 and 1944, causing thousands of civilian casualties. The Vatican maintained a strictly neutral policy and Pope Pius XII took to the streets to hand out alms to those worst affected. Eventually, he successfully pleaded with President Roosevelt to declare Rome an "open city"—one that had abandoned all defensive actions—which ultimately protected its people and its greatest treasures.

While my father struggled to keep the business going, his wife focused on their sons, whom she'd raised to be bilingual and planned to take home to visit her family in England as soon as she could after the war. The boys all attended the Mater Dei school, run by Irish nuns, and were close companions with the usual sibling rivalries. Giorgio, the eldest boy, developed a stammer and was a somewhat nervy child. Paolo, a typical middle son, was noisy and gregarious, while Roberto was adored as the baby. In the absence of the man they called "Daddy," with whom Olwen was locked into a loveless marriage, it was she who also fed their sons' emotional life.

It seems strange these days to think that less than a hundred years ago, divorce was not only unheard of in Italy but considered a direct violation of the canon law of the Catholic Church, which it still is today. It wouldn't be sanctioned legally until the 1970s. Even Protestant Britain frowned upon it. Unless Olwen went back to Shropshire to live on rationing without her children, she had little choice but to stay in Italy and bring up her boys as best she could. She resigned herself to the fact that my father would largely be absent from her life as he continued on his all-consuming quest for professional, personal, and commercial gain.

When the war ended and the partisans killed Mussolini, the despondent Nazis in Rome were replaced by triumphant American soldiers smoking cigarettes and handing out chewing gum. The GIs' seemingly limitless supply of dollar bills was welcomed nowhere more warmly than at Gucci. As Papà tallied up each day's takings, he must have been mightily relieved that what some had regarded as his reckless adventure was paying off at last.

Brimming with new ideas and hoping to build up an international reputation, he quickly increased production of easily transportable accessories such as gloves, belts, lapel badges, and key fobs. He also began grooming his children to take their places in the Gucci dynasty he hoped to create, something his father actively encouraged.

Such was his passion for his trade that my grandfather reputedly liked to wave a piece of leather under his grandchildren's noses soon after they were born, telling them, "This is the smell of leather, the smell of your future!" I'm not sure how I would have reacted as a baby if my father had done this to me, but as an adult I can appreciate the natural, almost primitive quality of rich hides, evoking memories of the finest moments in life.

Like his father before him, Papà also fostered stiff competition between his fresh-faced teenage sons, encouraging them to take a keen interest in the business he was determined they'd one day inherit. He enlisted them in the stockroom and with deliveries—just as he had been employed at their age. My father couldn't possibly have known as he cheerfully sent them out on their bicycles in those heady early days that, between them, they would bring about his ruin.

FOUR

A myth is defined as "a traditional story, especially one concerning the early history of a people." It can also mean "a widely held but false belief or idea." As someone who grew up shrouded in secrecy, I was well accustomed to the truth being disguised, so when I discovered that there was a little reinvention surrounding the Gucci name long before I was born, it came as no surprise.

Since his earliest days at the Savoy Hotel, Grandfather Guccio appreciated the importance of tradition when it came to creating a status symbol. Ancestral titles, family crests, and embossed initials were the marque of the gentry, so if the Gucci label was to become synonymous with luxury and attract the rich and upwardly mobile, then my father knew he had to downplay his family's humble origins and invent a more illustrious heritage. It certainly wasn't in their interests to reveal my grandfather's lowly start as a page.

As Papà once declared, "A status symbol is not born. It becomes one when accepted by a certain elite and everyone then becomes eager to buy it." So in the years immediately after the war, he and his father set about devising an ingenious plan to create a better backstory for the Gucci name. Having grown up in the era before motorcars and with so many of their clients horse-riding aristocrats, they based their remodeled history on a "presumed" line of descent from Florentine saddlers to medieval nobility.

This gelled with the durable equestrian-themed line of products they began to produce that would come to include red-and-green-striped webbing inspired by girth straps, fabrics the colors of racing silks, metal hardware and handles modeled on stirrups and bits, and the kind of double stitching usually associated with the finest leather saddles.

The clever twist was the upgrade of the tiny Gucci insignia hand-stitched into every bag that left the factory. It now incorporated a modified crest, which featured a shield beneath the family name adorned with a rose and a wheel. A noble knight in armor replaced the lowly servant carrying luggage.

And so this particular myth was born.

When I was a little girl my father presented me with a tiny signet ring bearing this Gucci crest. Crafted in eighteen-karat gold, it fit perfectly on my pinkie. Too young to appreciate its significance, I wore it with pride and still treasure it today.

My father had other ideas to keep trade brisk, too. During the difficult postwar years when Italy suffered a depression and leather was still a controlled commodity, he continued to experiment with other materials in order to produce financially viable goods. They say that from necessity comes invention, and in 1947, the Bamboo Bag came into being. Nobody is certain who within Gucci first came up with the idea of a distinctively shaped pigskin bag inspired by the contours of a saddle with a handle made of burnished bamboo cane, but I've always thought it was a stroke of pure genius.

The bag was an immediate success and even featured in a

Roberto Rossellini movie adorning the arm of Ingrid Bergman. After so many years of financial ruin and Fascist rule, Gucci's brave little Bamboo Bag represented something new and exciting. Emblematic of the country's revival, it was a signature motif that would be adopted in many later incarnations and remains an iconic status symbol with vintage models still highly sought after. I had one of my own in black, a gift from my mother, which was stolen years later along with a hoard of Gucci bags that were among my most prized possessions.

By this time, my father and both my uncles had become involved in the business full-time. Having spent much of the war entertaining the troops, Rodolfo's stage career collapsed. Unemployed, he somewhat reluctantly took up his position on the floor of the Via del Parione store while devoting his spare time to creating a lengthy autobiographical film featuring his greatest movie moments. He, too, was creating his own myth.

Easygoing Vasco, who'd overseen the wartime military boot production, was put in charge of the Florentine factories, including a new one built on the success of the Bamboo Bag. To reward them for their efforts, my grandfather awarded directorships to each of his three sons, giving them an equal number of shares, although everyone accepted that he and Papà were in the driver's seat. The move inspired confidence and family pride nevertheless. Skilled leather workers flocked to the firm, which was gaining a growing reputation as both a steady employer and one that encouraged innovation with commensurate rewards.

In a clever move that I suspect my grandfather copied from Franzi, each artisan was given his own identifying number—stamped inside everything he made—to encourage responsibility, creativity, and provenance. Anything found to be faulty could be traced directly back to the individual, which helped ensure the highest possible standards.

All hands were needed to fill the rising number of orders as the Rome store continued to bring in new trade. Eager to cash in on Gucci's growing international cachet, my father coined the motto "Quality is remembered long after price is forgotten" and had it gold-embossed on leather plaques placed strategically around the stores. Indeed, the products were so well made back then that my friends' mothers still comment on how bags bought then are timeless and look like new after decades. My grandfather, obsessed with craftsmanship and durability, would have been proud.

In his restless manner, which my mother and I were all too familiar with, Papà traveled farther and farther afield seeking new materials and visiting trade shows across Europe. In London he ordered a large quantity of ginger and brindle pigskins from specialist tanners in Walsall, Staffordshire. These butter-soft hides became so crucial to the Gucci business that he would visit the factory personally to choose them. The more he traveled, the more he appreciated that the company needed to expand to take advantage of the worldwide boom. He set his sights first on Milan, which was recovering well after being carpet-bombed by the Allies.

My grandfather remained nervous about any further expansion. He and my grandmother Aida still lived in the same house and had acquired few of the trappings of wealth. One of his mottos was "Stay small to remain great," and he was determined not to let my father get too carried away. Sensible Vasco, whose job it was to hire staff and supervise production, was also wary of Papà's naked ambition. Uncle Rodolfo, the baby of the family, known as "Foffo," had a slightly different take. Having been a matinée idol and seen something of the world, he'd mixed with sophisticated people and knew there was an untapped market for quality goods. Even though he'd been forced to give up his Hollywood fantasy, he could see that my father had dreams too and soon became his chief ally.

With his younger brother's support, Papà was able to get his own way in 1951 and acquire new premises at number 7 Via Monte Napoleone, known colloquially as "Montenapo"—Milan's most fashionable street. With what was becoming uncanny prescience, my father located the store in just the right place at the right time. He put Rodolfo safely at the helm of the smart *bottega*, knowing that he'd draw on his connections in the movie industry. Before long, the cream of the Italian film studios was clamoring at the door of Gucci Milan, with the likes of Marcello Mastroianni from Fellini's *La Dolce Vita* and Gina Lollobrigida snapping up the latest designs.

Papà, however, had even bigger plans. Long before my grandfather had been carrying bags at the Savoy, a vast tide of some three million Italians had headed to American shores in what was known as the "New Immigration" to become a vital part of the US economy. When GIs started returning to the States as unofficial ambassadors for stylish leather goods, they created a fresh hunger for all things Italian. My father was eager to transform the American image of Italy as a nation of poor pizza-eating immigrants into something much more prestigious, making it synonymous with quality and design. He had a sixth sense that he should take Gucci to New York, the commercial heartland of his favorite clients. These were pioneering days, and just like the miners of the gold rush in the previous century, he knew that there were fortunes to be made for those who acted boldly. Booking himself a passage on a transatlantic liner in 1952, Papà was determined to be among the first.

The city dubbed "the Big Apple" was all that he hoped for and more. From the moment he disembarked at Luxury Liner Row in the Port of New York, he was infatuated. With the name of a lawyer in his breast pocket, he stood in awe, taking in the spectacle before him. Everything from the skyscrapers to the scale of the streets and the tail-finned cars powering in all directions oozed enthusiasm and commerce. He was spellbound. It was the start of a love affair with America that would last for many years.

Accompanied by the attorney he hooked up with, Papà viewed a number of potential premises in midtown Manhattan. As with the shops he picked in Italy—and as I would see him do many times over the years—he'd stand across the street from each building and half-close his eyes as he imagined the distinctive Gucci lettering above the door. If the layout didn't look right or frontage didn't blend seamlessly with its surroundings, he'd shake his head and move on to the next.

One particular store caught his eye. It was situated on the ground floor of his hotel, the prestigious Savoy-Plaza (from which he would write my mother letters, but more on that later). On the corner of East Fifty-Eighth Street and Fifth Avenue, the iconic luxury hotel with the auspicious name towered over Central Park. The stores in its ground-floor premises may not have opened directly onto Fifth Avenue, as my father would have preferred, but they were within view of the luxury department store Bergdorf Goodman, a nine-story Beaux Arts monument to shopping that described itself as "the pinnacle of style." By comparison, the place Papà liked at number 7 East Fifty-Eighth Street was relatively modest, and at $1,500 a year it was too good to pass up. He was sold.

Keen to keep my uncle Rodolfo on his side, he urged him to sail to New York to view the property for himself before the two of them entered into negotiations with bankers about setting up Gucci Shops Incorporated in America. In what must have seemed like a brazen act of defiance to my grandfather, the two brothers sent a telegram informing him of the move only once the lease was signed and the deal was done. Helpless four thousand miles away, Guccio—who'd thought they'd only gone to the States to get a general feel for retail trade there—accused Papà of foolhardiness that could ruin them all. He demanded via cable that they cancel the lease and return home immediately. They didn't.

Few were privy to the conversations that ensued when they walked back into the offices of Gucci & Co., but they must have been tumultuous. For my grandfather, who'd lived through near financial ruin and two world wars, the pace at which his eldest son was pushing the business must have seemed terrifying. On January 2, 1953, he dropped dead of a heart attack with my stalwart grandmother Aida by his side. He was seventy-one years old. The indomitable woman who'd defied convention by having an illegitimate baby before persuading Guccio to set up in a business she'd help him run would follow him to the grave in less than two years.

It was to my grandfather's credit, I think, that the man who'd started the company and seen all his dreams come true did accede to his sons' wishes a few weeks before he died. Having listened to my father's persuasive arguments, he gave him his blessing for their ambitious new American venture. The baton had been handed on.

Ten months after Guccio was laid to rest in the marble family tomb at the Soffiano cemetery on the outskirts of Florence, which I would come to know so well, my father masterminded the grand opening of his first store on American soil in November 1953. A pioneer of Italian design, his was the first shop to sell high-quality Italian products in the United States.

Although officially a joint shareholder with his brothers, none doubted that Papà was now the de facto head of G. Gucci & Co. To mark the occasion, the company launched a new range, which included the first Gucci loafer—a personal favorite of mine as a young girl. The elegant slip-on shoe made of crocodile hide, leather, or suede with a metal snaffle-bit detail was an item that would help transform the future of the business.

With the opening of the Manhattan store, my father's passion was unleashed. He took great pride in the fact that all three of his sons were by then working for the family firm. Giorgio and Roberto plodded away diligently behind the scenes while the more colorful Paolo—a chip off the old block—was encouraged to draw on his creative impulses and set to creating new designs. As he watched each of them bring his own unique talents to the company, Papà knew he had created not only a myth but also a legacy.

The New York premises were the most elegant and aspirational yet, exuding sophistication, luxury, and glamour in a trend that would be echoed worldwide. As the camera shutters clicked, he stood beside his favored son, Roberto, and was flanked by my uncles Rodolfo and Vasco in a touching display of Gucci unity. They were sending a clear signal that this company would be run by the men of the family.

My aunt Grimalda, born of the wrong gender, had worked in the Florence store all her life. A loan from her fiancé had saved it from folding early on. Nevertheless, she received nothing from my grandfather's three-way split of the business as set out in his will. Instead she was gifted some land and twelve million *lire* (approximately $20,000). It was a decision that sparked the first legal action within the family when she challenged the unfair division of spoils. Attorneys acting for her brothers crushed her move ruthlessly in court, a result that would embitter her and her family for years.

This critical lawsuit in the history of Gucci happened ten years before my birth, but the internecine battles had begun.

Life for our family would never be the same.

FIVE

There are pivotal moments in all our lives when choosing a particular path leads us to a future we might otherwise not have had. I can think of several such instances in mine and often wonder how things might have panned out had I gone the other way.

In the story of my family, I suppose the moment Guccio decided to leave Florence and seek his fortune in London was a critical juncture, and for Papà it must have been the day he boarded the ship to New York. For my mother, Bruna, it was surely the moment she stepped over the threshold of the Gucci store at 21 Via Condotti, Rome, on a balmy Friday morning in April 1956.

It was, she said, "like entering another world." Eighteen years old and the daughter of a widowed seamstress, Mamma tried to conceal the trembling of her hands by tightly clutching what she suddenly realized was a very inferior purse. In her best dress, a shift of powder blue she paired with black court shoes, she had left her mother's apartment in Viale Manzoni in the west of Rome that morning excited but anxious. Her boyfriend Pietro had arranged an interview with his brother-in-law, who was the floor manager at the flagship store, and for days she'd been deciding what to wear and rehearsing what to say.

"I knew that if I could get this job I'd have my own money to buy whatever I wanted," she told me. "It was a good opportunity, otherwise who knows what might have become of me."

The youngest of three children, Mamma was conceived amid New Year's Eve fireworks in 1936 and born exactly nine months later on October 1, 1937, two years before the start of the Second World War. My grandfather Alfredo Palombo was a middle-ranking civil servant and devoted Fascist. Grandmother Delia was a liberal and, according to my mother, an "angel." The baby of the family, Bruna was adored unconditionally by her mother, who breast-fed her until she was two. With the dark hair that had inspired her name plaited into pigtails, as a child my mother was happy yet clingy—a personality trait that would dog her for much of her life and affect her relationships with my father and me. Afraid to be alone, she slept in her parents' bed until she was six and was permanently glued to my grandmother's side.

The advent of World War II changed everything for her family. Once Italy swapped sides and its government was dissolved, my grandfather Alfredo was divested of the job he'd expected to keep for life. Mussolini was arrested and imprisoned in a mountain resort until Nazi commandos swept in and audaciously rescued him in a glider before reestablishing him as a puppet leader. His new regime was set up in Gargnano on the banks of Lake Garda in the northern district of Lombardy. Eight hundred former government employees, including my grandfather, were summoned to work there. Virtually unemployable in Rome, they had little choice but to accept, and Alfredo was especially happy to serve his Duce once more.

Aged five, my mother was bundled onto a train with her older brother, Franco, and sister, Gabriella, as the family left Rome and relocated to a small house in the resort town of Maderno, near Gargnano. Aside from her delight at seeing snow for the first time, she found the transition difficult in a place where much of the town had been requisitioned for the sudden influx. The locals, who looked down on people from the south, resented the newcomers and my mother was teased at school for her Roman accent, making her feel inadequate and self-conscious.

Guarded by soldiers and surrounded by bomb shelters, this hitherto peaceful region also endured frequent Allied air raids. When several of Mussolini's soldiers were killed, the people of the town, including my mother, were ordered to line the streets as the corpses were paraded in open caskets. Missing their home and never settling into their new surroundings, the Palombo family remained there until the end of the war and the arrival of American troops. After the execution of Mussolini they had no choice but to return to Rome, all of them changed by the experience.

My grandfather could only find a much lowlier government job on less pay. His rancor affected his health, exacerbating an existing stomach ulcer and kidney condition, the pain of which only worsened his moods. Mamma frequently found herself on the receiving end of his temper, beaten for the smallest indiscretion. My uncle Franco kept out of the way and my aunt Gabriella, who was pretty, smart, and something of a "daddy's girl," was the only one to escape his constant carping. Gabriella was also someone to whom my mother was often unfavorably compared, which left her feeling she had little in common with either sibling. Lonely and self-absorbed, she learned to play in a world of her own. I can certainly relate to her childhood isolation.

At least she had her mother's unconditional love, or so she thought. At eight years old, she accidentally overheard my grandmother telling a girlfriend, "I didn't want Bruna to be born. We couldn't afford another child and I tried everything to get rid of the baby." Too young to comprehend the reasons, my mother was shattered by the news, which scarred her for life. Soon afterward, she developed a quirky habit of carrying a handbag everywhere as a kind of comforter. She still does it. In her childhood purse she kept her few precious belongings and began to trade them when anyone offered her a gift. Whether it was a piece of candy or something equally trivial, she felt she had to reciprocate, even if it meant plucking a button from her blouse. My grandmother thought the gesture amusing without recognizing the underlying emotional conflict about my mother's worth that it foretold.

In spite of the discovery that she wasn't wanted at first, my mother's only happy childhood memories revolve around my grandmother. Delia's sunny disposition illuminated their apartment as she sat at her sewing machine singing while she created the kinds of dresses she could never afford. My mother would watch her create a stunning garment from pattern to completion in a matter of hours and daydream about the lives of the people who might wear such extravagant gowns. "I loved dressing up and wearing makeup. I'd borrow my mother's eyeliner and apply it carefully until I looked just like Cleopatra. I imagined myself as an exotic woman, wearing those beautiful clothes and living a very different kind of life."

My grandmother was something of a psychic who claimed to have frequent premonitions. One day she looked up from her sewing machine to announce, "Your sister, Gabriella, will have to work hard to get what she wants, Bruna, but everything will come to you on a silver platter." Privately, my mother thought that highly unlikely.

By the time she was a teenager, Mamma had acquired a mischievous best friend named Maria-Grazia who encouraged her to rebel against her father's strictures. She began by trying items he had banned, such as chewing gum and cigarettes, and then she started staying out late—risking a beating if he caught her. By the time she was fourteen, however, her chief interest had switched to boys, or to one boy in particular. His name was Pietro and he was three years older than she with thick dark hair, exceptionally long eyelashes, and "a beautiful mouth."

As sweethearts, they did all the usual things young couples do, like taking part in the nightly *passeggiata* on the piazza, spending time with friends, or watching dubbed Hollywood movies such as *High Noon* and *Singin' in the Rain*. Pietro was an only son who worked for his family's thriving foods business, a job that often took him out of the city. He was better off than most, and with a Fiat 1100 (known as a Magic Millecento) as an eighteenth-birthday present, he became the first in their circle to own a car. Taking my mother for romantic drives, Pietro would park somewhere isolated, turn the radio dial to some ambient music, and then try to caress her while she resisted anything more than a kiss.

Happy enough with her boyfriend, Mamma was not so happy at home. Although my grandfather's mood had been lifted by an unexpected lottery win (of around $5,000), under his rule my mother and aunt Gabriella were expected to dress conservatively and adhere to a nightly curfew, both of which they resented. It seemed to her that his life's ambition was to make everyone around him miserable and she couldn't see how this would ever change.

Then on a hot day in June 1953, it did. My mother arrived home from school to be informed by a neighbor that her father had collapsed and been rushed to the hospital. As her father had been dogged by ill health for years and had recently undergone surgery to remove some kidney stones, my mother wasn't unduly worried.

She sat at the kitchen table and began flicking through the newspaper, which was full of photographs of the coronation of Queen Elizabeth. As she studied the pictures from London, she helped herself from a bowl of cherries that had been left for her. Eating one after the other in a reverie, she listened to the clock ticking on the wall and waited for her mother to come home. It was less than an hour later when the same neighbor who'd let her in with a key burst back into her apartment and shrieked, "Your *papà* is dead! Your *papà* is dead!" An *ictus cerebrale*, or stroke, had killed him. Mamma just sat there numbly finishing the bowl without saying a word as she stared at the clock. The taste of cherries would always remind her of that moment.

I never met any of my grandparents but I do know that my mother had few fond memories of my grandfather and didn't especially mourn his loss. Mercifully, his death left the family better off than they'd been, thanks to both the lottery windfall and his government pension. Then, soon afterward, my aunt Gabriella moved out to marry a dentist and my uncle Franco found a position with BP. My mother wanted a skill of her own and she started a course to learn stenography, where she met other young people and started to go out more. All seemed brighter until Franco assumed the role of head of the household and continued to enforce his father's codes of conduct, especially where Mamma's behavior was concerned.

"I did everything I could to escape Franco and the apartment," she told me. "He still watched my every move, though, and was on me like a dog if I stayed out beyond his curfew. He was a tyrant!"

This tyranny was mirrored in Pietro, who also decided that he didn't want my mother wearing makeup anymore, something that every pretty young *signorina* did, especially one who took such pride in her appearance. "And I don't like you wearing high heels unless you're with me," he insisted. He also wanted to know her whereabouts at all times. Their constant quibbling led to arguments over the telephone that invariably ended with her slamming down the receiver.

Then one night as they sat canoodling together in his car, Pietro unexpectedly proposed. Before she could even think what she was saying, she heard herself say, "*Sì*." So confident was he of her answer that he immediately produced a small velvet box containing a pearl engagement ring. She slipped it on her finger even though she hated pearls and had private misgivings about swapping a life under Franco's rule for one under Pietro's.

My grandmother was crestfallen. She had her own doubts about Pietro and immediately shared them, informing Mamma that she'd made a mistake in marrying her father. "Think carefully about what you're doing, Bruna," she warned. "I don't think Pietro's right for you. In fact, if you do go ahead and marry him, I predict you'll be home within three days."

Mamma was torn. She'd promised herself that she'd never end up with an authoritarian like her father, but then it seemed to her that most Italian men behaved like that, so what choice did she have? Pietro was essentially decent and conscientious and he clearly adored her. Her friends repeatedly told her he was a "catch" who'd make a steady husband and a fine father.

Unaware of her reservations and already making plans for their future together, Pietro began to give Mamma half his weekly wages, which she kept in a shoe box hidden under a chest of drawers in her bedroom. Their life together seemed preordained. Just as she'd pulled a button from her blouse as a child in exchange for something, so she'd pledged herself to him in return for his protection. There didn't seem to be any alternative.

After finishing her stenographer's course, my mother was told in no uncertain terms by my grandmother that if she wanted her own money then she had to get a job. Pietro agreed only reluctantly but he chose both the job and the venue once his brother-in-law Laurent told him there was a suitable position behind the scenes at Gucci.

It was a bright Friday morning in the spring of 1956 when my mother found herself at a pivotal moment in her life as she walked into a shop she'd never heard of before. Oblivious to the importance of the day, she gazed about in wonder at the luxurious but understated store with its wooden display cases redolent of new leather. When Laurent beckoned, she followed him to a first-floor office, noticing how the heels of her shoes sank deep into the green carpet. Pietro's brother-in-law was sophisticated, tall, and slim, and seemed extremely relaxed. He revealed that the job that might suit her was in the storeroom with a starting salary of what felt to her like a staggering sum of twenty-five thousand *lire* a week.

"If you do well, you could work your way to the shop floor," he added. Reeling from the idea of being one of the chic "front of house" girls she'd just passed downstairs, she almost tripped over him as he led her along a corridor to another office with a glass-fronted door. Turning the handle, he smiled and said, "First I have to introduce you to the boss."

Just before he opened the door, he whispered, "Don't speak until spoken to, and then don't say too much." She was suddenly so nervous that she felt dizzy.

They stepped into a surprisingly basic office arranged with artful informality. A secretary sat typing away in a small anteroom. Behind a large wooden desk stood a slim, smartly dressed businessman with thinning hair elegantly slicked back.

"Dr. Gucci, this is the girl I spoke to you about," Laurent said breezily. He used the title "*dottore*," commonly employed as a mark of respect, regardless of qualifications. "Her name is Bruna Palombo. She's trained as a stenographer, but with your approval, I'd like to start her downstairs."

My father stepped from behind his desk to shake my mother's hand and flash her a disarming smile. Her eyes lifted to meet his as he asked how old she was. When she told him she'd be nineteen in October he looked her up and down and replied, "Very good. You can start next week." She lowered her gaze, hardly believing her ears.

The few moments she'd spent inside the Gucci store were all she could talk about once she reached home, as she regaled my grandmother and her friend Maria-Grazia with details of how opulent everything was, exclaiming, "You can't even imagine!"

"And what was the boss like?" Delia asked.

"Kind," she replied thoughtfully. "And with the bluest eyes ... *such* eyes!" The job he'd offered her was, she told me, the most exciting thing that had ever happened to her in her young life. "I couldn't wait to get started!"

It was certainly one of the happiest days of my mother's life when she took the orange M bus to work that Monday. Her life seemed to have taken on a filmlike quality as she rode past the Colosseum to Piazza di Spagna and imagined playing a young girl about town. By chance and good luck, she had somehow slipped through a portal and entered that other world she'd dreamed of as a little girl, the one inhabited by women who were free to do as they pleased and wear gowns like those her mother crafted.

For her first few weeks she worked on inventory, stocktaking and pricing in a back room, and was delighted to be there. Whenever she could, she'd peer out onto the shop floor and watch with fascination as the cream of high society gathered beneath the crystal chandeliers. "The store attracted such interesting, elegant people, all of them clearly very well-off, many from the nearby embassies, and some movie people too. I was fascinated by how they dressed and the beautiful jewelry they wore."

Secretly, she studied their body language too, as well as the poise and grace of the staff, who hovered discreetly, ready to enthuse about the products and offer customers any assistance. *"Buongiorno, posso esserle d'aiuto?"* (Good morning, may I help you?) they'd politely ask, exhibiting the kind of etiquette insisted upon by the Gucci family since my grandfather's days.

My mother may never have heard the name before she started working there, but she quickly came to understand that it was one of the most esteemed luxury brands in all of Italy, with film stars such as Ava Gardner, Joan Crawford, Kirk Douglas, and Clark Gable frequently passing through its doors. The queen of England had even been a customer; as a fresh-faced princess, she had dropped into the Florence store. With a lady-in-waiting in tow, the young British royal was served personally by Dr. Gucci's father and apparently told him, "There is nothing quite like this in London!"

Before long, it was my mother's turn to take to the shop floor, an event she regarded with as much trepidation as a model regards her first step on the runway. Although she made mistakes at first, she quickly endeared herself to staff and customers with her demure manner and sweet smile. When I look at photographs of her back then I can see why—she was stunning and her presence must have caused quite a stir. One Iranian diplomat apparently took such a shine to her that he became one of the shop's most frequent visitors and informed her that, with her dark hair and porcelain skin, she had "the complexion of a Persian beauty."

Back home, she told my grandmother that working at Gucci was a dream come true, adding gleefully, "Every day there I feel like I'm in a movie!" As her confidence grew, she mimicked the more experienced girls and began to engage customers in conversation.

My father, whom she knew only as "Dr. Gucci," came and went—always at a breakneck pace. He worked at least six days a week and flew around the globe in what seemed like a punishing schedule. Papà didn't even pause for the month of August—a long-standing Italian tradition. While the majority of Romans left the city to relax by the sea or in the cooler climates of the mountains, he remained at work, complaining that the rest of his countrymen were *fannulloni,* or "layabouts."

His fedora hat firmly on his head, a leather attaché case under his arm, my father sprinted from place to place but never failed to scrutinize everything as he passed through his stores. In a manner I have witnessed many times myself, he'd spark a tremor of fear among his staff whenever he stopped to adjust the slightest misalignment or check that a surface was gleaming. Every now and again, he'd lose his temper and flare up, bawling out some poor underling who'd been sloppy with a display or dared leave a fingerprint on glass.

"Are you blind?" he'd shout. "Have you learned nothing here?" My mother told me that, before he mellowed with age, my father could be formidable. "He was like an earthquake. You could hear his voice throughout the store. People would quiver in their shoes!" She wondered at his outbursts but had been quite accustomed to them with my grandfather so she bit her lip and prayed never to be on the sharp end of his tongue.

The moment a potential customer walked through the door, though, it was as if a veil had lifted and my father once again became the epitome of charm. Always willing to engage with those who appreciated what Gucci stood for, he'd shepherd them toward his latest creations. He left the mesmerized men and women in no doubt that—for a few moments at least—they were at the center of his world. "That man could sell his own mother to the Bedouins," Mamma told my grandmother when she got home. "It's incredible to see him in action."

What she didn't realize was that my father was also watching her. Although he was hard on others, he was uncharacteristically gentle with her. Every time he saw her, he'd call out in his distinctive Tuscan accent, *"Ciao, Nina!"* endearingly using the tail-end of his nickname for her—Brunina. Sometimes he'd stop to see what she was doing or lift his fedora to greet her and ask how she was getting along.

Happy in her work, Mamma blossomed both as a young woman and as a member of the sales force. With her own money and a growing sense of her own worth, she found Pietro's controlling nature increasingly irritating, especially when he started warning her not to become "over friendly" with the customers. His insinuation angered her. She always behaved properly both in and out of the store and had never done anything untoward. After four (celibate) years together, surely she could be trusted! Their increasingly bitter arguments often ended with her dramatically calling off their engagement. Other times, she'd tearfully slip his ring from her finger and put it in the shoe box along with the nest egg they'd saved for a future she no longer wanted.

She didn't even have anyone to talk to about her concerns, as her best friend, Maria-Grazia, had moved to America for love, and she missed their conspiratorial times together. A salesgirl named Lucia was friendly but they weren't yet close enough to discuss affairs of the heart. Then one day, somebody walked into my mother's life who was to become her dearest friend.

She was at the counter when she first spotted the handsome young man with dark hair in a very British-looking plaid duffel coat loitering outside the store. She stepped outside to ask if she could help. His name was Nicola Minelli; he had experience with retail in London and had recently returned to Rome. "I'd so *love* to work here," he said with a mischievous smile that Mamma and I would come to know only too well. "Who should I approach about applying for a job?" Nicola spoke fluent English and had a certain flair about him. My mother was immediately impressed. She suspected from the start that he wasn't interested in her, or any woman for that matter, and she was right. She invited him in and then let my father know that there was a presentable young man downstairs looking for work. She was told to send him up. Soon afterward, Nicola appeared in front of her beaming with gratitude. He would start the following week.

Nicola was a godsend for Mamma—and ultimately for me too. With his wicked sense of humor, his shop-floor gossip reduced my mother to fits of giggles. "See that man over there? He thinks that buying a woman the most expensive bag will make her love him. With a face like that, she'll be gone as soon as she gets it!" It felt good to laugh again. There hadn't been much of that in my mother's relationship with Pietro lately.

My father, meanwhile, continued to take an interest in his youngest salesgirl and one day, having stopped to see how she was faring, he suddenly reached out and stroked her cheek with the back of his hand. It was a spontaneous, affectionate gesture and one that made her blush, but she didn't shy away. In fact, when he next came down to the shop floor on his way out to another meeting, her eyes found his and they locked for a moment in a way they never had before. He held her gaze and then he left.

In December 1957, the staff was told by Laurent that a special customer would be making an appearance. Dr. Gucci was abroad but his wife, Olwen, was traveling the short distance from her home at Villa Camilluccia in the district of Monte Mario, one of the seven hills of Rome, to select some Christmas gifts for her English family and friends. Like everyone else who worked in the shop, Mamma was curious to see what the boss's wife looked like. She was pleasantly surprised by the unassuming middle-aged Englishwoman, who seemed almost abashed by the attention everyone paid her. She didn't personally serve Signora Gucci but said later that she seemed like "a wonderful lady" and "extremely nice."

One day in the early part of 1958 my mother was summoned to my father's office and was immediately alarmed. "I worried that I'd done something wrong," she told me. With great trepidation, she knocked on his door and found him sitting alone behind his desk. Alarmingly, his secretary was not in her customary position in the corner, as if he wanted a quiet word.

He quickly put my mother at ease by telling her, "Ah, Bruna, my secretary Maria is getting married and will be leaving soon. I need to replace her and Laurent mentioned you trained as a stenographer, no?" She nodded. With that unnervingly beguiling smile of his, my father assured her that she'd be perfect to take up the position and could start the next day. He gave her no option but to accept.

My mother, who was twenty years old and had worked in the store for a little over a year, rushed home that night to tell my grandmother the good news. "It will be greater responsibility and more money," she assured her. "I think I have the skill set and I am sure I can learn a great deal from Dr. Gucci."

She needn't have worried that she wouldn't be up to the job. As soon as she sat at her narrow desk against the wall with its telephone, Olivetti stenotype, and narrow spools of paper, all that she'd learned in her course came flooding back. Sitting to one side of "Dr. Gucci," she typed whatever he dictated. These were mostly reprimanding letters to the factory or to managers he didn't feel were doing a good enough job. There were more considered missives to lawyers and banks, and many curt notes to his brothers or to his three sons—usually to berate them for missing a delivery deadline or overstocking raw materials. She noted that his letters to his family were always brisk and businesslike and that he never added anything warm or personal.

She also came to understand that Papà was a man of routine who only stopped work for *un caffè* or lunch. He kept himself busy from dawn 'til dusk, but every time she looked up, she'd catch him gazing at her in a "gentle but special way." She added, "I was very shy at the time and I didn't know what to do." His glances, she said, weren't overtly sexual; it was more as if she entranced him somehow. Whenever his scrutiny became too intense, though, she'd find an excuse to leave the room and take a breather. "I had never received this kind of attention before and I just couldn't concentrate on anything."

In time, it became apparent that she hadn't just been chosen for her stenography skills and she began to feel uncomfortable about where this might lead. Having prided herself on efficiency, she was upset when her work suffered and many of the letters she typed needed correcting, but my father didn't seem to mind a bit.

My mother desperately wanted to keep her job but was wary of his glances. Nevertheless, she found herself arriving for work earlier and taking even greater care with her appearance. Pietro didn't like that and became unreasonably possessive, which only sparked more rows. Before long, my father began to notice how often my mother wasn't wearing her engagement ring, which secretly amused him, for he believed it showed his shy little "*Nina*" had some spirit after all. In time, he came to regard that ring as a temperature gauge for how her relationship with her fiancé was faring.

The first gift my father left for Mamma on her desk after a trip to Florence was a bottle of perfume. More presents soon followed—silk scarves, cashmere sweater sets, the kinds of luxury items she would have loved to own but couldn't possibly afford.

"I cannot accept these, *dottore*," she told him politely. "It wouldn't be proper." She also knew that there would be too many questions if she ever took them home.

Flirting outrageously, my father teased her and refused to take them back. With a sigh, she began to stack them in a cupboard in his office where she hoped no one would find them. Before too long, that little cupboard was crammed full with one little package after another—a veritable treasure trove of my father's growing affection. It became like a game to him. He'd bring her something home from every trip and then wait for her to decline it.

As the sexual tension mounted, they accidentally bumped into each other one day while she was opening the mail by his desk. Taking her by the elbows to steady her, he suddenly pulled her toward him and kissed her passionately on the lips.

"There was," she told me, "a strange but not unpleasant feeling that I'd never felt before—not with Pietro anyway." Caught unawares however, she dropped her bundle of letters, then stepped back and cried, "No, *dottore*! What are you doing?"

"*Mi fai soffrire! Mi fai sudare!*" Papà announced boldly. (You make me suffer! You make me sweat!)

Mortified, she ran from his office. As she splashed cold water on her face in the ladies' room, she looked at her reflection in the mirror and touched her mouth with her fingertips. "I didn't know what the kiss meant. What if anybody had walked in on us? Would Dr. Gucci dismiss me for not kissing him back?"

She felt terrified and exhilarated all at once—an unwelcome mix of emotions in one so young. Smoothing down her dress and straightening her hair, she took a deep breath before she opened the bathroom door and headed back along the corridor.

As she turned the handle and stepped inside to resume her secretarial duties, she sensed instinctively that nothing would ever be the same again.

SIX

*E*ven though I was raised in a Catholic family it still aston-
ishes me to think that the year my father first kissed my
mother, adultery carried a prison sentence under Italian law.

Infidelity may have been quietly accepted as an integral part
of the male psyche (especially in a country that forbade divorce),
but it still had to be hidden. If any indiscretions ever came to the
attention of the general public, then they often became a matter of
high drama, pored over in the tabloid press.

A few years earlier, news had leaked out that the married
Swedish actress Ingrid Bergman was having an affair with the married Italian film director Roberto Rossellini and had borne him a
child. The scandal that ensued led to Bergman's denunciation by
the US Senate as "an instrument of evil" and banned her from
many public appearances. Rossellini too fell out of favor and when
Bergman fled to Italy to be with her older lover—and gave him
two more children—details of their respective divorces became
the stuff of tabloid legend, which haunted them both for years.

In a similar scandal, Fausto Coppi, one of the most idolized names in Italian sport, was the subject of public opprobrium because of his affair with a married mother of two. Coppi, who was known as "Il Campionissimo" (the Hero) after winning the Giro d'Italia and the Tour de France cycling races in the same year, was dragged out of bed along with his mistress, although only she—not he—would end up in prison.

Even the Vatican became involved, publicly criticizing Coppi and orchestrating attempts to repair his marriage if only for the sake of his child. When he was tried for adultery in 1955 and the couple's children were summoned as witnesses in court, Coppi was Campionissimo no more. The guilty parties were sentenced to two- and three-month prison sentences, though these were later suspended.

Aside from her own high moral principles, my mother was only too aware that her boss was a public figure and that his feelings for his youngest member of staff would not only be condemned but widely publicized if they ever came to light. His persistent wooing was endangering them both, a dilemma that occupied her night and day.

She was spooked from the moment he kissed her, something my father must have sensed. Her body language became tense to the point of rigidity, there were no more conspiratorial smiles, and she avoided eye contact and any physical proximity. He couldn't get her out of his head, though. At fifty-three years of age and feeling trapped, he was no stranger to infidelity, but this time it was different. He had fallen hard for a woman young enough to be his daughter. It was an infatuation that ran bone deep and one that he seemed unable to fight even though he was aware of what he was risking—for him and for her.

Disappointed with her response, he left Rome on one of his business trips and tried not to let the distance between them torment him. Thankfully, by 1958 he was able to take advantage of the new jet age, which changed intercontinental travel for good, making the rest of the world accessible within a single day. Never seeming to tire, Papà was one of the first passengers to travel to New York nonstop, using the first commercial flights such as BOAC's de Havilland Comet and Pan Am's Boeing 707. These suddenly shaved an astonishing nine hours off transatlantic crossings. Jet travel also offered the ultimate in luxury, with fine food and wines and even a chance for him to smoke his pipe or enjoy one of his Toscanello cigars.

Sales were going well at the East Fifty-Eighth Street store but international communication was cumbersome and my father knew he had to keep on top of things. Being the perfectionist he was, he couldn't rely on telegrams or echoing long-distance calls and had to keep checking on the Manhattan store himself, even if his travels kept him away from the object of his desire.

A month after their kiss, he returned to Rome and hurried to the office to tell my mother half under his breath, "I *have* to speak with you." When she ignored him, he left a handwritten note on her desk demanding that she meet him that evening at six o'clock in the Parioli Quarter. It was an upscale residential neighborhood northeast of the city, where, as the secretary in charge of all his paperwork, she knew only too well that he also kept a bachelor pad, known as a *garçonnière*. What he used it for she'd tried not to imagine—until now.

As the hour approached, and having told my grandmother and Pietro that she had to work late, she was filled with dread about where their secret rendezvous might lead. By the time she stepped out of the taxi that took her to Piazzale delle Belle Arti and spotted my father's green Jaguar Mark 1, she felt physically unwell. "When I got into his car I was so afraid that somebody might spot us that I was trembling. Your father saw and he told me to calm down."

Taking her hand in his, he told her again how fond he'd become of her and then he stroked her cheek. Still shivering in her seat, she reminded him once more that his feelings weren't reciprocated. As he moved closer, her eyes darted left and right and she broke into a sweat. "Don't worry, Bruna, I won't bite!" he said, laughing, before leaning over and kissing her full on the mouth.

Mamma responded at first, confirming my father's conviction that she, too, felt the chemistry between them. Then she suddenly pulled away, and on the brink of tears, she demanded to be taken home. When he dropped her in an alleyway not far from her apartment, she fled from his car without saying a word, her heart "beating like crazy." She was, she said, "confused and upset, and still so very afraid."

My father's heart was also beating fast, but in triumph. His coy little "*Nina*" had kissed him back!

Mamma barely slept that night and dreaded going into work the next morning. Unable to confide in anyone, not even my grandmother, she had no choice but to show up as usual but then found any excuse to leave the office to deliver something to the shop floor or stockroom. Even though she'd done nothing wrong, the strain of keeping what she thought of as her "dirty little secret" began to make her sick. She lost weight and couldn't sleep. Before long, those closest to her, especially Pietro and my grandmother, noticed a change.

My father wasn't a man who took no for an answer. Nor was he someone who liked to wait. He quickly planned a second outing with my mother, this time in the company of Vilma—his most devoted and longest-serving member of staff. My father assured Mamma that a chaperone would put her more at ease and that everyone would assume these outings were nothing more than ordinary business dinners.

My mother felt she had to accept but insisted that the dinner be on a night when Pietro was out of town. The Antica Pesa restaurant was in an old customs house in the bohemian district of Trastevere. I have been there a few times, if only to imagine my parents meeting there during this tricky phase of their courtship. My mother paints an unhappy image of them arriving together and says she trailed miserably behind when they were led to a table at the far end of the terrace. Even after they were seated she was so worried that she'd be spotted that she barely ate a morsel.

Papà was the consummate host. Laughing and telling tales, his eyes twinkling in the candlelight, he regaled her with stories of his travels, describing what it was like to fly four thousand miles across the Atlantic in a jet. "You can't believe the luxury, Bruna!" he told her. "They have such comfortable seats and stewardesses in smart uniforms serve martinis and gourmet dinners. You'd love it." The implication was always that—one day—she would accompany him. He went on to speak glowingly of New York with its supersized buildings and refreshingly honest people whose lives and enterprises were unaffected by the kind of political constraints he faced in Italy. He raved about the city's buzz and bustle, and told her how much she'd enjoy the freedom America offered.

Softened by alcohol and ambience, my mother began to relax, and—little by little—she came out of her shell. Sipping *prosecco,* she began to show my father the inner lighthearted side he'd always suspected she was hiding from him. "There was a woman in the store today who had a coat that perfectly matched her poodle," she confided. "It was all we could do not to laugh!" Those early glimpses of the mischievous, giggling girl typical of her age only made him adore her even more.

And so the courtship continued, albeit against my mother's wishes. Her only respite came when my father went away and she had a few weeks' peace. Or so she thought. Sifting through the mail one morning she came across an envelope from New York addressed to her. She recognized my father's handwriting and immediately suspected what it was. Afraid to open it in the office in case someone walked in unannounced, she hurriedly tucked it into the waistband of her skirt. It wasn't until later that evening when she was sitting alone in the back of the bus home that she reached for the first of his secret love notes, slid it open with her finger, and began to read.

Papà's words—and the strength of feeling they conveyed—stunned her.

> *Bruna my dear,*
>
> *It's the third time I put pen to paper, having destroyed the first two letters. I promised myself I would express just how strongly I feel the need to communicate with you, to tell you what I am feeling at all times, the tiny pleasures, the immense pain!!! It's all due to this insatiable desire to love you and the endless suffering of our secret that I ask your forgiveness and permission to love you, forever, before I am overcome by sorrow and delirious with grief.*
>
> *My sweet Brunicchi, I hope you don't think I'm exaggerating. I am just madly in love with you! As far as I am concerned, so long as I have the certainty of your affection and feel that I shall never lose you, I consider you my one big love; I swear I will do anything you ask! We don't have to go out. I won't torment you, nor will I do anything to agonize or embarrass you, all I ask is that you love me as if our hearts belonged to one another and our souls were fused into one, like an*

eternal embrace. I love you Bruna, I really, really
love you and I will not stop telling you because
it is the truth, above and beyond everything and
everybody. —xxxx A.

In these modern times of hasty emails and instant messaging, no man has ever written me a letter like that, sadly. What must it have felt like for my mother to hold that flimsy piece of paper in her hand and appreciate the weight it carried? She told me later, "It was incredible. I felt I was important."

No one had ever laid himself so bare to her. His use of language and sweeping declarations of love struck a deep chord. She had to pinch herself to believe this was from Dottor Gucci—a man of stature and the living epitome of style and grace. A successful entrepreneur, he was equally at ease with royalty as he was with a man in the street. Now here he was pouring out his soul to "an innocent creature" just out of her teens and from a modest background. How was that even possible?

She sat stock-still in her seat for several minutes staring out of the window at passing street scenes. Dazed, she watched mothers shepherding young children and old people struggling through the rush-hour crowds. She saw couples walking hand in hand, openly showing their affection for each other. She said to me, "I remember thinking that not one of them was worried about the consequences, like me."

In *Roman Holiday*, one of the most popular movies of the era, which Mamma had seen with Pietro and watched with me many times years later, the unhappy princess played by Audrey Hepburn falls for the mere mortal—a reporter played by Gregory Peck. Yet even in such a Hollywood fantasy the two lovers couldn't be together. After a magical time together they are forced to part, brokenhearted. My mother couldn't help but think back to the ending, which always moved her to tears, and wonder what possible hope of happiness she could have with a man like Papà. "I assumed that was how it would be for your father and me, too," she said. "The whole thing seemed so impossible."

Sliding the letter into its flimsy envelope and slipping it back inside her clothing, she tried not to dwell on the tenderness it conveyed or the passion it barely concealed. My father's words were etched on her heart but after she'd finished reading them she had to decide whether to keep it as an enduring token of his affection or burn it—as she was tempted to. When she reached home, she hurried straight to her bedroom and secreted it at the bottom of the shoe box under her chest of drawers—underneath the dowry for her future with Pietro. She would never allow herself to look at my father's handwriting again for fear of the emotions it might stir within her. Nor would she even mention to him that she had received it, choosing the path of least resistance.

If she'd hoped that his letter would be the last, then she'd underestimated how obsessed he'd become. Having found a fresh outlet for his feelings and one in which he could reveal them to her without being contradicted or interrupted, my father took pen to paper again and again. He prayed that the avalanche of mail he'd send her would eventually serve its purpose and sweep my mother off her feet. It worked.

She was flattered not only by his attention but also by his unconcealed jealousy about the time she spent with Pietro—someone Papà only ever referred to as "*him*." This intense rivalry made her realize that, crazy as it might seem, there was a possible alternative to marrying the man she seemed inexorably bound to for life. Furthermore, my father insisted that if she married Pietro, she would be throwing away her chance for happiness and opportunity. "*I want you to know how beautiful everything is here*," he wrote her from his suite at the Savoy-Plaza in Manhattan. "*The hotel [and] this dream of a room. New York really is the high life; it's what I often talk to you about—how wonderful it is to live like this!"* He added poignantly, *"The lovelier the frame, the more I feel the absence of a beautiful painting."*

His words planted a seed in the mind of a young woman who'd known nothing but shortage throughout her childhood, beginning with a scarcity of love from everyone but my grandmother. She didn't imagine that she would ever visit somewhere like New York or experience the life my father was talking about. He probably represented her only chance to see more of the world.

In another letter, Papà tried to frighten my mother by suggesting that if she kept turning him down he might be forced to give up his pursuit of her. He wrote, *"I have tried in vain to make you see the light but my advances will come to nothing if your intention is to seal your love with him and throw away your future in the process . . . Any other miserable soul would have given up long ago faced with such circumstances."*

He repeatedly spoke of *"the burning and spontaneous calling"* of his *"aching heart"* and of the waste of not seeing what he called their *"beautiful and sublime love"* come to something. He said in another note (written at three a.m. when he couldn't sleep for thinking of her), *"[It is] as though the air I breathe is no longer the same as when you are there."* He wrote frequently of his internal *"agony"* and the *"torture"* of not being with her. *"Love me, Bruna. I pray that you love me more and more and that you will consider me worthy of your affection . . . of the desire of our souls to be together and to grow into something undeniably wonderful . . . indelible for the rest of our lives. . . . Allow me to love you forever. I swear you will not regret it—I will prove it to you with each passing day."*

His time away from my mother began to weigh heavily on him and Sundays were the worst. Wherever he was in the world, the offices would be closed, there would be no one to berate, and instead of improving on trade, his employees would be indulging in the kind of personal time he hadn't regularly enjoyed with his family in years. Those were idle, wasted days, he always thought, especially in Rome. Left to his own devices, he'd lunch with Olwen, their sons, and their sons' families at Villa Camilluccia. Elsewhere, he'd don his fedora and wander aimlessly around the streets, imagining my mother with Pietro. Was she holding his hand as they strolled somewhere together? Was she locked in his embrace and kissing his lips? *"How I envy him!"* he wrote, adding that the very thought pained his heart.

On another Sunday he wrote again to his beloved from abroad. *"I want to know everything you've been up to and where you've been . . . what were you up to, I ask myself . . . I want you to know how much I love you and how terribly I suffer from this."*

As soon as he was back on European soil he'd send a telegram or—more daringly—call her at home. Pretending that he needed to speak to his secretary on an urgent business matter, he'd apologize politely to my grandmother or uncle Franco so as not to arouse their suspicions. Standing awkwardly by the telephone as they half listened in, my mother could only answer, *"Sì, dottore,"* or "No," to his barrage of questions about how soon he could see her again. These brief monosyllabic exchanges were deeply unsatisfactory for him and only served to panic her more.

On a train back from Florence, Papà wrote, *"Tomorrow morning I will rush to the office . . . It couldn't possibly be business that arouses such passion; it's the burning desire to see a . . . jewel— the essence of virtue, form and grace with such gorgeous eyes and a penetrating expression that does little more than glance at me before turning away because she insists it's all in vain."*

As soon as he could, and on any pretext, he'd try to snatch time alone with her, begging for "just five minutes of kindness."

On good days he'd take her for lunch to Ristorante Alfredo on Via della Scrofa, famous for its eponymous fettuccine. Once at their table he'd whisper again how much he loved her and longed to be alone with her. He affectionately called her *Nina,* or Nicchi (short for Brunicchi).

Beguiled by his charm, seduced by his letters, and entranced by the places he took her to, she agreed to start accompanying him without Vilma, and safe from prying ears, her resistance weakened.

"I love you, Bruna," my father sighed one day, his hand tantalizingly close to hers across the tablecloth. She could almost feel the electricity. "Don't you see that we were meant for each other?"

Lifting her eyes from the table, she whispered, "And I love you, Aldo," as she watched his face shine with joy.

The next letter he sent spoke of how the *"unrelenting weight on his heart"* had been lifted and how by choosing to ignore the *"harsh reality"* they faced, he was suddenly overcome by *"explosive sensations . . . of love and loyalty."* He added, *"How glorious it is to love you, my adorable Bruna . . . I am wildly in love with you."* He assured her that now he knew her true feelings for him, they *"owed it to each other"* not to rush into anything and *"drown"* their love. *"You are so young and beautiful and your sacrifice is no doubt greater than mine . . . I know our destiny is to be together . . . You have conquered my heart and I belong to you."*

As she read his words, a seed was planted from which would grow their destiny—and, eventually, mine.

SEVEN

I'm sure we can all remember those heady days when we first fell in love with someone and our thoughts about them consumed each waking moment. I know I've certainly felt that way more times than I care to recall.

My parents were no different, it seemed. Papà had clearly been smitten for a while but my mother now began to look forward to their romantic encounters with just as much excitement. Laughing at his jokes, half leaning against his shoulder as he murmured affectionately to her over dinner and wine, she relished the experience of feeling cherished and adored without any of Pietro's brooding undercurrents.

"I was Alice in Wonderland," Mamma told me, daring to believe that even though their love was "shrouded in secrecy" it offered the chance of a different life. Sadly, her happiness was colored by her growing anxiety that their relationship was ultimately doomed, coupled with her constant fear of being discovered—especially by Pietro. That very nearly happened one Friday when her fiancé was out of town but called the house shortly after her brother's nine p.m. curfew only to discover that she wasn't home. The following morning, when he arrived to pick her up he seemed preoccupied and told her he'd have to stop by his house before going out for the day. Once there, he locked her in the garage and hovered over her, demanding to know where she'd been the previous night.

Trembling with fear and stammering a reply, she claimed she'd been to a local pizzeria with a friend but quickly realized her mistake when he reminded her that it was closed. My mother had never seen Pietro so incensed as he grabbed her by the arm, demanding to know who the "friend" was and threatening that she would never leave there alive unless she told him the truth.

"It was Vilma, the lady I work with!" she cried. "When we found the restaurant closed we went for a dress fitting instead. I swear! I swear on my father's grave!" When he insisted that she take him to Vilma, she begged him not to embarrass her. At one point, when he put her in the car to drive her there, she tried to run but he grabbed her and dragged her back. "I was terrified."

It took several minutes to calm him down, but once she did he gave her an ultimatum. "We're getting married!" he declared. "Pick a date in October, sometime around your twenty-first birthday. I've waited long enough." That was less than three months away. It meant that by the end of 1958—the most tumultuous year of my mother's life—she was destined to become Pietro's lawfully wedded wife.

Afraid of how he might react if she refused, she reluctantly agreed. "What else could I do?" she told me. A year earlier, she'd accepted his marriage proposal and she knew that keeping her pledge was the only honorable thing to do. The time had come to put an end to the madness of her dalliance with my father. She was lucky it hadn't gone too far.

The dread of having to break the news to Papà almost gave

her a nervous breakdown, however. Debating in her mind all the reasons why she should end their affair, she played a game of devil's advocate I was to become all too familiar with, toying endlessly with the pros and cons. After all, if Dr. Gucci was the kind of man to betray his wife, then surely he'd cheat on her too eventually. And if they did choose to be together and were discovered, they might both end up in jail, forever shamed.

With so many conflicting thoughts racing around inside her head, she could hardly sleep once more. In a pattern of disturbed nights I so often witnessed, her dreams were only further tormented by her fears and she would wake, shivering and afraid, unable to share the cause of her nighttime terrors with anyone.

Papà sensed something new was troubling her and tried to reach out once more. He wrote to her in the early hours of the morning after one disastrous dinner during which she'd hardly said a word. His letter was lying on her desk the following morning as he headed back across the Atlantic.

> It's only been a few hours since I wished you good
> night. . . . [Y]ou turned and were on your way like
> a stranger in the night, as if our hearts had never
> touched. My precious treasure, how agonizing this
> is, what a torture! I know you love me. I know
> it because you told me so and it made me so
> indescribably happy, filling my soul with joy, that's
> why I understand your trepidation and I feel the
> distress in the mute language of a loving heart . . .

She had to wait an agonizing month for my father's return and then she plucked up the courage to tell him that his feelings for her were "preposterous" and that they had to stop seeing each other. Distraught, he asked her what had changed and so she told him of her fiancé's fury. After reiterating that their relationship was immoral, illegal, and ultimately impossible, she announced, "I'm marrying Pietro in October," before hurrying from the room.

Unable to reach her by any other means, my father flooded her with another wave of letters to try to keep her close—in spirit at least. In them he implored her *"not to let the curtain fall on [them] so soon."* He warned her that she was settling for a future that would deprive her *"of the fundamental ingredient of happiness"* and that she had to carefully consider the drawbacks. He was, he told her, miserable and *"alone in a storm,"* determined to *"fight for a life worth living."* He assured her that their future together was not as impossible as she imagined, especially with *"the means at [his] disposal."* Without her company he would return to his villa—*"a cold, empty castle, deprived of the oxygen and the atmosphere to enable [him] to breathe."*

He concluded, dramatically, *"I solemnly swear before God that if my soul is denied the opportunity of spiritual growth then I shall become cynical, mean and ruthless . . . I never will be able to erase you from my heart."*

Secretly, she loved his romantic overtures and relished each amorous note she pored over on her bus ride home. Once she read it, she'd fold it carefully and place it inside her blouse, close to her heart. Whichever path she chose, she knew she would always have his beautiful, if unanswered, letters.

Each time she spurned his advances and reminded him of her ongoing wedding preparations, he'd write her another note, the tone of which became increasingly desperate. He even tried to shock her into being with him by not communicating with her at all but this truce lasted precisely ten days. His desperation was such that my mother feared he might even turn up at her wedding to create a scene. Before either of them faced that day, though, he made a final attempt to convince her to be with him, while there was still time.

> *Forgive me if, despite my promise not to revisit this argument, I express once more just how important it is for me to put pen to paper . . . I love you Bruna, I love you in a way you may not yet understand. . . . What we have is a gift from God. . . . You must reflect very carefully . . . this is an important decision, think it over, do not commit, put everything on hold, this is critical, Bruna, critical.*

This time, something he said hit home. As October loomed and doubts continued to crowd her head, she knew that her marriage to Pietro could lead to a lifetime of regret. Hadn't her mother already warned her that she'd be back home in three days? Was choosing to be with the man she loved any worse than marrying a man she did not? My father cited his own experience, having spent the best part of his life in a marriage that had only come about because of what he called "an error of judgment" made in his youth.

He wrote to her somewhat bitterly, "*Happiness is a spiritual blessing that one does not necessarily find in marriage. It is up to us to recognize and interpret this divine gift. Everything else is nothing more than compromised, often bitter coexistence, which can be depressing to the point of eradicating love altogether. I know this from personal experience. . . . I gave in to social pressure without first consulting my heart. That vital source which feeds our hearts is all dried up in me now. How difficult it is to live this way, how sad! Sometimes, material wealth can compensate . . . but not always, indeed, hardly ever."*

That summer Papà threw a party for his staff at home while his wife was away visiting her family. "You must come," he urged my mother. "It will be a fun evening. Everyone else will be there. It will look strange if you don't."

She'd never been anywhere like Villa Camilluccia. Accompanied by Nicola, Lucia, and other colleagues, all in cocktail dresses or suits, she wandered openmouthed around the gardens, marveling at the grandeur of it all. "It was one of the best nights of my life," she told me. "There was a live band and white-coated waiters serving champagne, canapés, and cocktails by the pool." Guests danced under colored lights to popular songs such as "Nel blu dipinto di blu" and "'A tazza 'e café." Huge platters of hors d'oeuvres were laid out on tables spread with white linen and decorated with flowers.

Toward the end of the evening, my father went up onto the dance floor, stopped the music, took the microphone, and delivered a fine speech about how far Gucci had come since its early days. "With your help, we can take this company still further and ensure a great future for us all." It was a rousing, rallying call and everyone applauded as my mother stood in the center of the crowd proudly watching the man she wasn't sure she could give up.

The next morning there was a small package waiting on her desk. Inside was a cassette with an accompanying note explaining that it was a selection of the music from the party as well as a recording of my father's speech. She couldn't wait to get home and listen to it again on her brother's tape recorder. Once she'd established that the cassette didn't contain any compromising messages, she played it excitedly to my grandmother as my uncle Franco sat idly by.

A few days later, my father telephoned my mother at home from his hotel in New York. He was eager to tell her how much he longed to see her again. My mother listened in silence and then told him, "I have to go now, *dottore*. It's getting late."

"Ah, you're going to bed," he sighed. "I'm jealous. Soon you will be in the arms of Morpheus."

Neither of them was aware that there was a crossed line and that Franco—who'd telephoned the house to bid my grandmother good night—had accidentally dropped into their conversation and was listening in. He immediately recognized the voice with the Tuscan accent as the man on Mamma's tape and knew then that there was something going on between his little sister and her boss.

If it wasn't for the presence of my grandmother in the apartment the following morning, I am convinced from the account of what happened next that my uncle Franco might well have beaten my mother senseless. I only ever met Franco once (and all I remember is that he was fat), but from what I have heard I imagine him to have been much like my grandfather Alfredo—moody and unpredictable. The concept of family honor has been a tenet in Italian families since long before Romeo and Juliet, but it is still hard to imagine that it could lead to physical punishment.

Having arrived home from his shift, the young man who regarded himself as head of the family and protector of his sister's virtue bolted the front door and then made a beeline for her room. *"Puttana!"* he cried, calling her a whore, and slapped her repeatedly. She fell to the floor under the rain of blows but still he continued until my grandmother burst in and pushed her way between them, screaming at her son to stop.

"Franco! No! You'll kill her!"

Sensing that he may have gone too far, my uncle reined himself in as my grandmother knelt on the floor next to Mamma, who had protectively curled up into a ball. Standing over her shaking with fury, Franco accused her of bringing shame on the family. "She's engaged!" he yelled. "Yet she's messing around behind Pietro's back!" Seeing that my grandmother wasn't listening, he warned Mamma, "Now, I will teach that Dr. Gucci of yours a lesson he'll remember. I'll kill him!" before storming out.

My mother was in bad shape, with a bruised face and a split lip. Her left eye was already starting to swell. Sobbing, she tried to explain herself, but my grandmother urged her not to speak. Helping her to her feet, she supported her weight as she hobbled to the kitchen, where she could tend to her wounds.

In spite of her injuries, my mother's only concern was for Papà. She had visions of my uncle Franco bursting into the store or attacking him on the street and insisted that she be allowed to call the shop and warn him. Only then did she take to her bed, where she remained covered in bruises for a week.

When Franco eventually returned to the apartment a few hours later with no indication of where he'd been, my grandmother was assured that he hadn't visited Gucci after all. A few hours later the telephone rang and Delia was surprised to hear the voice on the end of the line.

"This is Aldo Gucci," my father announced coolly. "I would like to speak to Franco Palombo, please."

As my mother lay in bed holding her breath she heard her brother take the call and agree to meet Papà outside the Mediterraneo Hotel on Via Cavour. A few minutes later he left the apartment, slamming the door behind him. My father told her later that when they met, Franco's bravura dropped away the moment he came face-to-face with the distinguished gentleman in his fedora sitting in a Jaguar. Instead of "teaching him a lesson" as he'd threatened, Franco meekly accepted his invitation to sit in the passenger seat.

Turning on his legendary charm, my father assured my uncle that he'd got it all wrong. He added, "I am very fond of your sister and highly appreciative of her skills but I have the utmost respect for her and would never take advantage." Outwitted, Franco had no choice but to believe him. He even apologized to my mother when he got home.

She told her brother she forgave him, but she never did. Nor could she risk seeing my father again in secret. After Pietro's attack and Franco's assault, it was clear that if she and Papà were ever exposed the consequences would no longer just be morally and legally disastrous but—potentially—a matter of life and death.

By the time he tried to broach the subject of their love "one last time" she'd had enough. "You've created nothing but turmoil in my life!" she cried. "You are the cause of all my unhappiness. *Basta!* [Enough!]"

No, her love affair with Aldo Gucci was over, and the sooner he accepted that, the better it would be for everyone.

EIGHT

*M*y mother says that I can talk for England. She claims I've inherited my father's gift of communication and clever use of words in a way she never quite mastered.

"You're so eloquent, just like Aldo," she tells me. "You express yourself so well with a vocabulary that is impressive. If you'd been a lawyer, I honestly believe you could have convinced a jury of anyone's innocence!"

Like most daughters, I love it whenever she tells me that there's something about me that reminds her of my father, that I walk and talk like him and even look a little like him. It is a comfort to me now that he has gone. His command of language was certainly remarkable. With me he only ever spoke in English but with my mother it was always Italian. In whichever tongue, he was erudite, articulate, and quick-witted. Like me, he could turn a phrase to strike a chord or twist a heart.

His letters were undoubtedly what most impressed my mother at first. And in those pivotal days after Pietro insisted they set a date for their wedding, it was my father's words that would come to make all the difference.

From the Savoy Hotel in London, where the spark of Gucci was first ignited, he sat at his desk utterly dejected the day after their latest argument and wrote her perhaps his most serious letter of all.

> *Dear Bruna,*
>
> *Sadly I have come to the realization that yesterday was probably the last time we would discuss your predicament. While I do not want to make things worse than they already are, I must point out some serious flaws in your character that will hamper your development as a human being. It is plain to see that over the last twenty years, you have not truly understood the importance of self-respect and . . . the value of freedom of thought and freedom to make your own choices. . . . You have clearly been denied such principles and have allowed others to intimidate you and submit you to their will.*

He went on to remind her that her imminent twenty-first birthday would herald a *"bright new phase"* of womanhood and yet she was destined for a *"gray outlook"* as a servant to an egotistical man who needed to *"possess a woman without the kind of equality that makes relationships and life worth living."* It would be, he said, a *"humiliating course"* and *"tantamount to suicide."*

Perhaps it was that last dramatic expression that won her over—*tantamount to suicide.* A living death with a man she didn't love, someone who shared many of the same controlling personality traits as her late father. Or perhaps after Pietro's latest outburst it was the realization that Papà was indeed telling the truth. By contrast, my father was her "anchor," the one who adored her and who could give her a life beyond her wildest dreams. His letters had undoubtedly stirred something in her. They made her feel as if she was worth something for the first time in her life.

With these thoughts in mind, my mother came to an epiphany. She saw that Papà was right and that she needed to make a courageous decision. "I knew then what I had to do," she told me. "Even though I was still so afraid."

She decided to telephone Pietro rather than risk facing him in person, telling him coolly that their engagement was off. "I am not the wife for you," she told him. "Our characters will never get along. There is too much fighting and I'm tired of it." He'd heard it all before and didn't believe her for one minute—until she returned his savings, right down to the last *lira*, and the pearl ring that she'd never much liked. To her surprise, the young man she'd been tied to since she was fourteen years old mutely accepted her decision, spent their savings on a sports car, and moved to the Netherlands to start anew.

Mamma was on her own.

As if to mirror the turbulent events in her personal life, a few days after her birthday, Pius XII—the only Pope she'd ever known and the first to be born in Rome in over two hundred years—died at the age of eighty-two. After his near-twenty-year rule, the passing of the much-loved supreme pontiff shocked the nation. Following the announcement of his death from the papal summer residence of Castel Gandolfo, the capital was effectively closed. Nine days of official mourning were declared, with altars and buildings draped in purple. Hundreds of thousands of people lined the route of the papal cortege as Pius's funeral heralded the largest procession the city had ever seen.

Italians up and down the country gathered around their radios and television sets as they followed the latest developments from the Vatican, where a new pontiff had yet to be elected. With stores and offices closed and the city mourning for the Pope who'd stood by them during the war, there was little to do but sit at home and ponder. In normal circumstances my father would probably have flown to America, but having learned of my mother's momentous decision to leave Pietro, he chose to stay put.

It was during that extended period of public grief in an unusually warm October in 1958 when Papà invited her to meet him at his apartment. The lies she told my grandmother about where she was going only added to Mamma's growing sense of guilt as she jumped in a taxi and asked the driver to take her to the Parioli Quarter. She knew exactly what would happen when she got there. However nervous she may have been, she went anyway.

Papà was attentive and welcoming as he opened a bottle of wine while church bells echoed through the empty streets. The atmosphere between them was electric and her hand shook as she took the glass. To break the ice, he showed her around the apartment. "It lacked character, as if it was used for one purpose only," she told me later. Then he led her into the bedroom.

On that portentous day, my father took my mother's virginity, or as he euphemistically put it, "picked a rose without thorns." In four years with Pietro, she had preserved her chastity against all odds. Determined to remain pure until marriage, she had successfully fended off her fiancé each time he pounced. After such a tempestuous courtship and having finally chosen to be with my father, she appreciated that this time was different and she felt the weight of expectation on her shoulders.

"He was my first," she told me coyly. In her mind and in her heart, from that day forward she and my father were inextricably bound together—husband and wife in their hearts, if not by law.

For my mother, the experience proved both painful and

distressing. Afterward she felt dirty and sinful, especially on such a sacred day. The moment surely felt sacred for my father—albeit for different reasons—as he held her in his arms. Although he'd always admired her demure manner, he had been astonished to discover that she was a virgin, and the responsibility affected him deeply. He appreciated then that he'd taken something precious and, in turn, felt that she was "his forever." It was as if a switch had flicked in his head and his feelings for her had moved to a higher plane.

His Brunicchi was pure. She was his. He would never allow anyone to touch her.

To her enormous relief, my father's passion for her didn't wane. On the contrary, he inundated her with ever more fervent messages of love and tokens of affection. In the coming days, they met whenever they could—often in his apartment—and he never once gave her cause to question his devotion.

When he set off on one of his trips, he sent one telegram after the other continually declaring his love. She could be in no doubt of his ardor, and his stream of messages helped to appease any fears she might have had about what he got up to when he was abroad. As she still tried not to think too much about where their relationship would lead, her life unfolded in a way that she would never have imagined possible.

All seemed near perfect until the day in November 1958 when my twenty-one-year-old mother realized she was pregnant. It was only a month since the Pope had died. As the consequences of what this meant dawned on her, she began to unravel. The disgrace of having his baby would be devastating, and in the repressive climate that they lived in, the damage to their reputations would be irreparable.

In these enlightened times when a woman's right to choose is widely respected and abortion is no longer taboo, it is astonishing to think of the dreadful predicaments unmarried women faced in those days. Although abortion was legalized in Britain in 1967 and in the US in 1973, it wouldn't be legal in Italy until 1978. Even then, women were excommunicated from the Church for carrying out the operation. Prior to that, and in virtually every country, newspapers ran scaremongering stories about women who'd died having the operation illegally. Even today in Italy a high percentage of doctors refuse to perform the procedure on the grounds of conscientious objection.

What all this meant for my mother in Rome in 1958 was that if she'd chosen to get rid of the baby and had been reported to the authorities, she could have been sent to prison for up to five years. Papà might have been similarly incarcerated for fathering an illegitimate child. Mamma had already paid a heavy price for being with him but from that moment on this emotional debt was about to increase tenfold.

When she ended up losing the baby anyway she was almost relieved. Afterward, back at home, she was doubled up in bed with pelvic cramps and a rising fever from an infection. When my grandmother saw the state she was in, she put it down to food poisoning, and it was only when she went out that my mother was able to telephone a friend to get some help.

By the time she was reunited with my father several days later, she looked pale and exhausted as she described what she'd gone through. "It was terrible, Aldo," she sobbed. "I have never known pain like it." Breaking down completely, she added, "Why did this happen? What is to become of us? How can we ever be happy?"

He was so horrified that he kissed her repeatedly and promised everything would be all right. "Bruna, I will never allow you to suffer like that again," he assured her. In spite of his words, something inside my mother changed forever. My father had robbed her of her innocence in so many ways that she no longer recognized herself. Where was the sweet smiling *"Nina,"* the young woman who'd hoped for so much but now seemed locked into a relationship with no future?

Her sense of helplessness was compounded by the sudden reappearance in Rome of Pietro, who'd returned briefly from Holland. He looked more handsome than ever and when she accepted a ride in his little red MG convertible, driving through the streets of Rome without a care in the world, she realized how much she'd given up.

Full of emotion, she went to my father's apartment and told him, "I'm living a lie, Aldo. I can't take it anymore. This is not who I am. I should have stayed with Pietro and lived an honest life."

His response was so heartfelt that she didn't know what to say. Dropping to his knees and bursting into tears, my father told her that he couldn't face the prospect of a life without her. "I promise, Bruna, *farò di te una regina*" (I will make you a queen), he told her emphatically. "With you at my side I can conquer the world. Without you I am nothing."

Once again his colorful prose melted her heart. No one else loved her like he did. None other could express himself so beautifully. She knew that come what may, he'd protect her. Flattered as she'd been by Pietro and the brief fantasy of a carefree life, there was really only one man for her and his name was Aldo Gucci.

NINE

*H*aving an affair with a married man must surely be one of the more complicated and heartbreaking situations a woman can find herself in. Helplessly at the beck and call of a lover, she has to wait for him to slip away from family commitments to spend a few precious hours with her before he returns to his other life.

In Italy a mistress is referred to as *l'amante* and that is precisely what my mother became, although she'd be the first to say that my father was married more to his work than he ever was to his wife. It was the business that demanded most of his time and attention. "Gucci was the other woman," she told me. "It was always Gucci, Gucci, Gucci."

Meanwhile, she carried on working in the office from which he ran his growing empire but they would soon relocate to larger premises a few doors down at number 8 Via Condotti. Similarly, in New York, he acquired the space he'd had his eye on for some time at 694 Fifth Avenue, on the corner of East Fifty-Fifth Street.

The new store was in the prestigious Beaux Arts building that was also home to the St. Regis Hotel, sister to the Waldorf-Astoria.

Occasionally, he took my mother with him on trips, always careful to book separate rooms to avoid any unwelcome gossip. More frequently, he took her to lunch or dinner at their usual haunts, followed by evening trysts at his apartment. Young and in love, she accepted whatever time he could offer even though most of her friends were getting married to men their own age and starting families. Her life was on hold.

The irony was that although she hated the cloak-and-dagger nature of their relationship, she was never happier than in Papà's company. Nor did the age difference seem to be an issue. He was so charismatic and young at heart and had such boundless energy that the fact he was in his fifties didn't bother her in the least. Neither did she demand anything more from him, appreciating that he could never divorce. Not only was it legally impossible (divorce wasn't fully ratified in Italy until 1974), he and Olwen were parents and grandparents at the head of a family he'd spent years portraying as dynastic, noble, and beyond reproach. The scandal would have been unthinkable.

Long before my mother knew any different, if she ever worried about Olwen my father would reassure her that his wife had all she could possibly need. "She lives in a comfortable house, has a summer home in England and three boys who adore her. What more could she want?"

Similarly, he made sure that his sons, Giorgio, Paolo, and Roberto, were adequately provided for, even if it was clear to her that he rarely showed them any affection. Employed by the company and destined to take over one day, these young men were much nearer her age—between five and eleven years older than she and by then with seven children of their own. Giorgio lived and worked in Rome but the others were in Florence. My mother saw them occasionally when they visited the Via Condotti store, when she would nod and say, "*Buongiorno*," along with everyone else.

"I never gave them much thought," she said. "They were part of your father's life and I had nothing to do with them. He kept it that way—entirely separate—and never discussed them with me unless it was in connection with a business matter or a letter I had to type."

And so, almost a year into their affair, my mother had settled into the strange routine of her tangled love life. She woke each morning in her childhood bed, caught the bus to work, and spent her days in the office, seeing my father whenever she could. He made their affair seem so effortless after such an extensive chase that as long as she didn't fret about the future or worry too much about being found out, she could manage. Mamma had become reconciled to her strange new world. Or so she thought.

To renew his commitment and honoring a promise made to her after she had told him she'd have had a better life with Pietro, my father bought her a new apartment in the Balduina district of Rome, not far from Villa Camilluccia. With a huge terrace and several bedrooms and bathrooms, plus a smaller room for a maid, it was more than double the size of her family's apartment and was hers to do with as she pleased.

"He went and bought it for me without thinking twice, just like that!" she said. "I was amazed and it made me feel special, but really, it was too much."

Excited as she was about her new home, she knew that she'd then have to confess the truth to her mother. With my aunt Gabriella busy being a wife and mother and my uncle Franco relocated to Sardinia, there was only my grandmother left to lie to. She needn't have worried, though. My grandmother Delia was anything but foolish and had suspected for some time. "I've known all along," she told her daughter. "And I knew you wouldn't be happy with Pietro. The only question I have for you, Bruna, is—are you happy now?" When she saw her face light up as she was able to speak freely of the man she loved, she had her answer. Showing nothing but compassion and understanding, the woman I never had a chance to meet promised to keep my mother's secret.

When Mamma took Delia to view the Balduina apartment for the first time my grandmother was quite overwhelmed by the prospect of living in such a beautiful, airy place with so much space and light. "It was beyond my mother's wildest dreams," Mamma told me. "She wandered around feeling lost. She said being there would feel as alien as living on the moon. She knew then that I was in good hands and was happy that this was now my life."

It was certainly different from the somber atmosphere they had left behind at Via Manzoni. For propriety's sake, they decided to tell friends and family that, as a valued member of staff, Mamma had been offered the use of a manager's apartment at a discounted rate. It was behind those doors that my grandmother met Papà for the first time, and—much to my mother's relief—they liked each other immediately. They had been born in the same year, which must have felt somewhat strange. When my grandmother saw how he behaved with her daughter she sensed his total devotion.

"That man will only leave you when he dies," the amateur clairvoyant predicted, yet another prophecy that would ultimately come true. When my mother told me what she said I remember thinking how amazingly insightful she must have been. Of all my grandparents, she was the one I would have liked to meet the most.

Once my parents happily settled into their new home, this period marked a whole new phase in their lives. Thanks to my father, they were worry-free and far more relaxed with each other now that my mother no longer had to invent the truth. When Papà gently suggested that she leave her job at Gucci, she had flash-backs to Pietro's desire to control her, but my father was very per-suasive. He insisted it would be easier for them away from prying eyes in the store and he promised to take care of her financially. "It would also mean you'd be free to travel with me," he reminded her, "and you'd be able to wear all the things you've been hiding away all this time!" In the face of such assurances, even though she was reluctant to give up her independence, she eventually agreed.

My father continued to shower her with gifts: handbags, shoes, clothes—he even bought her a record player so she could listen to her favorite singers, including Domenico Modugno, Claudio Villa, and other Italian singers of the time. He bought her jewelry and rings—"So many rings! I love rings," she said, adding wryly, "Except the pearl one Pietro gave me."

In what seems to me now like such a romantic gesture, my father flew her to Paris for the weekend, booking a suite at the Hôtel de Crillon off the Champs-Élysées. He drove her to Naples in his Jaguar and they took the ferry to Capri, where—during the island's "golden years"—they lay by the pool at the Hotel Qui-sisana and strolled through the streets, stopping in the famed Piazzetta for an *aperitivo*. Starting a tradition he maintained for years, my father bought her a tiny gold charm in virtually every city they visited, which she used to create a charm bracelet that I eventually received for my forty-fifth birthday. Like my father's signet ring, I treasure it.

He mentored her and made her feel like his wife in every respect—other than in name—and even though he took her to the most beautiful places in the world she still felt like she was on the outside looking in. "I was like an ostrich. I spent the best part of my life with my head buried in the sand," she told me. "I was there but I wasn't there. I saw but I didn't see. I never really appreciated the value of these experiences until I was much older."

My father continued to profess his love for her, which he described as "pure and vast." Nor did he stop buying her presents, everything from furs to jewelry, the likes of which she'd only ever seen on customers in the store. Most of it, however, remained packed away in boxes or on hangers in her wardrobe, never to be worn in public.

"Where's the gold and diamond necklace I bought you, Bruna?" was my father's all-too-familiar refrain; he was irritated that she only wore it when he asked her to. "Why don't you put it on?" Then he remembered that she'd never been the showy type, preferring simplicity to anything too flamboyant. Even her new apartment proved too much for her, so she had half of it closed off, downsizing it to suit her needs and to make the place *accogliente,* or "cozy." When my father offered to buy her a new car, she spurned the idea of a coupe or luxury sedan, opting instead for a used Ford.

Her modesty was a refreshing change for a man so often surrounded by ostentatious, overdressed women in the glamorous circles in which he mixed. Whenever he returned from a cocktail party or black-tie dinner he rarely talked about it, preferring to focus his attention on her. Despite his position as head of an emerging luxury brand, he didn't consider himself a "celebrity" in the modern sense and always lived quite frugally. I suppose that, as the son of parents who'd known hardship, he'd inherited some of their judiciousness.

In fact, there was little about my father that was what most people might think of as "Gucci" at all. He happened to create an extraordinary phenomenon but he didn't do it through any kind of notion of, "Look at me, aren't I fabulous?" He did it through his own vision and by maintaining the high standards his father had insisted upon. He had an instinctive flair, a mix of creativity and entrepreneurship, that found its perfect time. Like an artist born to paint, his canvas was fashion and his brushstrokes were the products he knew how to coordinate with a unique sense of style.

People often find it hard to separate what they see in one of our stores from our day-to-day life. Although my father had Villa Camilluccia with its staff and formal dinners, it was more for his family and entertaining than anything else. He wasn't a snob and he didn't flaunt what he had. Generally speaking, his private life had little in common with the glamour and opulence associated with the brand. Once he came home, he'd take off his jacket and settle down to a plate of pasta. He was perfectly happy with a glass of Chianti and simple, honest food rather than caviar and champagne.

Wherever he happened to be, whenever he was apart from my mother in those early days he'd miss her so badly that he would pick up his fountain pen once more. A loving note would arrive with a huge bouquet of flowers, or he'd pour out his heart in blue ink. *"I feel your presence in everything I do and the decisions I make,"* he wrote from Manhattan. *"You once told me to stop writing 'nonsense' and that I should tell you about what I was doing etc. Well, what I am doing is thinking about you incessantly, wanting you, and dreaming of all the things I would like to do with you."*

During the especially warm summer of 1960, he was back in Rome by her side while most everyone else fled the heat of the city as usual. The hottest day of the year was August 28, when the mercury reached 99 degrees Fahrenheit. It was also the week that the games of the XVII Olympiad opened in the Eternal City. Highlights of the games had been televised since the Berlin Olympiad in 1936 but this was the first time they were broadcast in the United States and around the world. A new stadium had been built for the occasion and several sites, such as the Basilica of

Maxentius and the Appian Way, were used for sporting events to show off the city's most historic treasures.

While much of Rome remained closed for the annual holiday—including the Gucci store—my mother had the luxury of watching the world's greatest sporting extravaganza on a brand-new black-and-white television set. Papà had bought it for her so that she and her mother could watch their *sceneggiati*—popular Italian films based on classic books broken down into bite-size episodes.

My grandmother, who no longer needed to work, lay listlessly on the couch, weakened after a virus that had debilitated her for several weeks. Pale and suffering from the heat and with high blood pressure, she nevertheless insisted that she was on the mend. It was only when she deteriorated dramatically during one of the hottest afternoons, September 1, that Mamma fully appreciated the gravity of her condition.

"Bruna—I'm not feeling well," my grandmother panted breathlessly, so my mother telephoned my father's office immediately, only to discover that he was in a meeting and couldn't be reached. By the time he received her message and sent his own doctor, Mamma was found collapsed by my grandmother's side.

Delia was dead. After a lifetime of hard work and a difficult marriage, her heart had simply given out. She was fifty-five years old. She'd buried her husband and seen her children grow up and make their own way in the world. Living with my mother in Balduina was meant to be a bright new start and her sudden demise must have come as a terrible shock.

Orphaned and effectively without any family to speak of after her estrangement from her sister and brother, my mother wouldn't be comforted. Dosed up with sedatives, she took to her bed and was far too distressed to attend the funeral, which was held at the same cemetery where my maternal grandfather, Alfredo, was interred.

My father had taken care of all the arrangements and, in my mother's absence, made sure the day went smoothly. Franco flew home from Sardinia and Gabriella was there with her family. They took one look at the sharply dressed gentleman who'd paid for the service and immediately understood why he'd gone to such lengths, and why their sister and mother had been living in Balduina. Curious glances were exchanged but nothing was said and after the short service, they all went their separate ways.

The sudden awareness of her total isolation in the world was enough to unhinge my mother. Within a relatively short space of time she'd lost both parents, become estranged from her family, given up her fiancé, been pregnant, relinquished the job she loved, and begun living in constant fear of exposure. The previous twelve months with my grandmother may have been her happiest, but now the woman to whom she'd been morbidly attached since childhood was gone and she couldn't envisage a world without her.

All she had left was my father, who she now feared would almost certainly predecease her. "From that day on, I lived in mortal dread that he too would die suddenly, leaving me homeless and bereft. He kept assuring me that he was in excellent health, but I knew that he'd never be as dependent on me as I was on him and the thought terrified me."

Rendered almost insensible with grief, my mother remained in bed under the care of a doctor and a discreet *governante* (a companion-cum-housekeeper), a young Spanish woman named Maria whom my father had previously hired as a domestic at Villa Camilluccia. No matter what he did for my mother, though, she couldn't seem to shake off her depression.

Toward the end of the year he became so concerned— especially as her first Christmas without my grandmother approached—that he booked her a passage to New York on the SS *Leonardo da Vinci*. Maria was sent as her chaperone and he promised to join them soon after Christmas.

Incredibly, my mother was transformed within days of stepping aboard that luxury liner. The sudden shift in perspective completely altered her mood. Relaxing in her sumptuous cabin, the youngest girl in first class escaped into a fantasy world in which she completely reinvented herself. As a child, she'd watched her mother sewing pretty dresses and imagined a different, more glamorous life. On the high seas and free from expectations, she was able to put on those kinds of outfits and act out her daydream at last.

I find it hard to believe when I think of her now, but the story she told her fellow passengers was that she was the fiancée of a successful lawyer who'd marry her once she arrived in Manhattan. Pretending to be someone she wasn't was surprisingly liberating and allowed her stifled imagination to run free. All her young life she had simply been Bruna Palombo—the obedient daughter of a dominant father and somebody whose life revolved around tradition and duty. Now she was cast adrift from all that paranoia and risk of scandal. She not only made new friends, she was given a prize for being the prettiest young woman on board.

Whenever my father telephoned to speak to her via the radio room he was bemused at first to hear that she wasn't in her cabin. Where could she be? he wondered, trying not to have jealous thoughts. When it happened once too often, he became irritated and eventually told the radio operator, "It can't be that difficult to find one of your passengers, are you suggesting she's gone overboard for a swim?" While he protested long-distance, the woman he continued to describe in his letters as *"a whirlwind that unsettled [his] entire being"* was winning new hearts without him, sitting at the captain's table, where she'd been all along.

On a chilly mid-November morning, my mother's fantasy abruptly came to an end as her vessel sounded its foghorn and entered the deep waters of the Hudson River on its approach to Manhattan Island. Just as my father had instructed, she pulled on a warm woolen coat and went up on deck to see the Statue of Liberty loom through the winter mist. Like many Italians, she'd dreamed of going to the United States one day. She'd heard my father talk enthusiastically about how special New York was and how much he thought she'd love it. Now here she was—she'd made it.

Seeing the iconic statue on Liberty Island, however, only made her mood plummet. There would be no handsome young lawyer to meet her quayside and no wedding to prepare for. In fact, she doubted she would ever be a bride at all. Papà would not be there to greet her. She wouldn't see him for another month. She was alone but for a taciturn companion, in a far and foreign land.

"I never loved America the way your father did," she admitted later. "That was *his* dream, not mine." In spite of the brief hiatus from her cares on the journey across the ocean, her first glimpse of "the land of the free and the home of the brave" did nothing to inspire courage. Nor did it release her from the ghosts of her past or the dark shadows over what often felt like an impossible future.

Her new, temporary "home," which he had rented from an acquaintance, was distinctly old-fashioned and oddly kitsch, with frescoed ceilings and a lavatory that resembled a throne. Grotesque ornaments were taped to the surfaces to prevent anyone from moving them and the furniture was covered in clear plastic. Even though the location was relatively central, she knew no one and had no idea where to go. The weather deteriorated into a typical East Coast winter with snow and ice, leaving them even more disinclined to go out. Trapped and friendless, the two women spent Christmas indoors eating take-out orders of fast food—pizzas, hamburgers, French fries, and Coca-Cola.

By the time my father arrived in late December, he found my mother weighed down physically and emotionally and realized that his plan had ultimately backfired. As New Year's Eve approached, he whisked her off to the one place he hoped might provide the tonic she needed—Las Vegas, in the middle of the Mojave Desert. The place known as "Sin City" was like nothing she had ever seen before, with palm trees, streamlined American cars, and big bright neon signs everywhere. Luxury hotels and casinos such as the Sands and the Desert Inn were buzzing with excitement. It was the era of the Rat Pack and *Ocean's Eleven,* with Frank Sinatra, Sammy Davis Jr., and Dean Martin playing nightly. Elvis Presley's *Viva Las Vegas* had just been released and the Beatles would soon be performing on the Strip. I only wish I was old enough to have seen Vegas in its heyday.

Gazing at the bustling gaming tables and martini-drinking high rollers playing blackjack, roulette, and craps just like in the movies, my mother's eyes lit up. My father knew then that he'd done the right thing taking her there, even if he was a little anxious about letting her loose on the casino floor.

Excited by all that she saw, her spirited side came out as she teasingly urged him to play roulette with her before dinner. Papà may have taken a few well-calculated business risks in his life but he was never a gambler, so he bought her a hundred dollars' worth of chips and adjourned to the bar for a cocktail. If he thought she'd soon be back at his side, he was mistaken. When she didn't appear, he finished his drink and went to find her. He was staggered to spot her at the head of a roulette table, surrounded by cheering admirers, her stack of chips increased sixfold.

"Bruna! *Come hai fatto?*" (How did you do that?) he asked incredulously, pulling her away before she lost the lot.

Laughing with glee, Mamma agreed to stop gambling on one condition—"Tonight, *I'm* going to buy *you* dinner!" she cried. It was a small but important victory. Ever since she'd given up work she'd been entirely dependent on my father. She wanted to treat him for a change, and her gesture touched him deeply.

She tells me that the expression on his face as she grabbed the bill from the waiter at the end of their meal was "worth every throw of the dice!" My father was astonished at this new side to Bruna, who was high-spirited, having fun, and taking control. He had never loved her more.

TEN

My father loved to haggle. A trader at heart, he liked nothing better than to beat someone down on price and cut himself a deal. I can remember him doing this when I was a child time and again.

There was one episode in a British liquor store where a hapless sales assistant was left utterly bamboozled. "If you were to offer me a ten percent discount for ten bottles of wine," my father told him, "I would buy ten rather than five, and you'd make more money." His logic was inescapable but the man still needed some persuading. When he eventually conceded, Papà put two more bottles on the counter and said, "So for twelve bottles, I get a twelve percent discount, right?" The man eventually agreed, although his eyes popped out when he saw my father's wallet, fat with bills. Papà laughed all the way home.

For him, it was not just about saving money but playing a game—a war of wits with a fellow merchant—something that drove my mother spare. She'd sooner walk out of a store than be embarrassed by what she called his "souk practices." Nevertheless she couldn't help but laugh whenever he emerged triumphant after making some clever transaction.

In their later years I found her embarrassment a little ironic considering how she ended up negotiating with him about everything from the time he spent with her to major lifestyle choices. It was a characteristic he always admired and that she first began to develop on her return from her trip to the United States. By her own admission, her experiences there altered her. No longer an inexperienced teenager, she was a worldly-wise young woman determined to make some major changes in her life and take better care of her affairs.

First she decided to leave the apartment in Balduina. It was too big for her on her own and being in those empty rooms without my grandmother was unbearable. She rented it out and Papà found her another, more suitable property close to his old bachelor flat in the Parioli Quarter, near the park of Villa Borghese. Another big change in her life was that she resolved to go out more. She'd so enjoyed her time on the ship and in Vegas that when she returned to Rome she made plans to meet up with Nicola or Lucia after the store closed, and other friends she hadn't spoken to in a while.

For the next six months or so, my mother was as carefree as she had ever been as my father continued to fly around the world, checking on his stores and planning new ones. He continued with his routine of spending a week in one city followed by a week in the next, a cycle that meant she usually saw him every four weeks. He'd long since set his sights on opening a branch in London and every time he went there to view a potential location, he'd check into the Savoy, where my grandfather had worked as a young man. From his room, he reviewed details of various stores for rent, eventually settling on premises in Bond Street.

At Mamma's urging, he'd appointed Nicola as one of the

managers. She knew that he was eager to return to London and this would be a stepping-stone for him to branch out and see more of the world. Nicola was delighted and my mother was only too happy to help.

My father's expansion schemes for America continued unabated when he opened a store in Palm Beach, Florida. Known simply as "150 Worth," the new shop on Worth Avenue became an instant landmark. Its opening coincided with the launch of a shoulder bag named after Jacqueline Bouvier Kennedy, the electrifying young wife of the new American president John F. Kennedy, who'd come to office in January 1961. In addition to the "Jackie" (which became an instant hit after she was photographed with it), my father also had matching shoes made expressly for her.

In May 1962, my parents went to Palma de Mallorca in the Balearic Islands off the coast of Spain. They spent a few idyllic days searching for a villa by the sea where my mother would spend the summer with the few friends who knew of her affair. Papà would visit whenever possible. He was in great spirits and at long last she had him all to herself, away from the frenetic pace of the business. On their way home they stopped off in Madrid for the weekend and went for a romantic dinner to celebrate his fifty-seventh birthday. It was a magical night, with a flamenco guitarist and Sevillana dancers, and they were swept up in the moment, far away from prying eyes.

"I don't think we'd ever been so happy," my mother said wistfully.

Soon afterward, that joy was shattered when she discovered she was pregnant again—this time, with me. In spite of all their precautions, I'd been conceived in one sublime moment in Madrid. It was a time in their lives when they were devoted to each other, but sadly, my arrival threatened to ruin all of that.

Remembering the ordeal she had endured with the loss of her

previous baby, my mother went into an emotional tailspin. They'd never discussed the possibility of another pregnancy and had no idea what they would do this time around. Imagine her fear. How could she contemplate having a baby under the circumstances? The risk was far too great and it could potentially destabilize everything she and my father had been working toward.

Close to hysterics, my mother had to be quite literally shaken to her senses. "It's going to be all right, Bruna," my father said, taking her firmly by the shoulders. "You are going to have this baby. You'll have the best possible care and when the child is born safe and sound, I will look after you—both of you. I promise."

"But how, Aldo?" she wailed tearfully. "Where? This is not possible!"

"We *will* have this child," my father said emphatically, adding with a smile, "And it will carry my name. *Tutto è possibile,* Nina." And so it would prove to be.

So calm and reassuring was my father that my mother instinctively knew she could trust him, but still she was frightened. How would they be able to keep it secret? What about his other family? Olwen and their sons had always remained on the periphery and rarely came into their conversations. Mamma wouldn't have dreamed of interfering with my father's decisions but still she fretted about how he planned to handle the situation.

In spite of the dramatic change in their circumstances, the two of them went ahead with their summer plans. Instead of looking forward to becoming a mother, though, she agonized over the very real possibility that someone might expose her for what she really was—the pregnant mistress of a married man. Having been pregnant three times, I know the feeling of expectation only too well. There is the excitement of creating a new life with the man you love and, after the third month, being able to announce it to the world. Then there are the first signs of movement, and a kick now and again. But my mother had none of that. For her, there were only problems, and the more I grew inside her, the more anxious she became.

By the time she returned to Rome she was covering herself up with loose-fitting jackets and multiple layers, but when five months had passed it was clear that she could no longer conceal me. This called for drastic measures.

"You must move to London," my father suddenly announced. Never a man to panic, he seemed quite relaxed as he imparted this momentous news.

Mamma was horrified. "London? But why? I don't know anyone there!"

"Nicola is in Bond Street and Maria can accompany you, as she did in New York."

It was soon apparent that he'd been planning this for a while. He'd certainly worked everything out with his customary meticulousness and had arranged for her to be cared for by a leading gynecologist at the London Clinic in Harley Street. With the new West End store and the frequent need to travel to Walsall to purchase hides, he assured her he had a legitimate reason to be in England more frequently. "I will come often and I shall be with you when our son is born," he promised, kissing her forehead and reiterating his conviction from the get-go that I would be a boy.

Not really able to take it all in, Mamma was at least relieved that Maria would be with her throughout. Although she had never regarded her as a friend, she knew she'd be grateful for her company. Nicola, however, would be a godsend, and she could hardly believe her luck that he was in London—thanks to her.

The timing of her departure for British shores was dictated by how far along she was in her pregnancy, so as the end of the year approached she made her nervous preparations to leave Italy. My father had just left on his foreign circuit so she'd be moving without him but meeting him in London in a few weeks. On an afternoon in November 1962, when my mother was packing up her apartment as she waited for Maria to return from an errand, the telephone rang. She hoped it would be Papà, wishing her a safe journey.

"*Pronto?*" she said, giving the customary Italian greeting.

It was Maria. "*Io non parto*" (I'm not leaving), she said. Then she hung up.

After Mamma replaced the receiver in shock, she went straight to Maria's bedroom, only to discover that her closet was empty and her belongings gone. Whether it was the time they'd spent together in New York that had changed her mind or perhaps the idea of yet another winter in a foreign land, no one knows. She gave neither an explanation nor the chance for my mother to talk her into it.

She had no choice but to board the plane to London alone to give birth to me in a strange land. For someone who had lived her entire life in comfortingly familiar surroundings, that must have been a terrifying prospect. "Can you imagine what it was like for me? Having to hide like that?" she told me years later, shuddering at the memory. "It would have been such a big scandal in the sixties. A single woman—pregnant! I left Rome like a thief in the night!"

Papà had once written to his Brunina, imploring her with "*hands clasped—not to succumb to formalities, to social conventions or to external influences that [would] interfere with [their] desire to love one another*" and saying, "*Believe in me my darling, you will not regret it!*" In that moment, looking out of the window as the wheels left the tarmac, she most certainly regretted it and she had never felt more abandoned in her life.

It was raining when the taxi dropped her off in front of the six-story red mansion block she would now call home. Situated in Cadogan Gardens, Knightsbridge, overlooking a gated square, her apartment had a big bay window and a long corridor linking the various rooms. The village feel of the neighborhood with its trees and cobblestoned mews was a pleasant surprise in the heart of such a big city. The knowledge that Papà had enlisted the help of a local couple for any emergencies—under a strict code of secrecy—put her further at ease.

Nevertheless, my mother was in an alien country where everyone spoke a language she hardly understood and was far too nervous to attempt. Then history started to repeat itself because—just as in New York—London fell into the grip of a severe winter. Only this time it was far worse. What started as snow flurries quickly deteriorated into what was dubbed "the Big Freeze," which began in earnest over Christmas with bitterly cold conditions continuing until early March. There were blizzards and gale-force winds, and in the southeast of England the sea froze in several places. London got off lightly by comparison but the pavement was still too treacherous for Mamma to go out in case she slipped.

Trapped inside her apartment just as she'd been in Manhattan, she couldn't help but resent being in this situation yet again, unable to live a normal life. "When you are treated like a secret, you tend to live like one," she told me sorrowfully. Alone in her flat, she waited eagerly for every long-distance phone call from my father and was saddened that he no longer wrote her the beautiful letters of their early courtship. How she would have loved to read his looped handwriting again, telling her how much he adored her—"*Our destiny is to be together—I feel it!*" he once wrote.

His destiny, however, seemed to keep him busier than ever, on a roller coaster he seemed unable to get off. Gucci was well and truly on the world map, just as he had planned, and he'd become too deeply involved to let it expand without his stewardship. His flowery promises of "*eternal devotion and nurturing*" seemed hollow when he was always so far away, leaving her afraid and lonely.

Mamma would have been inconsolable if it weren't for the companionship of Nicola. Ever since he'd come into their lives, the handsome young man she'd had a hand in hiring had become almost part of the family. So much so that my father suggested Nicola move into the apartment while she waited to give birth. His presence proved to be a gift to us both.

The fun-loving Roman whom my mother refers to as "the first angel to walk into [her] life" introduced her to the British soap *Coronation Street*. It was a show they both loved, not least because of their endless amusement at the strange northern accents and how much tea everyone seemed to drink. If she didn't feel like going out for supper, they'd cook pasta and curl up in front of the TV to watch old American movies and other shows. Nicola was obsessed with California and desperate to go to Hollywood, his dream destination. After watching films like *Gidget* and *Beach Party* about the surf culture on the West Coast, he developed a rose-tinted idea of living in Malibu surrounded by handsome young surfers. "That's where I'm headed one day!" he'd tell Mamma. Thankfully for her, he was in London, at her side, and she had never been more grateful.

My father flew into Heathrow at the end of February 1963 in preparation for my birth. Since he was the father of three sons, he and my mother both assumed that she would be having a boy. Ultrasound wasn't used widely in British hospitals in the 1970s and it was impossible to know for sure. They were convinced nevertheless and had even chosen his name—Alessandro. So certain were they of my gender, in fact, that they didn't even pick one for a girl.

Unlike today, in the 1960s men were rarely present during labor. My father was no exception. He hadn't been at Olwen's bedside for the arrival of any of their children and told my mother that he used to go dancing instead. As she told me, "I neither wanted him there nor expected it. The fact that he'd interrupted his manic schedule to be at the clinic at all said everything to me."

So, as she struggled through an especially painful labor, my father quietly established that she was in good hands, then went for dinner and to see a movie. Imagine his surprise when, on his return later that night, the nurse told him, "Congratulations! You have a daughter!"

With the help of forceps, I had fought my way into the world kicking and bawling at 9:25 p.m. on March 1. My weight was seven pounds, eleven ounces, and I was "all arms and legs with a big mouth," according to Mamma. My father delightedly checked me over in the nursery for himself before rushing to my mother's room with a huge grin.

"It's a girl! She's beautiful! Once again, you have given me something I have always wanted, Brunicchi!" He was over the moon.

Only a devoted father could have declared me beautiful after looking at my screwed-up face, purple with rage as I shrieked at the indignity of being born. Having given my mother a tough time during my delivery, I didn't stop there.

"I swear that all the fear, sorrow, and anguish I felt during my pregnancy transferred to you," my mother admitted. "You screamed so much you woke up the entire ward." Since I refused to be breast-fed and cried nonstop, a pretty Australian nurse named Patricia stepped in and took me in her arms, where I eventually settled down. Such was her tender care my mother decided to name me after her. For my middle name she chose Delia.

My father stuck around for a few days before flying off to Paris to finalize preparations for the opening of his first store there, near Place Vendôme. The flowers he sent her every other day quickly overwhelmed her hospital room and then her apartment. No amount of flowers now could make up for the fact that she was on her own, however. Barely able to take care of herself—let alone me—and without Delia to show her how, she still feared what would happen to us both. My father was ever kind and attentive but in the last stages of her pregnancy, when she was feeling less attractive, he hadn't been around as much as before. Was that a coincidence or by design? she began to wonder. Would he move on to someone new? Or abandon her in England?

"All I could think about was what would happen when we returned to Rome," she would say years later. Fear robbed her of the sleep she so badly needed and she found it difficult to care for me. She often struggled to get through each day and vowed privately that, if she could help it, she'd never fall pregnant again.

Our "angel" Nicola was the one who bore the brunt. After a long day's work, he'd come home to my tearful mother, who'd hand me over to him immediately. "Please, Nicola. She won't stop crying. I need to sleep!" Never having cared for a baby before, all he could think to do was put me in my pram and wheel me up and down the corridor to give my mother some rest.

My father flew back to London for my christening at St. Mary's Roman Catholic Church on March 12, almost two weeks after my birth. Built in 1877, it was a severe-looking Victorian edifice and one of the oldest Roman Catholic parishes in London. As the handful of guests—friends and neighbors who formed part of my parents' inner circle—gathered around the white marble font, the priest doused me in holy water. Nicola was there as my godfather, Lucia had flown in from Rome to be my godmother, and everyone else present was asked to turn to Christ, repent their sins, and renounce all evil.

Even though I was being "cleansed of all sin" by being baptized, my mother still knew that I was ultimately *illegittima*. The unsuspecting priest who signed my baptism certificate had no way of knowing that my parents were in fact not lawfully married—another lie perpetrated by my father.

He didn't stop there, and went on to officially log my birth at the London registry of births and deaths with his name and that of my mother written indelibly in ink. To legitimize my birth as he had promised, he wrote, *"Aldo and Bruna Gucci."* In his mind I honestly think he believed that to be true.

My mother's fears about the future were compounded by the fact that he still made no mention of our returning to Rome. It was only when she repeatedly told him how miserable she was so far from home that he conceded. At just twenty-eight days old, I was added to my mother's passport, cocooned in a blanket, and flown back to Italy.

"We'll have to be much more careful from now on," my father warned her. With me in the picture, my parents had no illusions about how secretive their lives would now have to be. There would be no family outings or walks along the street where people knew them.

"I'd rather keep a low profile in Rome than be alone in London," my mother replied, fed up as she was with the weather, the food, and the language. She hadn't considered how low her profile would need to be, however; she was unable to wheel me around in a pram in her own neighborhood without questions being asked. Instead, a Spanish nanny they'd hired would take me out and my parents would meet as before.

As someone who was once a young mother, I cannot imagine being unable to show my daughter off to the world and take her wherever I want. Yes, it was a different generation and my parents did what they had to under the circumstances, but the idea that they were so restricted saddens me no end.

They must have believed it was a price worth paying. And that was how they managed to keep me a secret—for almost one year.

ELEVEN

*C*onfrontation has never been my mother's style. Her general feelings of inadequacy and lack of confidence usually prevent her from speaking her mind.

I am exactly the opposite. Being a pawn in somebody else's game characterized my childhood to some extent, giving me no choice but to do what I was told. With age and wisdom, I was able to express myself and let others know how I was feeling.

Mamma never really discovered her voice in the same way and whenever she came up against any dispute she would often shrink back in silence. Imagine her discomfort then, when, alone with me in Rome one afternoon, she opened the door to her apartment to come face-to-face with a well-heeled emissary from my father's wife, Olwen.

"Signora Gucci knows all about you—and the baby," the woman announced through pinched lips.

Mamma's heart leapt into her mouth.

"Signora Gucci feels that it would be in everyone's interests if you gave up all claim to her husband, Dr. Gucci," she continued, fixing my mother with a steely glare. "You're still young," she added flippantly. "You can start again."

Unable to summon any meaningful words, my mother began to stammer something but was never given the opportunity to respond.

"If you can't care for your child on your own, then Signora Gucci is prepared to take her off your hands."

Mamma stepped back, physically recoiling from what she was hearing.

Ignoring her reaction, the woman assured her, "She would have the best possible care."

My mother's hand flew to her chest as she fought for breath.

"Think very carefully about this," her visitor concluded before twisting on her heel and leaving my mother gasping for air.

As she staggered back into her apartment and tumbled into a chair, she recalled the day she'd first set eyes on Olwen when she came into the store to buy Christmas gifts. She'd been struck then by the humility and sweet manner of the woman who'd been Signora Gucci since the 1920s.

"I was impressed by her," my mother told me. "She seemed so very nice and proper." Was it arrogance or desperation that led her to dispatch this cruel messenger? Either way, what kind of a callous mother did she imagine her to be that she'd give up her own child? Even though Mamma knew my father's marriage was in name only, she still felt guilty about their affair, but this latest move was both offensive and shocking.

We will never know exactly how or when she found out about us, but in all likelihood the news reached her through Giorgio, the eldest of her sons, who had recently been tipped off by a series of anonymous letters. The first was a single typewritten sheet, which arrived in an envelope with a local postmark. Its unnamed author knew all about my mother and me, and claimed my father lavished gifts on Mamma "like an Indian prince." More correspondence followed, giving the specifics of my christening in London, our address in Rome, and places my parents had visited together. Set out with forensic attention to detail, the evidence was clearly designed to let my father know that I, his secret love child, could be exposed.

My father wasn't easily alarmed and the poisonous letters undoubtedly angered him when his stammering son showed them to him, but he said little and didn't reveal his emotions. He knew Giorgio and Olwen were close and that Giorgio would be naturally protective of her.

My mother, however, completely lost her nerve. After all the years of hiding in plain sight, they'd been caught. "I became obsessed with finding out who had written those horrible letters," she said. "What did they want? They contained so much personal information that I began suspecting everyone, even Nicola."

After making a few inquiries, my father broke the news to Mamma that one of her trusted friends—a woman who'd known virtually everything about her—was the one who'd betrayed us. Worse still, she'd been collaborating with a member of his family and together they'd orchestrated the whole thing. There was an ulterior motive, of course, and when it came to light my father agreed to the proposition to avoid any further controversy and put an end to the whole affair.

The experience bruised my mother badly. Not only had she been deceived by a close friend, it damaged her trust in almost everyone. For the first time she came to realize that—aside from the dangerous legal consequences of being associated with my father—there were disadvantages she'd never even considered, not least jealousy from those she'd once considered friends.

If she feared that the ominous visit from Olwen's messenger had heralded the beginning of the end for her and Papà, however, she was wrong. As she tearfully recounted what had happened that day, word for word, my father's growing fury was apparently frightening to witness. Although she'd seen him snap at colleagues and heard tales of his losing his temper elsewhere, she had never seen him quite so incensed.

When he heard her tell him that Olwen had offered to take me off her hands, something inside him snapped. His face like thunder, he left immediately for Villa Camilluccia to confront his wife of forty years. My mother would never know precisely what happened during their heated exchange but she was later assured that he'd told her everything about us, reiterating in no uncertain terms his abiding love for Mamma and me.

"Don't ever try anything like that again!" he told Olwen conclusively.

She never did.

Traumatized by the whole affair and still petrified about the future, my mother resolved to start saving every *lira* my father gave her for expenses. "The jewelry was lovely," she told me, "but I couldn't buy food with it if I needed to." Instead of squandering the money he gave her to pay for food and the nanny, clothes, and furnishings, she made certain sacrifices—cutting back on household expenses or deciding not to buy a new pair of shoes. Without wishing to give her carte blanche to do as she pleased, my father gave her what he thought was enough, without knowing that she was putting it away for a rainy day like an ant saving all her crumbs.

It was around this time that that her second "angel" walked into our lives. Her name was Maureen, a pragmatic young woman from Sunderland in the north of England who had replied to an advertisement my father had placed in the *Lady* magazine. My parents liked her immediately and hired her on the spot. My father had always loved British decorum and wanted me to be raised by an English-speaking nanny so I could learn the language—although her marked Tyneside accent may not have been quite what he had in mind.

Our real-life Mary Poppins was about the same age as my mother with cropped ginger hair, a knowing smile, and sensible shoes. Mamma appreciated everything about her. She even spoke a little Italian, and with my mother's rudimentary English, they eventually switched effortlessly between the two.

As a baby I demanded lots of attention, which Maureen was only too happy to give me. She dubbed me her "Poppet" or "Little Flower" and looked after me in a way my mother simply couldn't. Demanding to be seen and heard and with more energy than I knew how to handle, at night I'd refuse to lie down, standing in my cot and rattling the wooden rails until they broke. Poor Maureen would sit patiently alongside me, her feet wedged up against the bars of my crib to keep it from breaking, trying to read a book until I eventually ran out of steam.

In the daytime I was equally restless, picking up whatever was in reach and ripping newspapers to shreds. Exasperated, my mother frequently exclaimed, "You are most definitely your father's child! It must be something in the blood." Inexperienced as she was, she could never have coped with me on her own.

At least now that my mother and I were out in the open there was less need for secrecy, which must have been a relief for everyone concerned, but my parents still had to be circumspect and keep up appearances. The one blessing was that, no matter how indignant Olwen might have been, she would never be so stupid as to alert the authorities. The effects of such a scandal would have been devastating for her and her children, whose livelihood depended on the success of the business.

My father had other things to think about, not least how to meet growing demand following an endorsement by Princess Grace of Monaco. The former Hollywood actress Grace Kelly—who'd flouted the plot of *Roman Holiday* by marrying her prince—was to become one of Gucci's most loyal customers, drawing swarms of *paparazzi* and cheering crowds whenever she walked through the doors of Via Condotti that they had to be held back by the *carabinieri*. On a visit to the Milan store she asked for a silk scarf with a floral print. Too embarrassed to say no, my uncle Rodolfo stepped in to tell her he was in the process of developing such a range and she would be the first to receive one. The "Flora" scarf specifically created for her became another international bestseller that helped spread the Gucci brand around the globe.

In response to the growing sales, my father decided to relocate the original Florence store to Via Tornabuoni, the shopping thoroughfare in the district, and organized a pre-Christmas opening to mark the inauguration in 1966. His son Paolo and my uncle Vasco meanwhile supervised the construction of a new factory in Scandicci, on the fringes of the city.

His plans were almost dashed however when, in early November, torrential rain caused the river Arno to burst its banks. Overwhelmed by a wall of water and mud, as many as a hundred people lost their lives, thousands were left homeless, and the city of the Medicis lost some of its finest works of art. Via della Vigna Nuova, replete with stock due to be moved to the new store in the coming weeks, was quickly deluged. As the waters rose and my father remained helpless in Rome, his sons Paolo and Roberto along with Vasco and several staff waded in heroically and saved what they could by carrying everything up to the second floor. They even managed to lift the furniture before the floodwaters burst through the shuttered doors, filling the shop with six feet of silt and debris.

All the while, my father was frantically watching the television news and trying to find out what was happening by telephone. When he rang my mother later that day, she had rarely heard him so unnerved. "This is a disaster! I only hope everyone's safe!" To his enormous relief, he eventually discovered that everyone at Gucci was out of danger and that, thanks to some fast thinking, they had even managed to salvage most of the stock.

Just as Papà had been raised to compete with his brothers, so he'd brought up his boys, but on this occasion, they'd put aside their rivalries and joined forces. "It can take something like this to bring a family closer together. I'm very proud of them!" he told my mother before leaving Rome on the next train to see what else needed to be done. The people of Florence also pulled together admirably, and helped by volunteers from around the world, including many celebrities, my father's home city was eventually restored to its former splendor.

My mother knew that the business was everything to Papà and she understood his need to be so personally involved, but each time he went away, he'd leave her feeling increasingly deserted. As before, she became an insomniac, lying awake worrying about everything from the path she'd taken to where it would eventually lead. Without a job and now with a baby in tow, she felt worthless. Her dependence on him was total—financial, physical, and emotional.

"I didn't have the courage to leave," she told me. "Where would I go? How would we live? What would people say about an unmarried mother? I was trapped." Swamped by a growing sense of helplessness, she felt she had lost the ability to make the simplest decisions and increasingly relied on Maureen for everything.

My father did what he could to cheer her up whenever he was in Rome but she became more and more distant, often spending the entire day in bed alone with her thoughts. One sweltering Sunday afternoon in the summer of 1965, when she was especially low, he had a bright idea. It was unbearably hot, so he suggested we all go to Villa Camilluccia and spend the day by the pool.

"Are you crazy?" my mother snapped, thinking of Olwen, but he assured her his wife was spending the summer in England and had left only a skeleton staff. She took some coaxing to return to the house she'd only ever been to once before for the company summer party, which felt like a distant memory. But, with Maureen's help, my father eventually got her out of the apartment and up to the villa in the hills with its sprawling lawns and swaying cypress trees.

How strange it must have felt for my mother to cross the threshold of Aldo and Olwen's family home. This place represented the other world he lived in, the part of his life that she was never normally allowed to see. No matter how much husband and wife may have grown apart, there was an undeniable sense that she was intruding on a shared intimacy within those walls.

At two years old, I was too young to remember that day, but when I look at the photograph taken of us sitting by the edge of the pool, I can see how happy my father was and how surprisingly relaxed my mother looked in her swimsuit and silk head scarf. To protect me from the fierce August sun, I was dressed in a little bonnet and a knitted jacket, while Mamma had a tight grip on me to make sure I didn't accidentally fall into the water. All of my focus, however, seemed to be on Maureen—my very own angel. And so she would prove when, within a few months, my mother simply vanished from my life.

Years would pass before I found out exactly what had happened and even then the details were patchy. Neither one of my parents was prepared to discuss what represented one of Mamma's most fragile episodes. "I couldn't sleep," was all she said later. "I had too much on my mind. I was living an impossible life."

By the time I was three, her doctor diagnosed her as clinically depressed. He urged my father to get her some psychiatric help. Unfortunately, the analyst he sent her to developed a crush on her and began to plot against her association with Papà, Gucci, and materialism in general. Susceptible to suggestion, my mother began to regurgitate some of his rhetoric. "It is *you* that has made me this way, Aldo!" she accused him. My father was so incensed by what he considered her "brainwashing" that he turned up at one of her sessions to unleash his fury on the therapist. He never allowed my mother to go back but her abrupt removal from the influence of this Svengali was enough to tip her over the edge.

Barely out of diapers, I had no understanding of what happened next and my mother refuses to talk about it, but she clearly seemed to have suffered a total breakdown. My father certainly feared for her state of mind and was horrified to see the woman he loved unable to function. In the end he had no choice but to follow the doctors' advice that she spend some time in a clinic for *la cura del sonno,* or "the sleep cure," until she made a full recovery. They further insisted she have no contact with the outside world and that she be left alone, at least to begin with. After a spell my father could speak with her on the telephone, they reassured him. My mother went along with the idea, no doubt looking forward to some relief from her personal torment. Knowing Papà, I'm certain that no expense was spared and I do know that she liked the clinic so much that, even after she came home, she'd voluntarily go back to "have a little rest."

The whole experience was probably more traumatic for my father, as it represented one of those rare moments in his life when he was powerless to effect the outcome and felt responsible for the state she was in. Mamma said she'd never forget his anguished expression as he prepared to leave her in the clinic. Close to tears, he told her, "I will give you the moon and the stars, Bruna. Tell me what to do to make things better!"

My recollection of this time in our lives would have been nonexistent were it not for the insight of a hypnotherapist I met in

California some forty years later. Retracing my life back to my childhood, he identified a trauma when I was three years old and asked me what had happened. Unable to provide him with an answer, I called my mother, who filled me in and explained that I'd been left alone with Maureen for several months. This episode had contributed to my own feelings of abandonment, my therapist explained, shaping my relationships in more ways than one.

All Maureen told me at the time was, "Mummy had to go away, Poppet. She's poorly." She devoted herself full-time to my well-being, taking me on outings, reading to me, and chattering away to the point where I even started to dream in English. She became the kind of mother I would have wished my own mother to be. That summer she packed me up and took me on a grand adventure—to Sunderland for her sister's wedding. I didn't mind one little bit. I was introduced as her "Little Flower" and everyone made an enormous fuss of me, talking in an accent I'd grown accustomed to hearing at home. She was, as she would have said, "right chuffed."

My eyes and ears agape, I couldn't believe the noise and exuberance of Maureen's enormous family. As an only child, I had mostly grown up without that kind of social interaction and being among such warm, colorful people was a real novelty. Maureen's friends and family pinched my cheeks, ruffled my hair, and scooped me up in their arms. They swirled me around the room and covered me in kisses. I giggled and shrieked with delight, soaking up all that love like a sponge.

That weekend was an eye-opener for me. Never before had I been part of a big, happy family, and thanks to Maureen, I would be able to feed off its memory for years to come.

TWELVE

bsessive behavior is something that we all recognize and can develop in varying degrees over time. It can often start with something small but, if left unchecked, can turn into a compulsion or something worse.

Although I was much more laid-back as a child, I think that the older I've become I have definitely inherited some of my mother's need for order. Those around me might tell you that I'm a perfectionist, which admittedly can be something of an obsession. I have learned to temper my need to have everything "just so" and learned to be more accepting of the deficiencies and shortcomings in my life. Sadly, this wasn't always true for my mother.

By the time she was discharged from her sleep clinic for good, she had a new diagnosis—one of a "guilt complex," something the textbooks describe as an obsessive disorder in which the sufferer develops a paranoid inability to cope with feelings of shame. They become obsessed with the idea that they've done something wrong and that they will always do wrong. They begin to blame themselves for everything.

My mother's guilt was visceral and, I think, probably stemmed in part from her Catholic childhood. It was undoubtedly exacerbated by her affair with my father and the need to keep the biggest and most important part of her life secret.

As a toddler, I was still too young to know what was going on and my routines were completely unaffected by her prognosis. Maureen would take me out for hours at a time to keep me out of her way. As he was based in Rome my father called more often, which I loved because he was always so full of life and ideas. He had recently identified a prime location in the hills of Rome where he planned to develop an apartment building and he thought it would be perfect for Mamma and me. His excitement was short-lived, however. When her doctors made a recommendation for her recovery, it was an announcement that would affect us both.

"She feels she has been hiding for too long and she cannot do it anymore," they warned him. "Rome has too many bad memories for her. She needs to be removed from the source of her unhappiness. In another country, another environment, she should flourish and be able to begin a new life."

My mother, who had complete faith in their advice, concurred. With her best interests at heart, my father wasted no time in making alternate plans. We would return to London and move into an apartment in our old neighborhood with Nicola Minelli as our live-in companion once again.

Once we'd settled into London life, Maureen continued to take me out every day so that my mother could rest. We'd stroll to Hyde Park to feed the ducks or hop on and off red double-decker buses to museums and movies. We went to the Tower of London and to Buckingham Palace, where I peered through the railings and asked, "Is the queen there now? Can she see us?" Maureen was an avid reader and soon sparked the same interest in me. I could read and write by the age of three, a fact that impressed everyone.

I especially loved the Ladybird books, the Penguin Readers, and the Famous Five stories by Enid Blyton, particularly if they featured family life.

"What's it like to have a brother or sister?" I'd ask Maureen, or, "Does everybody's mummy and daddy live together?" I'd read for hours during the day and then couldn't wait to finish my book with a flashlight at night. I loved the dance of words and the imaginary worlds and sense of adventure they created in my head.

My real world was proving to be just as much of an adventure, because within a few months we were on the move again. "Central London is no place to raise our daughter and we have to get her into a good school," my mother told Papà. "I'd like a little house of my own, with a garden." With the help of a member of his London staff, he found us a mock Tudor house in the suburb of Hendon, northwest of the city. The neighborhood he picked turned out to be in the center of an Orthodox Jewish community. We had a mezuzah with verses from the Torah screwed to the doorframe and our neighbors were Hasidic Jews with skullcaps and their hair in ringlets. I watched, fascinated, from my bedroom window as religious services were carried out in their garden, where they'd built a small temple, and every Saturday they dressed in their Shabbat best. It was a huge cultural leap from anything we'd known in Rome and although I found it exciting, ultimately I think it only added to my mother's sense of displacement.

Nevertheless, she was determined to adapt to her new surroundings and immediately set about making the house her own. Feeding her need for order, she organized the redecoration of every room while I was sent to a small local preparatory school. It was run by a principal named Miss McCartney, a prickly middle-aged spinster who seemed to constantly hover over me. "You can do better than that, Patricia," she'd say, pushing me in a manner that was, at times, heavy-handed for a four-year-old. I lived in dread

My grandfather Guccio,
founder of the Gucci
business

Left: My grandparents
Aida and Guccio Gucci,
in Florence in the early
1900s

Below: Papà in the
foreground having lunch
al fresco with his family
in Florence

Right: MAMMA AS A LITTLE GIRL IN ITALY WITH HER BELOVED MOTHER, DELIA

Below: RODOLFO WITH MAURIZIO (LEFT) AND PAOLO (RIGHT) AT MY FATHER'S RESTAURANT CLUB COLETTE IN THE EARLY 1980S

Left: Papà (center) flanked by my uncles Vasco and Rodolfo in Milan in the 1950s

Courtesy of GIRAFFA/REX Shutterstock

Below: My twenty-two year-old father and his teenage bride, Olwen Price, at their wedding in England, 1927

Courtesy of GIRAFFA/REX Shutterstock

THE GLAMOUR OF GUCCI BEGUILED
EVERYONE FROM PRINCESS GRACE
OF MONACO TO RITA HAYWORTH

Above: Reporters Associati & Archivi/Mondadori
Portfolio via Getty Images

Above: PRINCE
CHARLES AND ME
AFTER PRESENTING
AN AWARD AT A
POLO TOURNAMENT
IN WINDSOR, 1982

THE GUCCI SHOP
IN FLORENCE,
C. 1950

MAMMA ON THE SHIP TO NEW YORK
RECEIVING HER PRIZE FOR THE PRETTIEST
YOUNG WOMAN ON BOARD

Above: MAMMA SHOWING ME OFF
AT HOME IN ROME, 1963

Left: PAPÀ AND ME AT VILLA
CAMILLUCCIA, ROME, 1965

Above: Papà, Mamma, and me with my aunt Gabriella and friends, Capri, 1966

Left: Papà, Mamma, and me at Villa Camilluccia, Rome, 1965

MAMMA AND ME
OUTSIDE THE HOUSE IN
PALM BEACH, 1973

Left: OUTSIDE THE SUBURBAN HENDON
HOUSE IN MY HORSE-RIDING GEAR, AGE FIVE

Below: ME AT THE PALM BEACH HOUSE AT
AGE TWELVE

of her sharp tongue or being slapped on the back of my head and didn't understand why she took such a close interest until I realized that my surname represented money and prestige for her little establishment.

I was a diligent pupil and good at most subjects, especially English. When I got in from school Maureen would sit me at the kitchen table with a glass of milk while I read aloud in a language my mother hadn't yet mastered, despite her weekly lessons. As I read effortlessly from the Peter and Jane books, I'd look up and always be happy to see her smiling at me.

Our neighbors must have thought us a strange family—the sorrowful but beautiful young Italian, the redheaded Englishwoman, and a bilingual five-year-old in plaits. Stranger still when I played with the other children in the street and told them merrily, "I have two mummies—one sad and one happy." After that, I suppose everyone assumed that my mother and Maureen were lesbians.

Happy Mummy was soon unrecognizable as the woman who'd arrived on our doorstep. Thanks to my mother, Maureen's spectacles had been replaced by hard contact lenses, her hair was restyled, and her teeth were straightened. Her wardrobe was overhauled with more flattering clothes to show off her figure. Her practical footwear was replaced with more feminine shoes. The change was remarkable. As my mother said, "I always knew there was a swan within! She became quite lovely and was so incredibly good for us. She was our backbone, and she loved you, Patricia, as if you were her own."

As a child, I barely noticed Maureen's transformation. I only saw her good qualities. She was a fountain of knowledge and always listened to my never-ending questions. She became a part of our little family and whenever I needed her I knew I could count on her.

Maureen was always there for my mother, too. "Take a look at this," she told her one day, placing a newspaper article in her lap. It was about the violinist Yehudi Menuhin and how he'd discovered salvation from depression through yoga. Within days, Maureen had found my mother a Hindu retreat a few miles away in Hampstead. "Why don't you try it?"

Sari Nandi, a yogi from Calcutta who dressed like an English gentleman, came into my mother's life then and was her next "angel." Married to a German and with four children, he claimed that race and religion were irrelevant. "God is everywhere and in everything if only we look for him," he said. A kindly man with vibrant eyes who gave me a book of poetry the first time we met, he soon became my mother's mentor. "You have spent all these years in silence, Bruna, so now tell me your story." And for the first time in her life, she did.

"He was a miracle worker," she said. "He helped me find freedom from mental anguish." Try as she might, though, she could never master his yoga techniques and complained, "I just can't bend that way!" With the enthusiasm of an obsessive, she fully embraced his other teachings and couldn't wait to share them with my father, even though she appreciated that the pragmatic *dottore* was unlikely to take much notice. Papà was certainly bemused by her sudden enthusiasm for life on a spiritual plane, but mostly he was relieved she was taking an interest in something. Pleased to find her so uplifted, he took her with him on his next trip to California, where he planned to open a new Gucci store, having already written from New York telling her, "*I am counting on your collaboration!*"

The trouble was, he couldn't decide where the store should be. In Los Angeles he'd found the streets largely deserted and couldn't imagine how a retail business could survive without footfall. So he decided to explore San Francisco, the "City by the Bay," which had been described to him as the most European of American cities. My mother felt quite differently. San Francisco in the late 1960s revolved around the ethos of free love, psychedelic drugs, and a prevailing mood of counterculture. Shaking her head as they wandered streets seeing beatniks in jeans, T-shirts, and Afghan coats, she told him emphatically, "This isn't right, Aldo. No, not at all. You need to be in Beverly Hills. That's where all the movie stars are."

My father wasn't accustomed to anyone challenging his plans, especially as his intuition so far had proved spot-on. Mamma may have worked for Gucci but that didn't mean she understood the first thing about global commerce. On the other hand, her youthful enthusiasm for celebrities endorsing products was infectious and celebrities like Princess Grace had done wonders for business in Italy, so he decided that he should listen to what she had to say.

On her insistence, they flew to Los Angeles and checked into the Beverly Wilshire—the home away from home for stars like Elvis Presley and actor Warren Beatty. The hotel was situated on the corner of a relatively unassuming street named Rodeo Drive. It was at number 273 that, in 1961, the Swiss-born businessman Fred Hayman opened his luxury boutique named Giorgio Beverly Hills and began a trend. His shop featured a pool table, a bar, and a library for the amusement of husbands whose wives were busy trying on the latest fashions.

"*This* is the place, Aldo!" my mother cried as they linked arms and strolled along Rodeo Drive in the sunshine. It wasn't exactly buzzing and many of the stores offered the kinds of every-day goods and services to be found in a regular neighborhood, but the people were smartly dressed and there wasn't a hippie in sight. My father promised to think about it.

What he didn't know as he pondered was that she was also secretly manipulating him. Ever since she'd been holed up in

London with Nicola and me watching TV, she knew Nicola's greatest ambition was to live in California. If Gucci were to open in Beverly Hills then he could become one of the managers, making his dreams come true by way of thanks for all he'd done for us.

Her game plan worked and within months my father returned to the US to supervise the opening of a stylish two-story double-fronted store at 347 Rodeo Drive, with a delighted Nicola at his side. It was the start of a love affair between Gucci and Hollywood that exists to this day. Frank Sinatra was so excited that the company was opening in LA that he sent his secretary to buy him a new pair of loafers before the store even opened to the public. John Wayne, Sophia Loren, and Elizabeth Taylor became regulars and the celebrity cachet my mother had correctly predicted did wonders for trade. It also turned Rodeo Drive into a destination address, with the likes of Ralph Lauren and Yves Saint Laurent following on in the 1970s and Chanel opening its first American store there in 1985.

To his eternal credit, my father told anyone who was interested that it was my mother, not he, who had seen the potential. At the civic ceremony to hand him the figurative "Key to Beverly Hills" some years later, he told the gathered crowd, "I have to thank my young wife Bruna, because it was she who convinced me to open in this great city—and how right she was!" When my mother heard that she'd been publicly acknowledged, and as his wife, she was secretly pleased. "Your father really made me feel as if I had done something important, and I guess I had!"

The success of Gucci America paved the way for future expansion into the Far East and, in the coming years, pretty much every corner of the globe. While his countrymen were in the grip of economic and political turmoil, Papà's "Made in Italy" banner was flying high and fast becoming a marker for other brands to follow.

With him away so much again, my mother became restless and decided we needed more space, so she started looking for a bigger house in the countryside. Maureen was dispatched to the real estate department of Harrods to pick up some brochures and every day while I was at school, she and my mother went house hunting. Laden with maps, Maureen acted as co-driver as Mamma sped her little Mini Cooper around the leafy lanes of Surrey, Berkshire, and Hampshire. She was fearless behind the wheel, dodging hazards and navigating traffic like a true Roman.

Their property search was only interrupted by our long-planned trip to New York to spend Christmas with my father. By the age of six, I'd started to feel his absence as keenly as Mamma did and couldn't wait to see him again. I missed his bright face and the sound of his laughter echoing through the house. Best of all, my mother seemed to be in good spirits whenever he was around and suddenly there was a whole new dynamic.

As someone who loved Christmas almost as much as I, he went to enormous trouble to make us feel welcome and those two weeks in New York City were truly memorable for me. There was so much to do and see.

"What would you like to do today?" my mother would ask over breakfast. My father would have already gone to the office and we wouldn't see him again until dinnertime, but I did get to see him once or twice a day.

"Could we go to the ice rink?" I'd ask.

"Good idea! Don't forget your hat!" she'd say before packing me off with Maureen. Hand in hand, we'd wander the streets gazing into shop windows, dazzled by the displays and festive lights. We trudged through snow and watched ice-skaters twirling on the rink at Rockefeller Center. I saw my first real live Santa. One night, we even went to Radio City Music Hall—as a family—to see the Rockettes, which I adored. Christmastime in New York was more exhilarating than I'd ever imagined—the buildings, the buzz, the people, and the wonderful world of American television.

Returning to school after all that excitement felt like the most enormous letdown. Even the discovery of a brand-new dolls' house waiting for me in Hendon didn't cheer me up. Peering into its pink rooms, I'd pick up the tiny figures and put them into position one by one. "Happy Mummy" played with the little girl while "Sad Mummy" lay on her bed. Watching my solitary stage directions one day, my mother noticed how I took the man and placed him outside the house, walking away. "Who is that, Patricia?" she asked.

"That's the daddy going to work, silly!" I explained, wondering why she'd even questioned what seemed to me like the natural order of things.

"What happens when he comes home again?"

Picking up the recumbent woman, I had her rushing down the stairs to greet him with a happy dance.

Sadly, there were no such dances for my mother or me in those first few months of 1970 and there was worse to come when she sat me down one April afternoon to tell me some shattering news. "Maureen and I have to go away," she said. "There are some things we need to do. You'll be staying with Miss McCartney for a while."

I didn't think I'd heard her correctly. "Miss McCartney? But—"

"It won't be for long." She attempted a smile. "Two months."

Panic-stricken, I looked across at Maureen, who nodded awkwardly and then busied herself with something. Two months seemed like an eternity, and why couldn't I stay with Maureen? No amount of pleading could convince my mother to change her mind.

"I need Maureen to help me," she said, not thinking to

explain that we were moving to a new house she'd found for us in Berkshire and that she had become so dependent on Maureen that her need for assistance superseded my child care needs. "It's the middle of the school term and we can hardly leave you home alone, can we?" There would be no further argument.

With a heavy heart, I watched Maureen pack me a small bag. "I'll put in your favorite toys, Poppet," she said, trying to keep things light. "And what books would you like?" Biting my bottom lip until I tasted blood, I just shrugged.

Several days later, my mother drove me to Miss McCartney's apartment in an old Victorian building a few miles from our home. Then she fled with a quick peck on the cheek. "Be good and do as you're told." She couldn't get away from there fast enough.

I still had my coat on as I wandered into the living room in a daze, wondering what I had done to deserve this. I remember the wall was dominated by a life-size oil painting of King Charles II. Later, sitting beneath it in silence eating cauliflower with fish fingers on a tray, I gazed around the drab billet I'd been condemned to and feared my mother might never come for me. Fighting back tears, at such a tender age I couldn't comprehend what seemed like a deliberate act of cruelty.

The apartment was so small that there was no escaping Miss McCartney. I even had to share her bedroom, sleeping a few feet away from her in a single bed, where I lay awake each night tormented by her snoring. Every hour I spent there seemed interminable and the trauma of being abandoned stands out as my first and most vividly unhappy childhood memory. "When will Mamma come to see me?" I asked.

"I doubt she'll have time," came the reply. "She's very busy."

She never did. Neither did Papà. Nor did I hear anything from them, although I'm sure she or Maureen would have telephoned to check that I was okay. Helpless, I was trapped in a world in which my "jailer" presided over my every waking moment. My resentment for my mother only grew.

Those miserable weeks came to an end the afternoon I spotted her unexpectedly at the school gates. "Mamma!" I cried, running over. I was so pleased to see her but she seemed furtive. "I'll pick you up on Friday after swimming lessons," she told me. "We're moving and you'll be going to another school but whatever you do, don't mention anything to Miss McCartney. *Hai capito?*"

I was far too young to comprehend the need for secrecy, which revolved around her general fear of facing anyone in authority, her lack of confidence in English, and the certain knowledge that my guardian wouldn't be happy to lose a pupil or the extra income she'd earned from taking me in. All I knew was that I was being set free and the thought filled me with such joy that I blurted the news to a friend. Inevitably, the information found its way to Miss McCartney, who was as furious as my mother feared she'd be. Tight-lipped, she helped me pack my things and waited with me on the doorstep for Mamma to arrive.

I watched their confrontation sheepishly from the front seat of my mother's car as, red-faced and struggling to make herself understood, she apologized for the change of plans. When she eventually hurried back to the car, the first thing she did was smack me hard across the head. I was totally confused and sat in tearful silence as she drove me to what was to be my fifth home in six years.

The property my mother had found for us in Berkshire looked a bit like my dolls' house, only much much bigger. Instead of being painted pink, it was off-white and pebble-dashed. As we pulled to a halt on the gravel outside the house, Maureen appeared at the door with open arms and my happiness was complete. Looking around the place, I didn't know what thrilled me most—my bedroom or the acres of garden all around. My new playground had trees to climb, a tennis court, greenhouses, and a cottage for a live-in gardener. It even had a wooden Wendy house—just for me. All the distress of the previous two months melted away as I ran from corner to corner, squealing with delight. It was perfect.

After house hunting for weeks without success and very nearly giving up, Mamma had a vivid dream about a property with a rose-covered pergola and was convinced she would find the right property. Then when Maureen showed her the brochure for just such a place, her jade ring suddenly broke into three pieces. She immediately took that as an omen with the conviction of my soothsayer grandmother.

Within a few minutes of stepping into the oak-paneled hallway, she made a declaration. "This is the one!" Her "indescribable sensation" was galvanized when she wandered into the garden and spotted a pergola exactly like the one in her dream. From that moment on, she knew that living in that house was our destiny.

Telephoning Papà in New York as soon as she got home, she insisted that he be interrupted during a meeting. As she chattered breathlessly, long-distance, he interrupted her to ask one question—"How much?" She'd barely registered the price but when she read it aloud from the particulars she promised to refund him by returning everything he'd ever bought her. "Bruna, you don't have to do that!" he chided. "Any other woman would have demanded the moon and the stars, and you never asked for a thing."

He'd written when they were courting, *"I am wildly in love with your grace, your beauty, your manner, your temperament, your family values."* He marveled at the fact that she never took advantage of his position by asking for fancy cars, a townhouse, or a yacht. He was even more taken aback when she then told him she'd secretly saved enough to cover the deposit of £5,000. "Where on earth did you get that kind of money?" he asked incredulously.

Insisting that she make the down payment with the money she'd squirreled away, my mother spent all her savings in one go. Just as she'd bought him dinner in Las Vegas, it was a matter of principle. "I was a single mother in my thirties and I knew the house would always represent a safety net for us, no matter what," she told me. It was a gamble that paid off and my father was impressed.

Better still, he loved the place. Through all his frenetic years of traveling he'd lived out of hand luggage, shifting from one hotel to another. Villa Camilluccia had become little more than a place to sleep and pick up a change of clothes before setting off again. His New York apartment was merely a pied-à-terre. In England, Mamma was determined to create a home he could share with us, and—up to a point—he did.

Growing up, I don't remember his ever visiting us in Hendon but in Berkshire he came regularly. The whole time he was with us, he laughed and made up stories and he never once told me off. His enthusiasm was infectious. From the moment he stepped over the threshold he left his cares at the door, or so it seemed. Changing out of his suit, he'd head out to the garden to check on new trees he'd planted or to discuss the landscaping with our gardener-cum-handyman, Brian. He loved to wake up with the birds singing and leaves rustling in the trees. The English countryside offered a welcome respite from the craziness of his world, which had become ever more complicated as the rivalries between his sons and brothers sharpened.

Eager to capitalize on his status, my father's headstrong son Paolo had—with my father's encouragement—launched a ready-to-wear range. Recently promoted to chief designer in Italy, Paolo certainly had taste and a grasp of marketing, but with hindsight, I think he always thought he was better than the rest. He never possessed the same insight or business acumen as Papà, though, and with so much racing through his mind all at once, he found it difficult to channel his ideas. Relentlessly jockeying for position within the company, he saw himself as a worthy successor while his more reserved brothers, Roberto and Giorgio, seemed content with their administrative roles.

Paolo wasn't the only one with his eye on the "prize." My uncle Rodolfo, who'd married an actress who gave him his only child, Maurizio, had been recently widowed. He never remarried and devoted his life to his son, who he hoped might one day be fit for the job. Much to his dismay, however, Maurizio took up with a woman named Patrizia Reggiani, whom Foffo didn't approve of, claiming she was nothing more than a gold-digger. Maurizio left Gucci in a fit of pique and accepted a position in the haulage company run by Patrizia's father. The rift between father and son seemed unbridgeable.

Papà did what he could to keep the peace between his warring family members. From the earliest age he had been instilled with the notion that family came first, family was everything, and the clan had to work together to maintain the reputation of the business and build on its success. The petty jealousies that pitched brother against brother, cousin against cousin, and father against son pained him no end.

Back in England, my mother and I had our own sorrows to face. After seven years, Maureen decided that it was time to leave and create a life of her own. She planned to return to Rome and seek new challenges. I didn't even have the chance to say good-bye. All I know is that when I came home from school one day she was gone.

As a child, I found her decision to leave us difficult to understand. Had I done something to upset her? Was I not a good girl? In what became a pattern throughout my life, my mother never really tried to explain. "She missed Italy and wanted to do something else," was all she said. By the time I reached adulthood, I understood Maureen's decision far better, of course. Her duties were virtually over by then, leaving only my mother to nanny. I was happily ensconced at a new local girls' school named Hurst Lodge where I'd made friends with everyone in the playground within five minutes on my first day. Maureen's only companion other than my mother was the family dog, a West Highland terrier named Giada whom I always tried to dress up and who therefore didn't like me much. With less and less to do, and no one to talk to, Maureen was largely idle. It was time for her to start anew.

For seven years she had been my rock. It was she who had read me bedtime stories and who'd taken care of all my needs. We'd gone on such adventures together and she'd introduced me to the world of books. It was Maureen's smiling face beaming down on me last thing at night and first thing in the morning. She'd brought serenity and consistency to our chaotic lives and she had cared for me all the time my mother wasn't able to.

When she slipped into the back of a taxi, leaving me alone with my mother, she left a huge Maureen-shaped hole in our world that nobody else could ever fill.

THIRTEEN

Throughout my adult life I have found tremendous solace in friendship. Predominantly people I grew up with, my friends are all generous of spirit, from eccentric families, and tend to have similarly dysfunctional backgrounds to my own. Like me, their upbringing has been anything but ordinary.

One thing that seems to perplex them, however, is that I tend not to ask many questions. "You're very social and you're definitely not shy!" Whether it's a trait I picked up in my formative years or something more innate, I can't be sure. It's not that I don't care or that I'm not interested—I am—it's just that I don't like to meddle in other people's affairs. My inquisitive nature only really found its outlet with Maureen in those early years in England and once she was gone I simply followed instructions and focused on being a good girl—anything not to upset the fragile equilibrium at home.

My mother ensured I looked nothing short of flawless, in my pigtails, ankle socks, and the ubiquitous Start-rite shoes (worn by virtually all British schoolchildren), at all times. I was happiest among my classmates at Hurst Lodge, where I instantly took to the camaraderie of an all-girl environment. My best friend was Belinda Elworthy, and as was the norm with British schoolchildren, most of us had a nickname, so we were known affectionately as "Pee and Bee." We had so much fun together.

Back home and with no one to confide in anymore, it was a different story. In spite of my mother wishing that my father might visit more often, he still only came once a month, so the intervening weeks ticked slowly by. The house she'd found was lovely in the summer but cold and dark in the winter, so rooms were closed off and curtains drawn.

At least in Hendon, we'd had neighbors, and even though she never spoke to them, the idea of having someone nearby was comforting somehow. In Berkshire we lived in an area where houses were hidden behind gates and out of view. When we looked out of the window all we saw were trees and the occasional muntjac deer skipping across the lawn. Apart from one family that lived farther along the lane, we never became friends with anyone, and besides, my mother was never at ease engaging with anyone in English.

With a father who wasn't present and a mother who struggled to be, I often felt like little more than an appendage. Mamma went through the motions with me in the same way as with her dog, Giada. When I needed to be fed, she prepared my meals. When it was time for me to clean up, she drew me a bath. Then she'd plop me in front of the television until it was time for bed. She'd done her duty and that's where it ended.

I quickly learned to occupy myself in a way that bred lifelong self-sufficiency. Alone on weekends, I'd lose hours in the pages of *The Lion, the Witch and the Wardrobe* or *Peter Pan*—both stories that offered their characters escape into places of fantastical adventures. I played with my Barbie dolls or chatted with imaginary friends. It never occurred to me to ask for a pet of my own to play with. In fact, I never really asked for anything at all.

My mother filled her days with the teachings of Sari Nandi, whom she still visited in North London once a week. For hours on end, she'd lie on her bed practicing her *pranayama* breathing as part of her preparation for Transcendental Meditation, which had a calming effect for a while and became her only real source of contentment. I didn't appreciate it at the time but she was trying desperately to keep from slipping back into a black hole. While it may have been a form of escapism, she was just doing the best she could with the means at her disposal.

Whenever she was in her room meditating, I knew not to disturb her. On rainy weekends the water drummed on the roof and against the windows, keeping me from the garden I loved. As soon as the sun broke through the clouds I'd rush out to frolic with Brian's children or invite Bee over to the house. She and I played happily for hours, dressing up in my mother's old clothes while making up stories and characters to turn into little plays.

I was also thrilled to go to Bee's house, where her ever-cheerful mother, Liz, treated me like another daughter. I never once met Bee's father, whose absence I never questioned, such was the noisy, chaotic, and fun atmosphere of Rose Cottage. Bee was naughty, as were her sister and brother—the first boy to make my heart pound. Between us, we wreaked havoc, playing our silly little games and running wild. We left everything in a mess but at least it felt like a real home. At my house, there was an altogether different mood. There was hardly anything that didn't make my mother anxious, and she often developed obsessions. When she worried I was too skinny, she began to ply me with food from morning until night and fed me some sort of stimulant syrup to boost my appetite. Whenever she thought I looked pale, she'd pinch my cheeks to bring back some color. If my hair looked lackluster, she'd curl it so I looked more presentable. It seemed imperative that I was well turned out at all times.

Bee thought I was the "luckiest girl alive," with no siblings competing for attention and a big house all to myself. What I longed for more than a nice room, a smart dress, or pretty hair, though, was a kind word. Having come to know Liz, I longed for a mother like she, someone who'd take more of an interest in me and not just find fault where there wasn't any. After they became friends, I hoped that some of Liz's carefree nature might rub off on my mother but sadly it didn't. When Mamma was my age she'd been smothered with love by my grandmother, who'd led her to believe she was the center of her universe. For some reason I have never understood, she seemed incapable of doing the same for me.

In fact, I can recall only a handful of occasions when we did anything fun. One Sunday morning when I was about eight years old sticks in my memory. It was raining and cold outside and until we lit a fire, Mamma's bedroom was the only warm room in the house. With nothing else to do, she invited me to climb into bed in my pajamas and watch TV. Bored by the limited choice of programs, she said, "Let me show you some yoga."

She began with the lotus position as she explained how to twist my leg until my foot rested inside my knee. Then she showed me the tree pose. I was good at that, balancing on one leg a few minutes at a time. "Look, Mamma!" I cried. She was impressed.

"Well done, Patrizina!" she said, calling me by the nickname she used only when feeling especially pleased with me. "You're so flexible, you're like a rubber band!"

Thrilled that I had her undivided attention, I carried on trying out all the poses she showed me. I mastered them all, right up to the shoulder stand, as I tried to balance on my head and raise my legs to the ceiling. Losing balance, I toppled backward onto the carpet, taking my mother down with me. The two of us lay there, hands on our tummies, laughing out loud with tears streaming down our faces—a rare moment of silliness in our otherwise spiritless existence.

The rest of the time we lived for the days my father was home, when life seemed so much more vibrant. Our big old house was often silent and gloomy and he represented a welcome burst of sunshine. Rooms were reopened, curtains were pulled back, and flowers appeared. As soon as I heard the crunch of tires on the driveway, I'd rush out the front door ahead of my mother. Grinning, his eyes sparkling, he was never the kind of father to scoop me up or swing me around but he would pat me affectionately on the head or peck me on both cheeks.

Then he'd embrace my mother. No sooner had he stepped through the door than she'd start complaining. "Aldo, I cannot cope with her . . . ," or, "Look at her school report. What are we going to do?" Never did she say anything positive or show him one of the drawings I had done at school. She made me feel like an instant disappointment when all I wanted was to be special in his eyes. Papà didn't heed her comments much, telling me with an understanding smile, "We'll talk later, Patricia."

Then I'd be banished upstairs. *"Vai in camera tua!"* (Go to your room!) my mother would chide as she led my father into the kitchen and promised to call me when lunch was ready. I couldn't help but resent her possessiveness. I also had things I wanted to tell him. There were plays I'd been cast in at school, books I'd read, and dances I'd learned. I longed to boast about the time Mamma had the flu and I virtually ran the household, answering the telephone in my most grown-up voice and signing for deliveries. I even made her a breakfast tray, which I carefully carried up to her room. "I boiled two eggs, toasted two slices of bread, and made tea," I told him. "She congratulated me on remembering everything—even the honey for her tea."

My dream was for us to be a regular family for a few days. I wanted to create happy little bubbles of perfect times, even if I knew it could never be like that.

After weeks of seclusion, though, she was hungry for adult conversation. Knowing he was mentally preparing to leave from the moment he arrived, she'd compile lists and bombard him with a litany of problems as he sat quietly in abeyance. For her, each of his compressed visits represented her only chance to vent. And vent she did, which usually led to a row and then reconciliation all in the space of forty-eight hours. There was also lots of drama. "It was too much for me to handle," she admitted later. "It was mad chemistry, everything all at once. I'd have to be lover, mother, friend, listener, and cook all in the space of a few days. I was like his Florence Nightingale. There was no time to just enjoy one another. For much of the time he was with us, it was a sense of duty."

Eager to share what she'd learned from her guru, she quoted ad nauseam from her growing selection of books on mind, body, and soul. Papà had always encouraged her spiritual pursuits but one day he'd heard enough. "Bruna, Bruna, please stop preaching at me," he implored. "We have such little time together. You don't know as much as you think. I don't need to read your books. I experience real life every day." Softening, he added, "Thank you, but I have all that I need to know in my head."

For such an impatient man, I thought he responded to her needs with surprising forbearance. Mostly, he'd nod and listen and tell her with a smile how adorable she was. Speaking to her in Italian, he'd call her by her nicknames and tell her how *meravigliosa* she was for coping so well on her own. "*Brava,* Bruna!" Once he'd heard all her news, my father would fill her in on the latest developments in his world, careful not to divulge anything that might upset her. As he decompressed from his high-octane life, he'd gradually open up to her in a way he couldn't with anyone else. She became his confidante as he shared his anxieties about the family infighting or talked about the challenges he faced.

Most of all, though, he just loved to sit at the kitchen table and have Mamma spoil him. If he had a cold or a cough, she'd rustle up a few of her concoctions and lay her "healing hands" on his aching joints. He liked nothing more than to watch her prepare dinner. My mother was a wonderful cook who could make something out of virtually nothing, filling the house with the most delicious aromas. I don't think she was ever happier than when she was standing in her apron in front of the stove, stirring and tasting. One of Papà's most anticipated meals was *coniglio alla cacciatora,* a "hunter-style" stew made with rabbits from the garden, prepared with tomatoes, onions, peppers, wine, and herbs. Dragging his bread across the plate to savor every last bit of sauce—the final act of any home-cooked meal, known as *scarpetta*—he'd chatter and laugh as she fussed around him and ladled in some more.

Nowhere else in the world would a woman make him feel so nurtured. She was his safe harbor, offering the one place he could go to recharge. In the summertime, he and Mamma would swing back and forth on the *dondolo* seat on the terrace, taking in the sun and giggling conspiratorially. She teased him about his distinctive Tuscan dialect, famous for dropping the hard "c" and replacing it with a softer "h."

"Aldo," she'd say playfully, "*vuoi la Hoha Hola con la hannuccia horta e holorata?*" (Do you want a Coca-Cola with a short and colored straw?)

He, in turn, would mimic her Roman accent with its double consonants and truncated words, poking fun at the north-south divide that runs deep in Italy to this day.

Once he relaxed with her, so he began to relax with me. On Sunday mornings he'd take me to church and afterward we'd stop at a little bakery to buy cakes. Back home he'd sit by the fire puffing on his pipe while he watched John Wayne westerns. He never saw the whole movie, though, recumbent on the sofa and dozing off. I didn't mind. I was happy to be at his side just staring into his face. For me, these were moments that were as precious as they were rare.

That feeling of closeness ended as soon as he left. The days immediately after were always the darkest, as we knew it would be at least another month before he'd return. Mamma would disappear to her room like—in her words—"a cloistered nun" while I went to my dolls' house and walked the father figure back down the path. No matter how hard I tried to maintain the lighthearted atmosphere, I could never fill the vacuum.

Without his affection, my mother withered like an untended plant. When I went back to school the house would feel so silent that she could hear her own breathing. Like me, she lived for his visits. Like me, all she had to feed on were memories. "I'll be back soon," he'd cry with a cheery wave each time he drove away. Deep down I knew that he would and that he loved me, come what may.

My mother didn't seem quite so reassured and retreated further into the recesses of her mind, and soon he began to worry for her sanity once more. After one weekend home when she seemed especially lost, he came up with a solution. "If Patricia were to become a full-time boarder, then you'd be free to travel with me." She jumped at the chance—as did I.

Although I'd never asked to be a boarder and the decision was made in order to please my mother, from my perspective upgrading my day-girl status was one of the best things that ever happened to me. Eager to fit in, I immediately found kindred spirits. I loved my new regimen and the special feeling that came with being a boarder, playing pranks and whispering late into the night.

From that day on, the only time I went home was when my parents returned from their travels. I once went a whole term without seeing them, and although I missed our weekends together I had a life of my own and was as happy as a peach. My time at Hurst Lodge represents the best years of my childhood, and surrounded by all my friends, I wanted to stay there forever.

FOURTEEN

First events are important milestones in any child's life—the first smile, the first tooth, the first step. In normal families, parents joyfully relish these moments and proudly tell all their friends.

Once I became a mother I wanted to be able to talk to my daughters about my own childhood development but it must have been Maureen who witnessed all my "firsts," because getting anything out of my mother from those early years wasn't easy.

"How old was I when I first started talking?" I'd ask.

"I don't remember. One, I suppose."

"And what were my first words?"

"Oh, I don't know. . . ."

Something we do both remember, however, is my First Communion. Soon after my ninth birthday we flew to Rome especially for the event. Looking back, receiving the sacrament from the very church that would have denounced my birth seems rather ironic, but in my long white dress laced with daisies—my mother's favorite flower—and matching gloves, I felt like a princess. After the church service my father organized a luncheon for family and guests who'd come to witness my special day. Among them was my aunt Gabriella, whom I'd met on several occasions over the years. She and Mamma had become much closer since growing apart after my grandmother had died. Zia Gabriella was fun and lively, always giggling, and a stark contrast to her sister. Holding court with my first-ever glass of champagne, I was surrounded by people who seemed genuinely interested in me.

Another unforgettable first was the day I visited Gucci on Via Condotti with my mother for our very own after-hours shopping spree on that same trip to Italy. Up until then, I had only an inkling of what my father did for a living and where he went each time he left us. At school, I had come to understand that the funny Italian surname I carried—which some of the girls at school mockingly mispronounced as "Goo-ky" or "Goo-sie"—actually represented something not so "goofy" after all. I never appreciated the scale of my father's enterprise, though, until the day he arranged for a few trusted employees to stay behind as he walked us through the store where my mother had once worked.

The fact that everyone was so deferent gave me a fleeting feeling of excitement, but I sensed Mamma wasn't comfortable being back there, no doubt thinking about all the idle gossip as we meandered through the store. I, on the other hand, felt right at home, especially when my father told me I could pick out a few things. "Why don't you try on some shoes?"

I was boggled by choice until the manager showed me some soft white moccasins that I instantly fell in love with. They were my first pair of Gucci shoes, which I wore until they no longer fit me. Papà, laughing at me in his indigo suit with a spotted pocket square, was elegance personified. He had never looked more at home to me than in that store.

Without a doubt, the happiest "first" in my life was the time he took me on a trip to Switzerland. Mamma stayed behind, so it was just the two of us who went to visit my uncle Rodolfo at his chalet in the Swiss village of Suvretta, near St. Moritz. It wasn't a vacation exactly, as there was business my father had to attend to, but I didn't care. I was just looking forward to spending time with him.

"*Fai la brava,* Patrizina—behave yourself!" my mother told me before we set off. As if I would do anything else. Even when I was at such a tender age, people always commented on how I carried myself and how mature I was. Admittedly, the prospect of going on a long trip with Papà on my own was thrilling enough, but knowing that he had things on his mind, my mother thought it best to caution me for his sake. I didn't have a clue that he was battling with relatives desperate to assert their authority over the business. Or that his hopes of floating Gucci on the Italian stock exchange had been dashed by his brothers, who were concerned that he was moving too fast. My father had aspirations of appointing his sons as directors to reward them for their hard work over the years but Rodolfo and Vasco were opposed to that idea, too, on grounds of nepotism. It was also unfair to their own children, they maintained, regardless of the fact that they were too young to be considered for such a promotion. After years of working toward what he considered a common purpose, it must have been hard for my father to be burdened by his family in this way.

His chauffeur, Franco, drove us the seven hours from Rome to Milan, stopping every now and again for gas or a bite to eat. We then took a three-hour train ride across the border and through one tunnel after another as Papà read the newspaper and I sat next to him with my book. We had lunch in the dining car and I peered out of the window hoping to catch my first glimpse of the Alps.

The man my father called Foffo wasn't nearly as open or warm as I had hoped. He was polite enough but seemed rather sad and eclipsed in the presence of my father. After kissing me on each cheek, he showed me to my room and made sure I had everything I needed, but his manner was somewhat detached. He also appeared to be living in the past. His chalet, named Chesa D'Ancora, in a nod to his prewar screen name of Maurizio D'Ancora, was crammed with mementos from his films. In a separate chalet that was a shrine to his career, there was a screening room, where he watched many of his old productions.

We would have dinner together at one end of a long table but when we were finished he entrusted me to his son's former *governante,* who took me to the chalet next door so that he and my father could speak in private. The cause of Rodolfo's sadness, I later discovered, was his errant son Maurizio's ongoing relationship with Patrizia. The rift between father and son had deepened and they weren't speaking to each other at all. While I settled down to watch the movie *Camelot,* Papà offered his advice as the head of the family. People had always sought his counsel and Foffo was no exception. Even though my father had a reputation as a firebrand who could flare up at the slightest thing, I only knew him as calm and reasonable.

"*Together, we* could do this," he'd say, rarely using the word *I.* Or, "Maybe if *we* try to look at things from his perspective." He always made sure to stress the importance of inclusion when making decisions that affected the future of the business. Oversights and mistakes undoubtedly rattled his cage but when it came to solving a crisis he'd be cool as a cucumber. If anyone could bridge the divide between Rodolfo and Maurizio, it was my father, and that trip to Switzerland paved the way for their eventual reconciliation.

As for me, I just loved waking up and staring at the picture-postcard view of the mountains through my window, the first time I had ever seen them. My wood-paneled room was cozy, with a single bed and a duvet I could sink into. In the mornings after breakfast we would go on walks and one day we all went on a lengthy hike along a rocky path through the Engadine valley. When the sun is shining there, with its twisting footpaths and picturesque stone houses, nothing is quite so beautiful. There, for the first time, my father talked to me about being a young man. I listened attentively, trying to keep up with the punishing pace he set as he marched on using an Alpine stick.

"When I was younger, I used to ski in those mountains," he said, pointing to the distant peaks. "But then I had a bad accident so I turned to rock climbing instead." Seeing my surprise, he laughed. "It wasn't always about work! I used to love sports and was a keen equestrian too." I was astonished and wondered what else he might tell me about his childhood, but that glimpse was all and he said little more.

We plodded on with my uncle Foffo and the *governante* trailing farther and farther behind. When I asked if we should wait, he scoffed. "They'll catch up soon enough." Even though my legs were sore for days, I was so proud of the fact that I not only kept up with him but also managed to reach the end of the twenty-kilometer trail that day. Most of all I enjoyed spending time with my daddy. It felt like such an adventure and even though it was only for two or three nights, it was precious nonetheless.

Our time together was over all too soon, and once we returned to Rome he was off again. My father was never busier than in the 1970s. An Italian newspaper had recently dubbed him "Aldo the Great" in recognition of his latest achievements in America. Sales there were at an all-time high and there were more than five hundred staff catering to customers who lined up outside the stores eager to get their hands on the latest items. By then there were three stores in Manhattan, including one on the corner of Fifth

Avenue and West Fifty-Fourth Street. When he opened another right across the street, the area became known locally as "Gucci City." Then he attended the launch of an eighteen-thousand-square-foot store on North Michigan Avenue in Chicago. It was the most lavish by far, with its own artificial lawn laid on the sidewalk that wrapped around the entire corner. Standing shoulder to shoulder with my uncle Vasco, he answered questions about the future of the company and proudly described his sons as "three cannon blasts with common sensibilities," assuring reporters, "We all speak the same language."

Further stores opened in Tokyo and Hong Kong, and Gucci was becoming so popular that mass purchasing risked jeopardizing the integrity of the brand. When a Japanese tourist walked into a New York store and bought sixty bags all at once, my father decided to do something about it. All too aware that the man was taking them back to Tokyo to sell on the black market at three times the price, he limited purchases to one of each item per customer.

Then he had to deal with the next problem—counterfeiting. Nothing infuriated him more than to see imitations for sale. The idea of a knockoff being sold as genuine Gucci angered him so much that he was known to challenge hawkers on the streets before buying all their stock and throwing it away. He once bought a score of fake Gucci watches and would wear them from time to time to see if anyone could tell the difference.

Whenever he spotted someone with a fake Gucci bag he would point it out immediately. "You know that's an imitation?" he'd say disdainfully.

"But how can you be sure?" they'd ask, surprised.

He'd smile indulgently and reply, "My dear, how does a mother recognize her own children?"

Famously, he once noticed that a passenger was carrying a fake purse on a flight from New York to Los Angeles. Leaning across the aisle, he tapped her on the shoulder and asked with a smile, "Excuse me, *signora,* but what is an elegant woman like you doing with a Gucci imitation?"

She was visibly taken aback. "My husband bought it for me!"

Nodding sympathetically, Papà scribbled on one of his business cards and handed it to her. His note read, "Please give this lady a thirty percent discount on a *real* Gucci handbag. Signed, Aldo Gucci."

As well as his own personal crusades, my father set up an entire department whose job was to thwart the counterfeiters in every country where they appeared. Lawyers engaged by the company, who were to become an integral part of Gucci affairs, were rarely idle.

To unwind from the stress of keeping on top of such a vast enterprise, he and my mother began to escape to the sun whenever possible. Without doubt, their happiest times together were in Palm Beach, where he initially rented a two-bedroom bungalow with a pool. He loved the area so much that he bought a larger property close by. It took a bit of searching but eventually he found just what he was looking for—a Mediterranean-style villa with white stucco walls and a red-tiled roof on North Ocean Boulevard. There was a sweeping lawn that led down to the beach, past a guest cottage and pool with its own cabana. Sitting on the terrace listening to the sound of crashing waves, my parents thought they'd found their Shangri-la and few would disagree.

Busy with my studies and enjoying life as a boarder, I was still excited to go there during my school vacations. We'd wake up early, take a dip in the ocean, and wander barefoot through the garden picking grapefruits for breakfast. My father never sat still but occasionally I'd find him lying by the pool without a care in the world. The only thing we had to be wary of was encountering poisonous snakes. My mother was confronted one day with a four-foot-long diamondback, which slithered across the kitchen floor as she stood frozen to the spot. After reading up later on its symbolism, she was alarmed to discover that a snake often signifies an unexpected disaster befalling the head of the household. She prayed that wouldn't be the case.

Fortunately, our head of the household was in high spirits. When he was in the mood to go out we went to restaurants like La Petite Marmite, my personal favorite, where I had escargots for the first time and always ordered the same thing. Occasionally—and only when it was just the two of us—my father ordered frog's legs or cow brains, and whenever we had a whole fish, he'd eat the head, including the eyes, delighting in telling me how crunchy they were as I winced. My mother never would have allowed him to have those kinds of dishes.

Papà liked to tease the staff, too. A hapless maître d' might approach him and say, "*Buonasera*, Dr. Gucci. How many are we tonight?"

"*We?*" my father would say with a grin. "Why? Are you joining us?"

In Chinese restaurants, he'd suddenly start juggling plates or toss one at me, certain that I'd catch it. Or he'd take the order pad and jot down something vaguely resembling Mandarin before handing it back to the waiter and telling him, "With rice please." His humor was contagious and I'd cry with laughter while my mother kicked him under the table, imploring him to stop. The more she protested, the more capricious he became and we'd beg her to see the funny side. "Relax, Bruna!" he'd say mischievously. "It's just a bit of fun!" She'd shake her head and call us both crazy but I think she sometimes only pretended to be cross.

On special occasions, my father would take me shopping

to my favorite store on Worth Avenue. While he waited outside the dressing room, I'd try on outfits and parade in them for him. *"Bellissima!"* he'd cry, clapping his hands and making me feel like a million dollars. "Oh, I love that orange color on you!" He may not have been around very much in my childhood but when he was, he sure made up for it.

On Sundays, the three of us would curl up in bed and watch the American "Holy Rollers" on TV. Our favorite was the bewigged Christian evangelist pastor Reverend Ernest Angley, who broadcast from his Temple of Healing Stripes in Ohio. How we would laugh at his antics as he "saved" the sinners who collapsed under the "power" of his hands as he cried, "Praise the Lord!"

Florida was the only place in the world where my father didn't go to the office every morning. Instead, he'd spend a few hours pottering about and freeing up his mind for what he called "more profound matters." My fondest images of him are his watering the lawn in shorts, barefoot, the grass between his toes. Or sitting on the porch, filling his pipe with that distinctive blend of cherry tobacco. I'd often find him there, deep in thought and staring at the horizon with his pipe sticking out of the side of his mouth, left elbow on right forearm.

My mother loved Florida too and virtually lived in a bathing suit and pareo as she lay in the sun or puttered around the kitchen preparing lunch. We were there as a family far more than we'd ever been in Berkshire and it was the one place she came to think of as home.

Palm Beach was undoubtedly where Mamma and Papà were most openly affectionate and endearing with each other. I'd hear him calling out to see what she was doing or catch him taking her some iced tea on a tray. "Bruna! *Dove sei? Vuoi qualcosa?"* (Where are you? Do you want something?) he'd cry, and for a few precious moments I was able to enjoy that rare feeling of togetherness under the same roof.

I didn't appreciate it until much later on but whenever I think of our times there, I realize now that they were the best years of our lives.

FIFTEEN

*H*ome is a concept I haven't always found easy to grasp. As someone who grew up constantly on the move, it took me a long time to understand that home is wherever I make it.

Florence was my father's "home," and then Rome, where he was married with children before he met my mother. She has always considered Rome "home" but then she went to live in London—twice—and Berkshire, where she desperately tried to create a home. Florida became a home for us all and then there was New York, although Mamma never liked it as much as Papà. "I was so bored and had far too much time on my hands," she complained. "All I ever did was wander around Bloomingdale's and Saks Fifth Avenue buying things I didn't particularly need. I can't stand department stores now!"

By the age of ten, I'd been shuffled back and forth between England and Italy, never living in a place for too long before it was time to pick up and go. I spent month-long vacations in America and summer breaks on the Italian coast. Boarding school certainly felt like home, with Bee and all my friends. The longest spell I'd had anywhere was Berkshire so I suppose that was my true home. Certainly, when I think of my childhood "home," that's the place that springs to mind.

One Saturday in 1973, that sense of familiarity would be disrupted for good. On a weekend back from school my mother sat me down to tell me something. "We're moving," she announced as I drew a sharp intake of breath. "We're going back to Rome."

I could hardly believe my ears. My heart began to pound in my chest and my head went into a spin. She was tearing me away from the place I loved without so much as an explanation, but I knew better than to question her. Objecting to any decision always ended in tears, so quizzing her would be futile. Besides, I didn't think anyone would pay me much attention.

Even so, I couldn't pretend to be anything other than heartbroken. This would be the last time that I would allow myself to feel fazed by a move from one place to another. As a result of all this relocation I have never felt particularly attached or committed to anywhere and can now transfer from one country to another without much fanfare. I became a gypsy.

I didn't find out what had triggered this latest move until I was a grown woman. Much to my surprise, it had begun with a painter who'd been hired to redecorate the house. When my father came across a photograph of my mother in the man's belongings, he immediately suspected they were having an affair. Furious, he pounced on her when she came home from shopping, shouting, "What do you think you're playing at?" She was about to protest her innocence when she saw the rage in his eyes. Dropping her groceries, she fled from him screaming as he ran after her and slapped her. He stopped only when he remembered the incident with her brother and realized he might have gone too far.

My father eventually calmed down enough for Mamma to assure him that nothing had happened. He seemed to accept her answer and then he left for New York. Or so he said. Unbeknownst to her, he canceled his flight and checked into a local hotel instead. In the early hours of the following morning, he crept back into the house expecting to surprise her in bed with her lover. Instead, he was astonished to find her sound asleep, alone. She awoke with a start, turned on the light, and found him standing over her with a shamed expression in his eyes. "Bruna, my angel, *perdonami!*" he said apologetically. "I should have trusted you. *Ti prego,*" he implored. "Please forgive me!"

My mother was visibly stunned by the extent of his jealousy.

"How can I make it up to you?" he pleaded, sensing her shock. "Ask me for anything—anything at all."

"I want to go back to Rome," she announced suddenly. "I'm homesick, Aldo. I can't be on my own here any longer. It's time to go."

My father had no idea she felt this way. On the surface, everything seemed okay. I was doing well at school and they were traveling together more. He knew she struggled with her English and that she would have liked to feel more connected, but he never suspected she was so miserable. Knowing he was in no position to argue, however, he agreed without another word.

And so it was that in the late summer of 1973, I had little choice but to pack up my belongings and say good-bye to all my friends. My father decided that the house wouldn't be sold in case we wanted to come back for family holidays or even to live one day. That was my dearest wish.

Still trying to swallow the bitter pill I had been given, a few days before we were due to fly my mother sat me down on her bed and said she had something to tell me—never a good sign. Feeling my stomach tighten, I braced myself for the next bombshell.

"Your father has a wife in Italy," she declared as my mouth dropped open. "And three sons."

My ten-year-old brain was barely able to take in the news. He was married to someone else? With other children? I was utterly confused. "Wait, aren't you married to Papà?"

"No, Patrizina. I'm not," she said remorsefully, trying to soften the blow.

My mind swam. Like any child, I'd always assumed my parents were together to the exclusion of anyone else—that it was just the three of us in this world. The idea that my father had another family was difficult to envisage but one thing my mother had said stuck with me. "I have brothers?" I asked, my eyes wide.

"Yes," she replied slowly. "Their names are Giorgio, Paolo, and Roberto but they're much older than you. They are married, with children of their own."

My heart skipped a beat as I carefully stored away their names. Questions flooded my thoughts. What were they like? Did we look the same? Were their children my age? Instead, I asked a more poignant question: "Do they know about me?"

She nodded. Why hadn't Mamma told me before? I wondered. And if they'd been told about their little sister, why didn't they try to contact me?

"You have to understand that this isn't an ideal situation," she said as my face fell. "You can't presume that they'll embrace you right away. They're much older than you and have their own lives. You won't have anything in common with them. Besides, they don't care much for me and weren't too pleased when they found out about you."

Once she registered my expression, she insisted, "You are just as much your father's child as they are but they, well, they see it differently." She tried again. "It's nothing to do with you personally. It's all about money."

"When will I see them?" I asked, ignoring her pessimistic outlook. I was eager to set my eyes on these walking, talking brothers of mine, whatever they thought of me.

"At some point you'll be able to meet," she replied with a sigh. "Your father will arrange it."

Boarding the airplane to Rome not long afterward, I was filled with so many conflicting emotions. Sorrow at leaving my home, my school, and all my friends. Resentment that my mother had never thought to consult me or considered how painful it would be for me to move. Dread at the idea of starting at a new school where I didn't know a soul, and a frisson of intrigue at the concept that I wasn't an only child.

Staring out of the window as we took off, all I kept repeating in my head was, "I have brothers. I have *three* brothers!"

In spite of my hopes, however, it would be over a year before I'd meet them. First I had to settle into my new home and different routines, which began with my curriculum at St. George's English School. Having led a relatively insulated existence at Hurst Lodge, I was suddenly hurled into an exciting new environment where students spoke many different languages and I immediately learned a slew of Italian swear words. Best of all, though, there were boys.

I quickly hooked up with a girl named Andrea Bizzarro who'd also recently arrived from an English boarding school. When she sat down next to me in class, she had nothing to write with. "Can I borrow one of your pencils?" she asked, spotting the newly sharpened stack in my brand-new case.

"Only if you return it," I told her curtly. Fortunately she didn't hold my attitude against me and we soon became friends. In a school that was far more relaxed than any I had ever known, Andrea and I discarded our uniforms, wore whatever we liked, and ran wild. From speaking in a cut-glass English accent, I began to favor Italian with its gesticulations and inflections. I loved the freedom of not having to tie my hair up and being able to wear bell-bottom jeans with Fiorucci tops emblazoned with slogans. For a while we dated two boys who were best friends, smooching on the sports field and listening to records after school, but we soon dumped them and kept to each other—the start of a lifelong friendship.

Having been a diligent student in England, I now did the bare minimum required to get by. My mother was none too impressed but my rebellious nature had been triggered and there was little she could do about it. All I could think about was boys and I lived in virtual ignorance of the world around me, including the fact that Italy was going through a major economic slump and a period of militant extremism. The infamous Brigate Rosse had precipitated a wave of terror marked by sabotage, kidnappings, and murders. Among the fifty or so people they slew between 1974 and 1978 was the former prime minister Aldo Moro, whose bullet-riddled body was discovered in the trunk of a car in the center of Rome. Other victims were kidnapped, terrorized, or kneecapped to cripple them, along with the country.

On July 10, 1973, a few months before I'd arrived, John Paul Getty III—a former pupil of St. George's and grandson of the famous oil tycoon—was grabbed off the street, blindfolded, and imprisoned in a cave. His kidnappers—thought to be part of a Mafia sect from Calabria—demanded $17 million in ransom. When the sixteen-year-old's family refused to pay, his captors cut off his ear and sent it to a newspaper. After five months in captivity an estimated $2.9 million was paid and the boy was freed.

Even Andrea and I couldn't be oblivious to the incident, news of which gripped the world. Our school went into lockdown and from then on we had to be transported in and out by secure buses. Bomb scares became a frequent occurrence, although many were bogus—no doubt masterminded by St. George's pranksters. We didn't mind; it meant that we were sent home early and could spend the rest of the day lounging by the pool at a nearby hotel.

My father got on with Andrea like a house on fire. He loved her vitality and was always pleased to see her, especially when we'd show up at the Via Condotti store. In time, she joined us in Palm Beach for the holidays and he treated her like a second daughter. Ever the joker, at dinner he would make up stories whenever his business associates would drop by our table to say hello. "May I present you to Contessa Stuzzicadenti" (Countess Toothpick), he'd tell them, pointing to Andrea with a deadpan expression. "And this is Principessa dei miei Stivali" (Princess of My Boots), he'd add, referring to another of my friends. Invariably, his foreign colleagues would be impressed and would only realize he was having a joke at their expense when we could no longer keep a straight face.

One night my father told Mamma he wanted me to accompany him to a business dinner in Rome. Our sole dining companion turned out to be a stunning blonde. She seemed nice enough and paid a lot of attention to my father—as most people did—but I didn't speak to her much and my attention was firmly on Papà, who was in sparkling form that night and went out of his way to compliment me on my manners and how grown-up I seemed. When we returned home later that night still glowing, my mother was in one of her moods so I decided not to say much about our evening, other than briefly mentioning the name of the woman who'd joined us. Then I went to bed.

While I'd found a new best friend in Andrea, Mamma didn't make friends quite so easily. She didn't even meet Andrea's mother for years and she missed Liz and the close bond they'd shared. When she heard that Liz had developed breast cancer, she was devastated. Then one night she had one of her dreams, in which she saw a doll lying facedown in a bath full of water. When the doll turned, it was Liz. The vision haunted her all night and the following morning she received a telephone call to inform her that her dear friend had died. Her howls filled the apartment and she wept inconsolably for hours. I had never seen her so upset and no matter how hard I tried to comfort her, I couldn't ease her pain.

My father arrived and told me sadly, "She was like this when your grandmother passed away. We just have to give her time."

He soon had his own bereavement to deal with when his brother Vasco died of lung cancer in 1974. He was sixty-seven years old, one year younger than Papà. They'd never been especially close but still he felt the loss. Vasco's death created a new dynamic in the company when his widow sold his shares to my father and Uncle Rodolfo, a division of spoils that meant that Papà could no longer be outvoted. Even though he was approaching his seventieth birthday, he had never given up on his determination to stay on top and keep ahead of the growing competition. He was also keen to reward his sons for their hard work in some way, despite continued opposition. My father wasn't someone to let people get in his way, however, so by setting up a separate company called Gucci Parfums Inc. with his sons as directors, he finally got what he wanted. Ultimately, it proved to be hugely successful, too.

Rodolfo's only son, Maurizio, meanwhile, continued down his rebellious path and ended up marrying the controversial Patrizia Reggiani. My father sent a token gift but didn't attend the wedding. Nor did any other member of the immediate family. Uncle Foffo promptly disowned his son and for a while it seemed as if my twenty-four-year-old cousin would never return to the Gucci fold. Such a deep rift weighed heavily on my father after a lifetime of encouraging the family to adhere to Guccio's principles of legacy and unity. Eventually, it became too much for him and he felt compelled to intervene. After shuttling between the aggrieved parties he came up with a plan. Maurizio would move to New York with

Patrizia, where he could learn the retail trade under Papà's supervision. He wouldn't be entitled to shares or a boardroom vote until such time as he proved his worth and his loyalty to the business. The deal satisfied everyone.

Maurizio and his young bride moved into my father's spare apartment on West Fifty-Fourth Street but soon decided that wasn't good enough and relocated to a suite at the St. Regis Hotel. They eventually persuaded my uncle to buy them a penthouse in the brand-new Olympic Tower—the iconic black glass building next to St. Patrick's Cathedral developed by Aristotle Onassis. With floor-to-ceiling windows, the apartment enjoyed some of the most spectacular views of the city. They lived there in far greater comfort than my father or anyone else in the family, thanks to Patrizia's determination to have the best of everything. "I'd rather cry in a Rolls-Royce than be happy on a bicycle," she once famously said. Dressed in designer clothes and dripping with eye-watering jewelry, she set herself up as a Manhattan socialite and reveled in her newly acquired status as Mrs. Gucci.

With Maurizio settled in, my father got back to business, going ahead with his plan to design a range of cars. The $20,000 Cadillac Seville, manufactured by General Motors, came in three different colors and featured a vinyl roof patterned with the GG *rombi* design, a matching fabric interior, a twenty-four-karat-gold interlocking Gucci emblem, wheel trims, luxury seats, and the trademark red-and-green equestrian stripe. Anyone who paid an additional $7,000 received a color-coordinated set of luggage. Known as the "Big Daddy" of designer vehicles, it was one of the very first collaborations between a luxury brand and a car manufacturer, paving the way for many more to come.

Although he wasn't an ostentatious man, Papà reserved a midnight-blue model for himself, which he kept in Palm Beach and used to travel back and forth to the store on Worth Avenue.

My mother thought it too gaudy and refused to be seen anywhere near it, preferring to drive her sky-blue Seville, parked alongside it in our garage.

Around this time, my father decided to gift a 3.3 percent share of his half of the company to each of his sons, confident that they'd back him in the boardroom, no matter what. My brother Paolo did especially well out of the deal, as Uncle Vasco's passing meant that he'd also taken control of the main factory in Florence and now wielded a great degree of influence.

Perhaps because of the new arrangement or maybe simply because he thought the moment was right, Papà decided to ask his sons to assemble for a special meeting. "It is time to meet your little sister," he told them. "Patricia is part of our family and she is certainly keen to meet you!"

I had been waiting for this momentous day for so long but hadn't dared ask why it had taken all this time. Besides, I'd been busy settling into my new life. I wasn't nervous at all, but Mamma was apprehensive and went to unusual lengths to make me look presentable. My jeans and T-shirts were cast aside and swapped for a navy blue pleated skirt and flowery blouse. My hair was coiffed into luxuriant locks, and as my father arrived to collect me, she gave me a last check and pronounced, "*Sei perfetta!*"

During the two-hour car journey north to Scandicci—the nerve center of the company—my father spoke of the early days in Florence and the genesis of it all. As we approached the car park, he pointed to the long two-story building and said, "This is where it all begins."

As always with Papà, I couldn't help but notice how people behaved in his presence. From the security guard who swept us through the gates to the smiling receptionist, everyone treated *il capo*—the boss—with utmost respect. Placing a reassuring hand on my shoulder, he led me past room after room filled with artisans wearing identical smocks working quietly away on their sewing machines. The smell of leather pervaded the building and there were skins and huge bolts of fabrics stacked up to the ceiling. I was mesmerized.

We made our way upstairs to a light and airy office with sketches of products on the walls and scattered around the room. I was so fascinated by all the different designs that I almost forgot the reason we were there until my father invited me to sit next to him at a huge table in the middle of the room, opposite the door. That's when my nerves kicked in. Suddenly there was a knock on the door and my father cried out, *"Avanti!"*

When I first set eyes on the brothers I'd been longing to meet, I was a tad disappointed. My forced smile must have said it all— they looked almost as old as my father. In my mind I'd conjured up images of handsome, dynamic brothers, not average-looking middle-aged men. Papà sat back and observed us as if he were the director of a play whose characters were entering stage right. I think he assumed, ever the optimist, that as long as he wanted us to get along then that is exactly how it would pan out.

The men who appeared before me one by one were so very different from each other. Forty-six-year-old Giorgio came in first and kissed me on the cheek with an awkward, *"Ciao* Patricia." He was a mamma's boy, and his nervous, stuttering speech made me think of him as somewhat defenseless and vulnerable to bullying. He couldn't have been more different from Paolo, three years younger, who threw the door back on its hinges and came bouncing into the room like a cannonball. Hugging me and kissing me through a wiry mustache, the virtually bald middle son cried out in a distinctively Tuscan accent, *"Ciao, sorellina* [little sister]! What a pleasure it is to finally meet you!" He seemed manic and theatrical, exuberant and open. I liked him the best.

Then Roberto ambled in and suddenly made me feel as if I

were an applicant in a job interview. The youngest, aged forty-two, he was cold and distant and after only the lightest peck on each cheek, he sat down, lit a cigarette, and began to interrogate me in a rather disparaging tone. "How are you enjoying living in Rome? What are you studying? How is your Italian coming along?" Tugging repeatedly at his cuffs, he spoke in an affected manner. I later learned that he had married into nobility and acquired some airs and graces along the way, as well as becoming deeply religious. Strangely, my father—who called him "Sonny"—seemed to dote on him.

When the chitchat was over and an awkward silence fell, Papà suggested we all have lunch in the staff canteen. Sitting together at a long trestle table, everyone was far more relaxed. Gratifyingly, several members of staff came over to shake my hand and tell me how nice it was to meet me. It was clear that they knew of my existence, even though I'd never known anything about them or the brothers they'd worked with for years. Chatting with them all over lunch, I understood for the second time what it felt like to be part of a family.

Mamma didn't seem convinced when I recounted the day's events later that evening, reiterating how nice everyone had been. "They were just being courteous," she replied, wiping the smile off my face. Seeing my expression, she tried to make light of what she'd said but I could tell she doubted their sincerity.

Nothing could spoil my day and I went to sleep that night feeling strangely buoyed by the idea that there was more to my life than just my mother and father. It wasn't that I felt any sense of homecoming—just that I now knew there were people in the wider world who were connected to me, even if we didn't really belong together. I had brothers and they seemed to quite like me. For now, that was enough.

SIXTEEN

I never once felt that I couldn't trust my father. I knew intuitively that he could be relied upon to look after my mother and me and that—when he was around—he would give us his undivided attention.

In a relationship between two people, trust is essential; otherwise one risks living in a constant state of anxiety. I know that feeling all too well and it caused me great unhappiness for many years. Only a trusting relationship can bring peace and lasting romance.

I imagine Olwen must have given up the idea of trust years earlier and so, to a point, did Mamma. She had long since accepted my father's duplicity when it came to other women but she also knew deep down that she was "the one" and that he'd never forsake her. Or so she thought.

During my first few years in Rome, a dark cloud settled over our apartment that had nothing to do with me. Something much more serious was afoot, although I wouldn't discover exactly what it was for a while. All I knew was that things weren't right and my mother was floundering in misery once more. Papà visited less even when he was in the city and she feared he might have met someone else.

Her fears weren't entirely unfounded. The man who once claimed he'd seduced a nun was, after all, incorrigible, and— unbeknownst to me—she knew there had been dalliances in the past. One night, she'd picked up the telephone to overhear him tell a disappointed lover that he couldn't see her. "Bruna's arrived," she heard him whisper. At a dinner party some time later, she'd spotted another woman rubbing her foot up and down his leg under the table.

Each time her suspicions were aroused, she bit her lip and said nothing. Mainly, she was afraid that if she raised the issue their relationship might collapse. Like most of her girlfriends whose husbands were serially unfaithful, she also accepted that Italian men—especially those of my father's generation—believed it was perfectly acceptable to take a mistress or two. I was well aware of that custom from hearing stories about some of the fathers of my friends who seemed incapable of monogamy. As in France and across much of Europe, wives were expected to put up with the infidelity as long as they were otherwise well treated and their husbands eventually returned home.

Having witnessed my mother at her lowest ebb in the past, Papà could be in no doubt of her fragile, sensitive nature. He was keen to protect her from knowing that kind of pain again, even though he ended up being the cause of much of it. His logic was that no matter what he got up to, she was the only woman who truly meant something to him.

To lift her spirits and reassure her of his undying affection, he'd take her away with him every now and again. He loved to show her off and always reveled in the admiring glances she attracted. My mother was a beauty and, even now, looks younger than most women her age. What she'd never managed to become, however, was the kind of companion who'd fraternize effortlessly with his business associates, due to her lack of confidence. She knew that at times he wanted her to make more of an effort, so on one trip to spend Christmas with him in New York she bought some new outfits and resolved to be more social. Papà had taken her out on occasion with my cousin Maurizio, whose wife also called on her from time to time, even though the two women had little in common, so when Patrizia invited Mamma to attend a cocktail party at the St. Regis Hotel on a night when my father was away, she agreed.

"There are some people you simply must meet," Patrizia gushed. One was a woman in her sixties who worked in Gucci's VIP Relations department. Her name was Lina Rossellini, and she was the sister-in-law of film director Roberto Rossellini. My mother liked her immediately. Warm and open, Lina was easy to talk to and Mamma knew instinctively that they'd be friends.

Halfway through the evening Patrizia, power-dressed like a character out of the eighties television show *Dynasty*, joined their conversation. As soon as there was a pause, she said, "Oh, Lina, you *must* tell Bruna what you heard the other day."

My mother immediately sensed Lina's discomfort as she shook her head and feigned ignorance.

Patrizia pressed her. "Oh, *you* know—the latest on Aldo's new mistress." She then spoke the woman's name before telling Mamma, "He's now bought her an apartment and some expensive works of art. Apparently there's *nothing* he won't do for her."

The woman's name meant little to my mother but still her heart froze. Determined to maintain her composure, she forced a smile as Lina sputtered, "N-no, Patrizia! What are you talking about?"

Maurizio's wife studied my mother's expression closely before saying, in mock apology, "Oh, Bruna. I'm so sorry. Didn't you know?"

"Idle gossip!" my mother shot back before hurrying away. Lina chased after her, trying to reassure her that there was no substance to the rumors, but my mother had heard enough. She fetched her coat and went back to the apartment alone to gather her thoughts. Where had she heard the woman's name before? It was vaguely familiar. Then she remembered, with a jolt. I'd mentioned her the night I'd gone to dinner with Papà on my own. That was the moment he'd introduced his *amante* to his daughter, she realized. He would never, ever, have done that unless he had lost his head—and possibly his heart.

Mamma was beside herself. That evening's impact on her was profound. She was in shock and went into paroxysms of anxiety, wondering what to do. When my father returned to Manhattan a few days later, however, he had no inkling what she'd unearthed in his absence. Although the information was killing her, she decided not to spoil our Christmas holidays by confronting him with it. Instead, she became what she described as a *"tigre,"* actively seeking out further information in the coming months. "I was a masochist. I went in search of the information that would hurt me and then I dwelt on it. Sometimes I think I must have enjoyed the pain. I even kept a diary as a way of getting everything down on paper. I had all these hidden secrets . . . more secrets."

None of the information she gathered in her detective work did anything to allay her fears. On a trip to Palm Beach, she rummaged around in the back of a wardrobe and found photographs of the woman there—proof positive that my father had taken his mistress to their beach house and almost certainly to their bed. Still, she held her tongue.

The new mistress, meanwhile, seemed quite brazen about

being seen out with my father in public, so more and more gossip was drip-fed back to my mother. Young, sexy, and socially adept, the other woman turned out to be everything she wasn't. The threat she represented was real.

The day came when Mamma could hold back no longer. I happened to be in the kitchen in Rome when my father walked into the apartment that evening oblivious to the impending storm. As usual, he went to freshen up before dinner but she followed him into the bedroom to blurt, "You've been having an affair!"

He froze.

"I could see the change in his face the minute I said her name," she told me. "There was a twitch and a look in his eye." The argument that ensued was the most explosive I'd ever heard. I sat glued to my chair as it spilled into the living room. Never had I heard my mother so angry. I soon understood what she was accusing him of but naively trusted my father when he denied it.

"I know what's been going on!" she persisted, waving the photographs she'd found. "Tell me it's not true!" He remained on the defensive and assured her that they were headshots for public relations purposes. Still, she wouldn't be calmed. Her outburst shocked me so much that I remember thinking that I wouldn't honestly blame Papà for taking a mistress if she didn't change her tune.

Their fight only ended when my father suddenly picked up an object from a coffee table and hurled it against the wall. Then he stormed out, slamming the door so hard that the whole building shook. It would take me a long time to realize just how painful that whole episode must have been for my mother. If it weren't for her frequent telephone calls to her guru, who repeatedly assured her that there was a reason she was being "tested" and that she had a "higher purpose," I'm not sure how she would have survived.

If I'd hoped the argument would blow over, then I was

mistaken. My mother wasn't as helpless as she sometimes appeared. Furthermore, she was determined to get to the truth. It was almost as if hearing my father admit his guilt out loud would somehow diminish its power over her. Having never previously been comfortable with confrontation, she now accosted him at every opportunity, demanding to know more as the atmosphere between them grew increasingly toxic. This went on for months and included one hysterical row in a hotel in Hong Kong. Repeatedly, he denied being unfaithful, but my mother was a terrier worrying at a bone.

"He took whatever I threw at him," she said later. "He was like a statue, never saying a word." With stealth I never knew she possessed, she began to compile the evidence against him by seeking out those who knew more and who—like Patrizia—would enjoy filling her in on the details.

"I can get you the address of an apartment he bought her in Rome," one woman apprised her over lunch. Another so-called friend Mamma referred to as the "messenger from God" was especially eager to help after her own husband had also been having an affair. "She has jewelry you wouldn't believe," she confided. "This has been going on behind your back for quite a while." Being the last to know was humiliating, to say the least.

Painful as all this was to hear she registered every date and event until she'd amassed a dossier to confront him with once and for all. The evidence was damning. Looking back on the kinds of things he was prepared to do for this woman, she now says she thinks he went "a little crazy" during this period. Whether he was having some sort of midlife crisis or was genuinely infatuated, we will never know. "This episode definitely unbalanced him," she said. "It made him wonder who he was and what he really wanted." One thing is fairly certain—my father seemed beguiled by the new temptress in his life, who appeared to demand so much from him. My mother's pure goodness and what he often referred to as her "virtue" must have seemed such a sharp contrast.

I hated being a silent bystander to their ongoing dispute, especially when I recalled how happy they'd been in Palm Beach. I barely recognized them now. Even though I was only thirteen, I had moved into the studio apartment on the floor above Mamma's. I couldn't hear her but I knew she was crying her eyes out most days. Although I felt sorry for her, like most teenagers I also found my mother deeply irritating. She nagged at Papà for every little thing and her constant sniping was unbearable to be around. It is only with the wisdom of adulthood that I can see how distressing it must have been for her to be neglected in this manner.

As soon as he went away again on business, my mother took her frustration out on me, which only made me even more resentful. Our quarrels intensified and our relationship suffered to the point that I stayed away as much as possible to avoid her. She accused me of turning into a "nightmare" of a daughter, claiming she didn't know how to handle me anymore. In her angriest moments she'd tell me, "If it wasn't for me, your father wouldn't even know you!" I think I was supposed to be grateful to her for the life that I'd had.

I'm sure I was as much to blame. I was disrespectful and started answering back. "If you'd put half as much energy into raising me as you spent doing whatever your precious guru told you, then things might have worked out differently!" I'd counter. "I was the perfect little girl! I did my schoolwork and kept out of trouble, but it was never enough for you, was it?"

When everything else in her life was spinning out of control, it must have been dreadful to realize that she was also losing her grip on the one person she'd always been able to command. Then one day I went too far. In response to something I said, she went to slap me and then chased me out of her apartment with a broom.

Shocked, I locked myself in my room and turned up the music to muffle her shrieking at the door.

After that incident, I told myself I'd pack my things, move out, and live at Andrea's house. Her mother would happily take me in and with Papà away so much, there was nowhere else for me to go. I felt trapped. Yet in spite of my dreams of running away, I never did. Nor was there any need to. Mamma had other plans and when things had calmed down, she sat me on her bed and revealed them to me.

"I've had enough of your attitude, Patricia," she said wearily. "I'm tired of fighting all the time. Since we left England, you've become impossible!" She made it perfectly clear that she wasn't going to take any responsibility whatsoever for the breakdown in our relationship. "Your father has asked me to spend more time with him in the United States, and as we're also worried about these kidnappings in Rome we need to make alternative arrangements for you. Staying at St. George's is no longer an option. You're going back to boarding school—in Switzerland."

I didn't see that one coming.

Aiglon College was located in the village of Chesières high in the Swiss Alps. My future had been decided by Mamma's *pendolino,* a crystal on a chain that she dangled over the names of Aiglon and another Swiss school, Le Rosey, until it settled. Modeled loosely on the British "public" school system, Aiglon was established after the war by a former teacher of Gordonstoun, a notoriously tough school in Scotland. His avant-garde philosophy was that education should be about the "whole" self, including spiritual, physical, and environmental factors. Students were expected to respond positively to the disciplinary regimen, which included taking part in rigorous physical activity—even in the depths of an Alpine winter.

Although I was initially horrified by the idea of being

banished to the mountains, over time I began to appreciate my new environment. From the moment I arrived, I was made welcome. There were three hundred pupils from all over the world and Italy in particular. As one of my roommates said, "We already have a Pucci, now a Gucci. All we need is a Fiorucci!"

Admittedly, there were times when I wasn't so thrilled about being there, especially with the seven a.m. wake-up calls and having to do PT on a freezing-cold terrace first thing in the morning. None of this sat well with my inner city-girl. My days lying dreamily by the pool in Rome seemed a distant memory, especially during one particularly arduous trek in which our group was wading through waist-deep snow in a blizzard ten thousand feet up a mountain. I'm ashamed to admit that the extreme conditions brought out the worst in me and I refused to take another step. Flopping back down into the snow, my sealskin-covered skis sticking up vertically, I declared the expedition too dangerous and demanded an immediate helicopter rescue. "This is crazy!" I screamed above the winds, unable to feel my hands or feet. "Our parents didn't send us here for this!"

What they did send us there for was what happened next— the esprit de corps of my fellow classmates. "Come on, Patricia! Let's get going!" they said encouragingly. Even though every muscle in my body hurt and my tears were turning to ice on my cheeks, I pushed on through the pain. The sense of achievement when we reached our destination was phenomenal, and we clung to one another like the survivors we felt we were. The friendships I forged at Aiglon are among those I cherish most today.

While I was finding myself in the mountains above Lake Geneva, my father was still whizzing around the globe as the so-called Guru of Gucci. He showed no signs of slowing down and seemed unable to relinquish control of anything, from the design of new stores to the look of the latest advertising campaign. As part of his ongoing expansion of the company, he supervised lucrative new licensing contracts, including my brother Paolo's new ready-to-wear range. Then he launched his very own signature perfume. Full-page adverts for Il Mio Profumo were tagged with Papà's autograph above the strap line, "Inspired by and dedicated to women of love."

He also launched the first Gucci wristwatch—the Model 2000—whose multimillion sales would earn an entry in the *Guinness Book of Records*. It was a project that had first been suggested to him in New York when a Belgian-born salesman named Severin Wunderman rang the Gucci offices one day and was surprised when my father picked up and agreed that he could pay him a visit. Severin, a Jew who'd survived the Holocaust, spun Papà a hard-luck story on his arrival. After emigrating to California at the end of the war, he worked for a French watch company that was trying to break into the American market. Wunderman claimed that times were hard and he couldn't pay his rent so he was prepared to negotiate a deal in which a Gucci watch would be manufactured under license. Noticing his scuffed shoes and frayed cuffs, my father took pity on him and placed a huge order. When Severin's company couldn't keep up with demand, Papà cut him a large check to set up on his own. Gucci Timepieces would go on to generate annual royalties of $150 million, while the company Wunderman created grew to gross more than $500 million a year, ensuring that he never again had to worry about meeting the rent.

My father's business was running like clockwork and someone was coming up the ranks who seemed to feel as passionately about it as he did. Unexpectedly, it wasn't one of my brothers. Although Paolo was showing flair and ambition and Giorgio and Roberto were plodding away quietly in the background, my cousin Maurizio looked to have inherited the Gucci acumen. The young pretender had thrived as an apprentice under Papà for seven years, and while he admitted that my father was "a tornado" who screamed at any member of staff who dared take time off, he was also quick to praise him for his courage and vision. "With Aldo it is not living, it is surviving," he said. "If he does one hundred percent, you have to do one hundred fifty percent. . . . From my uncle I really learned the business and the market."

Paolo must have envied Maurizio's relationship with Papà, especially as he repeatedly clashed with management over his own plans to woo a younger clientele. He had set his sights on creating a new company—Gucci Plus—funded by outsiders. My father and Uncle Rodolfo wouldn't hear of it and their objection infuriated him. He accused them of "medieval" practices and secretly decided to forge ahead regardless, confident that Papà would ultimately back him. None of them realized it then, but that was the beginning of the end for Gucci as a family business.

Packing me off to school in Switzerland might well have rid my mother of the conflict between us, but it left her even more beleaguered in Rome. I wasn't there the night she felt she'd gathered enough evidence against my father to confront him once more. On an otherwise uneventful evening, she waited until he was sitting comfortably after dinner before launching her attack. There was no shouting or broken *objets* this time. Instead, Papà sat in silence as she presented him with a dossier of his misdeeds, complete with dates, places, and times. It detailed virtually every trip, every hotel room, and every gift he had bought his lover.

"He sat stock-still, as speechless as the Sphinx. Then he said, 'But who told you?' A muscle in his jaw twitched involuntarily but there was no other response until he stood up, reached for his jacket, and quietly left the building."

Holding her breath, she watched him go, fearing she might never see him again. Still hell-bent on getting her confession, however, her relentlessness knew no bounds and she continued to plague him with questions, demanding, "Aldo, admit it! Tell me that it's true!" After more than two years of her hounding, my father felt the need to escape. In 1978, he flew alone to Palm Beach for some peace and quiet but one night he was woken at two o'clock in the morning by a phone call in which my mother wailed that she was tormented by the demons in her head. Tearfully, she sobbed again down the line that he owed it to her to tell her the truth.

Exploding with frustration, my father cracked. "*Basta*, Bruna! *Sì, sì. E'tutto vero*. It's all true," he shouted. "I admit everything— okay? Satisfied?" There was an eerie silence. He waited for her to respond but there was no sound. More gingerly, he called her name. It was his turn to fear that he'd gone too far. "Bruna? . . . Bruna?" he tried, before the line went dead.

Their roles were reversed in an instant. With my father's confession, my mother had what she wanted but felt as if she'd been punched in the stomach. This was it—the moment she'd dreaded for years. She was convinced that my father was lost to her now and that we were completely on our own with no legal rights. "I became paralyzed, sitting on the bed like marble," she said.

Reaching for the telephone in a daze, she called her guru in London, dialing a number she knew by heart. She realized the futility of that as he rarely answered, preferring messages to be left. But someone must have been on her side that day, because this time, Sari Nandi picked up. As soon as she heard his voice, she broke down and told him everything. "Mr. Nandi, I don't want to live anymore. My life is a mess!"

The significance of that call cannot be underestimated. There is no knowing what my mother might have done if she hadn't been able to talk to the only man she still trusted. Hearing the distress in her voice, he coaxed her back from the emotional ledge. "I will help you," he promised. "Please, Bruna. Calm down and pray with me."

She was comforted by his reassurances. "For reasons I can't explain, he gave me hope," she told me.

My father meanwhile was left hopeless in Florida. Unable to return to sleep and frantically worried, he called her back repeatedly but the phone was constantly engaged. When he eventually got through she didn't answer, no matter how often he redialed. He had no idea that her guru had insisted she leave the apartment and spend the rest of the day with a friend. Panicking, Papà continued to call every hour for the next eight hours without success. Terrified that she'd done something foolish, he called everybody he could think of—even her sister, Gabriella, and the porter of her building—but her apartment was found to be empty and no one had a clue where she might be. He was half out of his mind.

When she returned home late that night and picked up the ringing telephone, he was breathless with panic. "Get a ticket!" he cried. "You're coming to New York! We have to talk."

By the time she reached his apartment in Manhattan, he was figuratively on his knees. "I've been an utter fool!" he cried. "I lavished money and gifts on someone who wanted me more for the things I could offer her than for who I was. When she insisted I leave you, I was horrified and told her, 'No! Bruna is a part of me, like an arm or a leg. I can *never* leave her!'"

He assured her his affair was over. He promised to remain true to her forever. His words seemed heartfelt and Mamma longed to trust him. As always, though, her abiding concern was our security in case she couldn't. "You must promise me that Patricia will always be your priority," she told him coolly. "I don't care about me—you don't have to leave me a thing—but you must vow to provide for our daughter in the same way that you would provide for your sons." He gave her his word.

My father then became "an angel overnight," according to my mother. Struck by her tenacity and besotted with her all over again, he even lived up to his oath to be a better "husband." Spontaneously, she'd telephone him at the office to say, "Aldo, I'm making spaghetti. Would you like to come home and have some with me?"

My father would listen in silence before readily accepting the invitation. "*Sì, certo*," he would say, replacing the receiver and making up some excuse about an emergency he had to take care of. He'd then abruptly end his meeting just so they could have lunch together. This was the Dr. Gucci few could have ever imagined. As my mother said, "He was a man of many faces but the moment he walked through my door, he took off his mask."

He opened up to her in ways he hadn't since he penned her all those letters. "I've never known a woman like you," he told her over and over, "I owe you everything." No one else had the same hold over him. No one else understood him so profoundly. He continually expressed his regret for all the pain he'd caused her, adding, "I will spend the rest of my life making it up to you."

He was convinced that the unshakable connection between them was what he called "*miracoloso*" and that they were being driven together by something "supernatural" and bigger than them both. "It's absurd. Even if I wanted to leave, I couldn't!" he declared.

To my mother, it was anything but absurd. Sari Nandi's prophecy that she had a higher purpose in life had come true. Her prayers had been answered. Though it must have taken her a long time to trust my father again, no matter who or what came between them, their love for each other would prevail. His mistress may have temporarily borrowed Papà's heart, but it would always belong to Mamma.

SEVENTEEN

*I*n the words of George Bernard Shaw, "Imagination is the beginning of creation. You imagine what you desire, you will what you imagine and, at last, you create what you will." My father was first and foremost a businessman but he drew inspiration from his surroundings, which imbued him with a sense of culture and appreciation for the finer things in life.

Having grown up in the giant art gallery that is Florence, he lived and breathed architecture, sculpture, and paintings—an experience only amplified when he moved to Rome. I may not have inherited his flair for business but I like to think that some of his qualities have rubbed off on me—the ability to see the bigger picture, to innovate, and to find creative ways to express myself.

Of all his sons, I think Paolo was the most like him—prolific, restless, and with little regard for authority. Above all, he was talented, although my uncle Rodolfo didn't seem to think so. Their relationship had deteriorated to the point that Foffo fired him as chief designer and had him physically removed from the Scandicci factory. A handbag Paolo had been working on had been the catalyst and was so detested by my uncle that he'd hurled it from a window—where it landed at the feet of startled employees taking a cigarette break.

Papà stepped in to broker a truce just like he had with Maurizio and, as with him, suggested that Paolo move to America to work under his supervision. My uncle was delighted to have him out of the way and Paolo saw this as the opportunity he'd been waiting for. He was given a series of grand new titles, including managing director of Gucci Parfums and Gucci Shops as well as vice president of marketing. The position would involve creating new campaigns and coming up with bold concepts for displays. It came with a higher salary and a number of perks, including an office of his own in the Fifth Avenue headquarters.

Middle-aged and with a second wife in tow, Paolo believed he was getting the recognition he deserved at last. Eager to show my father what he was capable of, he set about implementing his plans, which he didn't like anyone interfering with. Whenever they tried, Papà witnessed how temperamental his son could be— attributes he couldn't tolerate in others. Then Paolo proposed a massive budget increase to promote Gucci far and wide. My father had never seen the need for too much advertising. Since the end of the war word of mouth had been sufficient to create brand aware- ness and when Paolo insisted on extra funding my father laughed in his face and told him not to waste money.

Feeling thwarted at almost every turn, my brother reverted to "Plan A"—Gucci Plus, his concept for a younger, trendier ready- to-wear line that had already been blocked once by the board. He was determined to find a way to bring about his vision, even if it meant resorting to an independent manufacturer.

Papà had a vision of his own—to elevate the Gucci image by combining art with fashion, two worlds he'd always felt were inti- mately connected. The Gucci Galleria was his way of expressing that. When the first one opened in 1977 at the Beverly Hills store to critical acclaim, a thousand patrons were each given an eighteen-karat *chiave d'oro*, or golden key, to unlock the door to the members-only area on the second floor. After gaining access via a dedicated elevator, the privileged few were introduced to luxury on another level.

The Galleria truly had the wow factor. VIPs were greeted with champagne as they marveled at the works of art displayed between rosewood and brass cabinets filled with precious gems, limited-edition jewelry, and crocodile and lizard handbags. Artisans from the factory were flown in so that potential customers could witness their skills. The space maintained a timeless elegance, warm and inviting, where guests could linger without feeling obliged to make a purchase. Whether they'd been invited or just dropped in to enjoy the ambience, the moment they stepped out of that elevator they felt like they were part of something special.

In an industry where trends are soon outmoded, especially when a brand becomes so ubiquitous, my father knew he had to keep ahead of the pack and offer customers something even more aspirational. The Galleria was a direct attempt to reinstate that cachet. Once it was declared a success, he set his sights on replicating the concept in New York in what would come to be considered the most astounding retail space in Manhattan—Aldo Gucci's message to the world.

It was around then that my father thought it was time to include me in company events. Aged just fifteen and on a school break, I accompanied him to Singapore, Hong Kong, and Japan— the first of my many trips to Asia on behalf of the company. Then, in the summer of 1979, I flew to Los Angeles to be his official representative at a major Hollywood benefit he'd sponsored at the famed Beverly Wilshire hotel. I sensed that this would be an audition of sorts so I had my hair done and wore a beautiful yellow off-the-shoulder chiffon Halston dress. I was placed at the top table with June Allyson and Rita Hayworth, in her day one of the most stunning actresses in Hollywood. Even in her sixties and with early Alzheimer's, she had the kind of beauty that never fades.

The evening went without a hitch, as I tried to speak with everyone present without appearing overwhelmed. For a teenager, I suppose I did okay. "Your father said you were brilliant!" my mother told me later. Praise from him meant more to me than anything else.

In June 1980, he asked if I could be given special leave from Aiglon to attend the grand opening of the new US flagship and Gucci Galleria in New York. He wrote to the headmaster that it was "imperative" I attend, adding, "The Gucci families will be here." Even my mother was going. She rarely attended these kinds of functions but I was glad she'd decided to make the effort. During my four years in Switzerland, she only ever came to visit me on occasion. I spent the summer holidays with friends, which meant we didn't see each other very often. The only time we were really together was when my father organized something special.

The New York opening was one such time and he insisted we both be there. It was especially important to him that he be seen with the woman most Americans assumed was his wife. His real spouse remained firmly ensconced in Italy. In her seventies with failing health, she was rarely seen in public.

My mother looked stunning that night but kept a low profile. Although she'd met Giorgio, Paolo, and Roberto before, she wouldn't have been comfortable with them in such close proximity. I'm sure she turned away when Patrizia posed for photographs in some outrageous getup and Maurizio held court, sending the message that Gucci would remain in family hands long after my father had passed on the mantle.

The plaudits for the latest Galleria were extraordinary, even by

American standards. "New Gucci out-Guccis itself!" said the *New York Times*, which described it as an "oasis of hushed but opulent luxury." It certainly was. The glass elevator ride to the hallowed space gave customers a bird's-eye view of a vast sixteenth-century seven-by-five-meter tapestry called *The Judgment of Paris* woven in silks and wool that had been commissioned by Francesco de' Medici. It took up an entire wall, as did a five-by-two-meter painting called *The White Tree* that my father had commissioned from the artist Roy Lichtenstein. The sheer scale of these pieces set the tone for what was about to unfold, as guests were able to stand before works by some of the biggest names in Italian contemporary art as well as others from around the world.

"I love to be surrounded by beautiful things," my father said, showing off the unique collection he'd put together. "And contemporary art speaks a language of its own." It was a language he understood and appreciated far more than yachts or other such status symbols. Fine art touched something deep inside him—his creative core.

Though dazzled, the media were quick to suggest he was being reckless in opening twenty thousand square feet of retail space during a recession. Shaking his head, he reminded them that the Galleria was reserved only for Gucci's most loyal customers— "the five percent who can afford it." He added, "Luciano Pavarotti wouldn't dream of singing in a café for all the money in the world. Pavarotti has a voice and an image . . . This is our voice—the voice [with which] we sing."

Of all the images I have of my father in my mind, the one of him that warm June night is among the fondest. Impeccably dressed, the man dubbed "the Michelangelo of Merchandising" moved energetically through the eight salons filled with orchids, art treasures, and—of course—plenty of Gucci merchandise. With a smile for everyone, he greeted society hostesses, politicians, celebrities, and movie stars with equal warmth as classical music played discreetly in the background. Looking twenty years younger, Papà was the master of his domain.

Whatever lay ahead for him and for Gucci, he couldn't have helped but be delighted at how far he'd come. My mother was at his side and I was playing an increasingly important role in his world. His family seemed to have settled their differences momentarily and the future looked brighter. That night represented decades of hard work and tireless dedication but I think even he would have stood with a glass of champagne at the end of it all and reflected on the magnitude of his achievements.

What he hadn't counted on, however, was the reckless ambition of my brother Paolo. Uncle Rodolfo had been keeping close tabs on him and when he discovered that he'd secretly gone ahead with his plans to launch Gucci Plus, he was incensed—as was my father. Four months after the Galleria opening, Paolo was summoned to the boardroom to explain. When he refused to apologize and tried making further demands, he detonated my father's temper. In a fit of rage, he fired him on the spot and sent him packing with a dismissal letter from the board.

Paolo had underestimated Papà. If he'd waited and then backed down, he might have been able to ingratiate himself. Instead, the hotheaded fool went to his lawyer and lodged a petition to establish the Paolo Gucci trademark. The move directly contravened a shareholder's agreement that specifically forbade the use of the Gucci name "for the exercise of any further industrial, commercial or artisan activity."

Nothing angered my father more than disrespect, and the idea of a sideline under the "GG" banner sent him into the kind of fury normally reserved for counterfeiters. He launched an immediate lawsuit citing trademark infringement, then threatened to blacklist any supplier who dared do business with his son. This would have sounded the death knell for those who didn't comply, most of whom relied on Gucci for the bulk of their trade. That ended the whole affair and Paolo's bitterness toward Papà soured their relationship forever.

Contact with my other two brothers by this time was a little more amicable. The atmosphere between us softened, although they always felt more like uncles to me than siblings. Ultimately, they remained largely as I had assessed them in our first encounter.

Giorgio was never too comfortable in a crowd and only when we were on our own, away from Papà, was he able to be himself. He hardly even stammered with me. I also discovered that he had a quasi-British sense of humor and that far from being timid and mild-tempered, he could be razor sharp.

Roberto, with his hair slicked to one side and his trademark rounded shirt collars, remained aloof and never once lost his sarcastic tone with me. I hadn't warmed to him. Nor did I trust him. He pretended to be nice to me in front of Papà but when we were alone, he was snide and rather cold. He and his wife started referring to me disparagingly as *"la lava"* because of what they considered my eruptive personality, which I took as a compliment. Not that I was eruptive, per se, just bubbly, I suppose.

His eldest son, Cosimo, was the only one from that side of the family I really liked. He would invite me to dinner with his fiancée and always showed the greatest respect for my father, so we had an immediate bond. Having worked in the business for a number of years, he also knew how everything came together, so whenever I was in Florence he took me under his wing and showed me around. He felt more like a brother than all of them put together.

On a visit to the Scandicci factory with my father when I was seventeen, I was taken to view the latest collection, which was being unveiled to buyers from around the world. By now, all my

childhood nervousness had gone and I felt quite at home surrounded by family and long-standing employees. With the growing
confidence instilled in me at school from a young age, I introduced myself in Italian or English to our franchisees from Japan
and North America, as well as representatives from our stores in
the United Kingdom, France, and Italy.

Watching the show from the back of the room with Cosimo
as models paraded the new season of ready-to-wear, shoes, bags,
and accessories, I saw how the buyers made their selections and it
gave me an early insight into the complexities of the retail trade.
Roberto was in charge of the proceedings that day, and taking
the microphone, he announced we would all be adjourning to the
canteen for lunch. In a final quip, he added, "Everyone except
you, Patricia!" singling me out from across the room. His failed
attempt at humor only served to embarrass us both.

As happy as I was to be included in the day's activities, I
never seriously entertained thoughts of working in the family business. Like my uncle Rodolfo before me, I had dreams of pursuing
a stage career. I'd loved studying drama at school, most recently
at Aiglon, where I was regularly cast in leading roles, including
Maisie in the musical *The Boy Friend*. Incredibly, my mother was
able to attend. "*Brava,* Patrizina! You were amazing," she told me
afterward, before taking me out for dinner with some friends. It
was another happy memory.

I would have loved for Papà to see my starring debut but he
was, of course, on the other side of the world. As disappointed as
I was, I soon got over it—especially as none of my friends' fathers
came either. At least my mother had come. Papà did send me a
note that I still have to this day, along with other encouraging letters he sent me over the years. In this one he wrote: "*I am sending you all my best love and always thinking about you and how
proud I feel of my daughter.*"

In the summer of 1980 it was time to leave Aiglon and return to city life. With my parents' blessing, I moved to London to prepare for my A levels and then university, where I hoped to continue my drama studies. Having a flat all to myself right opposite Harrods was a truly liberating experience. At last, I was free from rules and regulations and able to taste real independence for the first time. I certainly made the most of my newfound freedom.

London was an exciting place to be. Most of my friends lived there, including many who'd recently moved from Aiglon. There was my dear friend Maria Dahlin, as well as Enrico Marone Cinzano, who refers to me as "ninety percent perfect and ten percent mad." In those days, the ratio was definitely inverted. The three of us would stay out all night in clubs like the Blitz or Heaven, catching a taxi home at sunup with the sounds of Ultravox, Visage, and the Human League still ringing in our ears. On little sleep and with no one to make me knuckle down, I did virtually no studying and inevitably my grades suffered.

My mother and I were leading separate lives. We spoke periodically on the phone, especially when I needed new pasta recipes after growing tired of eating spaghetti with butter and Parmesan— the best cure for my all-too-frequent hangovers. "How do you make your *penne all'arrabbiata?*" I pleaded. "I have people coming over and it would be perfect." We still had our differences but when it came to food we were always on safe ground.

By the time I approached my eighteenth birthday in February 1981, I'd been in London for six months with no real plans to speak of. All I cared about was having fun. I was only halfmindful of my responsibilities or the fact that I might one day be asked to live up to them, a fact that was brought home to me when someone at Gucci suggested that my birthday could be promoted as a PR event. The idea of a debutante ball in Palm Beach and New York horrified me and I immediately told my father so.

"Okay, what would you like to do instead?" he asked.

I opted for a private black-tie dinner at the Savoy in London, where (unbeknownst to me at the time) my grandfather had first found his creative inspiration a hundred years earlier. I could have had any gown I wanted but instead found a 1930s long black sequined dress in a vintage store on the King's Road in Chelsea. I'll never forget that night. Regrettably, Mamma wasn't able to celebrate with me. Her excuse this time was that there would be "too many young people" and she wouldn't feel comfortable in such a crowd. Papà, on the other hand, enjoyed himself immensely. He loved being with my generation and was only too proud to lead me onto the dance floor for the first waltz. There was one perfect moment toward the end of the evening when he took the microphone, called for a hush, and gave a speech in front of all my friends. As I stood somewhat shyly to one side, I listened to him tell everyone that I made him the "proudest father in the world."

Two months later, there was another grand party to attend—this time in Palm Beach. Having spent so much time there and in New York, my father had decided to make America his official country of residence. Although Italy would always be his heartland, it was still going through tumultuous times and, for many, was an increasingly dangerous place to be. In contrast, America's frontier spirit and enterprising culture had truly allowed my father to fly. By registering as a resident of Florida he officially transferred his domicile status there, which meant that from then on he'd be expected to pay stateside income tax.

The decision further galvanized his love of Palm Beach. He had bought the vacant lot next to ours and created a fabulous new home with the help of the architect who'd designed the Gucci Galleria. Even though Papà was still haunted by the ongoing discord in the family and anxious about my brother Paolo in particular, he decided to take his mind off things and throw a housewarming party. He wanted my mother and me at his side for what he hoped would be a new era for us all.

By the time I arrived, preparations were well under way for what the local media described as "the hottest ticket in town." Dominating the garden was a huge white tent to cater for the two hundred and fifty guests, which included Luciano Pavarotti and the cream of Palm Beach society. While the staff bustled to and fro, Mamma descended into her own private hell. She loathed events like these—especially when she'd be the center of attention—and the idea of having to interact with so many strangers petrified her.

"Parties kill me!" she'd protest. "I can't bear all the smiling! It's so fake." Years later, she told me that she always felt "painfully inadequate" and ill at ease among my father's circles, as if she didn't belong. "I never knew if I was saying the right thing or if I looked the part. I felt ten times smaller than those sophisticated women who knew how to put themselves together and engage in conversation. I was the Cinderella."

She needn't have worried that night. When she emerged from her bedroom in an ethereal gray chiffon dress, my father and I gasped. *"Quanto sei bella!"* (How beautiful you are!) he cried, throwing his arms open to embrace her. I also assured her she looked sensational but of course she didn't believe either of us for one moment and begged us not to tease.

Incredibly, she carried herself like a star all evening— mingling effortlessly with the kind of confidence I'd rarely seen before. Observing her from a distance, I was mesmerized and couldn't help but wonder how she was managing. I watched her graciously accept kisses from Pavarotti, who was equally entranced. "Bruna! What a delight you are!" he cried, before enfolding us both in his big loving arms. As my father grinned at the playful spectacle with this larger-than-life character, I could see why he and the great tenor had become good friends.

My mother should have won an Oscar for her performance. Only Papà and I knew how much she must have been quaking inside. The only reason she made it through the night, I later discovered, was because a friend of the family had slipped her the first (and last) tranquilizer she ever took, which allowed her to relax and "float" through what I referred to as her "coming-out ball."

"It was as though I wasn't even there but I hated the feeling!" she told me. "Never again."

Probably her worst moment was when my father rose during dinner and insisted that she and I stand to either side of him while he addressed his guests. He was determined to let everybody know how important we were in his life as he pulled us close for photographs. I could tell she wanted the ground to open up and swallow her as all eyes fell upon us when my father started to make a speech. "I'm so happy to welcome you all to our new home, which started as a dream and has become a reality," he said, his eyes glistening. "And to be with my beautiful wife Bruna and my lovely daughter, Patricia, here in Palm Beach—our favorite place in the world."

We all smiled into the cameras as the crowd applauded, and in spite of my mother's embarrassment, it proved to be a night to treasure for always.

EIGHTEEN

The one thing my mother was naturally adept at was dealing with ailments. With her homemade soups and curative rice dishes, she was a real alchemist and had a remedy for just about anything. It was all part of being *una mamma Italiana*.

When I was a little girl and went through all the usual childhood maladies, she was nothing short of attentive and bordered on obsessive. She'd cover my head in a towel and sit me over a steaming bowl of eucalyptus to clear my sinuses, or dab my chicken pox with calamine lotion, putting me under strict orders not to scratch. She meant well but at times her compulsive manner was a little annoying. "Take this and go to sleep!" was about as close as she came to a good-night wish.

I'm sure she must have been present when I had my tonsils out in Berkshire, and I'm sure she was distraught the time I was rushed to the hospital in the middle of the night with appendicitis at Aiglon, but I must have filed away those memories. These days she still makes a huge fuss at the first signs of a cold, calling each morning to make sure I'm okay. *"Come ti senti oggi?"*

(How do you feel today?) she will typically ask before even saying hello. She was the same way with my father but had little sympathy for anything she deemed to be self-inflicted. Nor did she pay much heed to the fact that my father and I traveled across time zones and were frequently exposed to the afflictions of the outside world. So when Papà developed insomnia, she was cross with him at first, blaming it on jet lag. He'd always been a restless spirit but he generally slept fairly well for someone with such an active mind. When he really couldn't settle at night my mother—who was no stranger to sleeping disorders herself—started preaching about deep breathing to clear his mind. It rarely worked. She'd wake in the small hours in Palm Beach to find him gone from their bed. Pulling on her dressing gown, she'd wander out into the humid night to discover him watering the lawn barefoot under a star-studded sky.

"Aldo! What are you doing?" she'd cry.

"It's okay, Bruna. Go back to bed. I'll be there soon."

What he didn't know was that she often stayed watching him, noting that he was so engrossed with his thoughts that he'd stand in the same spot for several minutes at a time, flooding the ground and soaking his bare feet.

Hoping it was only a phase, Mamma knew deep down that the trouble at Gucci was behind his agitation, and no amount of deep breathing could rid him of one particular anxiety. My brother Paolo continued to be a thorn in his side and his antics demanded more and more of my father's attention. "He's never satisfied," Papà would complain in a subdued voice. "He always has to push for something more. And these lawyers he keeps bringing in! They're nothing but bad news. Why can't he be more like his brothers and just get on with business?"

"Can't *they* make him stop all this nonsense?" Mamma would ask.

"They've tried but it's no use."

"Aldo, you must try not to worry too much," she'd tell him, but she knew that with all the simmering tension it was easier said than done. When she was with me, it was another story. "Paolo's going to ruin us!" she'd cry with a growing sense of foreboding. "Nothing's ever enough for him. Your father's beside himself."

There were other problems too. My uncle Rodolfo had recently demanded a bigger stake in Gucci Parfums, the company Papà had set up for the benefit of my brothers but had since exceeded all expectations. At the time, Rodolfo had agreed to grant his nephews a 20 percent share in the fledgling operation and chosen not to allocate Maurizio a similar shareholding, as they were still incommunicado. Now that the business was doing so well, he wanted his own percentage increased threefold but my father refused.

The stress began to seriously undermine Papà's health, though he'd have been the last to admit it. He'd been fit and healthy all his life and rarely took time off work due to illness. But during the summer of 1981, when he was meant to be relaxing in Florida with us, he developed a horrible cough that wouldn't go away.

"I'll tell you how you got this," my mother chided as she fixed him some milk and honey. "It's all that shuffling in and out late at night. Don't you know how dangerous it is to go from the heat into an air-conditioned house, and with wet feet?" She feared that his immune system, coupled with his insomnia, was at risk of crashing so she also prepared her "miracle" chicken soup. Dismissing my mother's concerns, Papà insisted he was well enough to attend a meeting in Miami even though he was short of breath. "I'll be fine," he told her grumpily. "It's only for a few hours."

"No, Aldo, you *mustn't* go!" she insisted, wagging a finger. "I forbid it!"

She nagged him to the point that I sensed his growing

irritation and ended up intervening to try to prevent an argument. "Oh, leave him be, Mamma," I said. "He's old enough to make his own decisions."

Undaunted, my mother demanded a second opinion. The doctor she summoned suggested it was the flu and ordered some blood tests. "It's pneumonia!" she argued. "He needs to go to the hospital." Ignoring the only qualified medic there, she instructed our driver, Stanley, to take Papà to the local ER immediately. "Go with him, Patricia," she ordered. "I'll gather a few of his things and follow on." It was apparent she wasn't going to take no for an answer, so we all did as we were told.

Only when I was sitting in the back of the car with my father did my skepticism turn to concern and I recognized she might be onto something. As if he no longer had to pretend that he was okay, he turned ashen and was fighting to catch every breath. By the time we reached the hospital, he succumbed to the doctors' care like a child. Which was just as well because Mamma was right. They diagnosed viral pneumonia and when it emerged that he was allergic to penicillin they had to wait several crucial hours for a special antibiotic to be flown in.

It was frightening to see how quickly he deteriorated. One minute he'd been arguing with my mother and the next he was virtually unconscious with a high fever. These were life-threatening circumstances for a man seventy-six years of age. For the first time, I realized that I would one day lose him, and the thought shook me. I visited the hospital frequently but my mother never left his side as we waited for the drugs to take effect. She lived on bananas and coffee, and lost five kilograms in as many days. Sitting close by, she noticed that Papà clutched a tiny gold frame of the Madonna and baby Jesus in his hand. He must have picked it up before he left the house, which proved to her that he'd known that he was dangerously ill all along.

"You have your wife to thank," the doctors told him when he eventually opened his eyes. "If we'd waited another day, it may have been too late."

They didn't need to tell him, because during his semi-coma he had "touched the veil," as he put it. Speaking to Mamma of his out-of-body experience, he was full of wonderment and humility. "I was moving toward a bright light!" he told her tearfully. "It was so peaceful, Bruna! I wasn't at all afraid." Squeezing her hand, he said he only forced himself to come back from the brink because he had some "unfinished business" to take care of.

Throughout his delirium, he'd been aware of her constant presence at his side. The near-death experience had crystallized his thoughts and made him aware of how little time he might have left. Everything my mother had been trying to tell him over the years about the importance of a spiritual life suddenly made sense to him. She was right. We all had a higher purpose and it was our responsibility to do right by those who loved us.

Kissing the little gold frame in his hand, his face full of emotion, he told her, "I swear on this Madonna that if I leave this hospital alive, I will make you my wife."

"Oh, stop it," my mother scolded. "You can't make such a vow. You're already married!" Then she listened, stunned, as he told her something he claimed he'd discovered on a recent visit to a land registry office outside Rome. As far as he could tell, due to an oversight on his part, his marriage to Olwen in 1927 didn't appear to have been registered in Italy. If this was so, then as far as the local authorities were concerned, he was still officially single.

This meant that their wedding ceremony in Shropshire might have been the only official record of their union. Such a blunder could have been nothing short of calamitous for his sons.

My mother heard him out before placing her hand on his

forehead and instructing him to lie back down and go to sleep. She was pleased that he'd shared his news but she knew it didn't make any difference. He was delirious, she told herself, and his proposal meant little or nothing. The fact remained that Olwen had been his wife for the best part of his life and had borne him three sons. She would never grant him a divorce and my mother respected that. All she wanted was to bring Papà home.

My father was not someone to make such an oath without following through, however. Even if it would only be a token gesture, he wanted to thank my mother for all she'd done for him. There were, he decided, only two people in his life who truly loved him—Mamma and I. Ultimately, we were the ones he could count on. Love and loyalty were all that mattered, he said repeatedly. Love and loyalty.

In his mind, he'd survived thanks only to my mother's careful nurturing and his faith in God. He fully intended to keep his promise to both. When he called and asked us to fly to Los Angeles for Thanksgiving in November 1981, neither of us suspected he had a secret agenda. "I have a surprise for you," was all he told my mother, laughing.

She hated surprises and feared the worst. "What are you up to, Aldo?"

"If I tell you it won't be a surprise, will it?" By the time she arrived at the house in Beverly Hills a few hours ahead of me, he could no longer keep his secret. "We're getting married!" he cried. "We're going to the Ingleside Inn in Palm Springs in two days' time and a minister will marry us the following morning. Everything has been arranged." She shook her head at the impossibility of it all but he enfolded her in his arms and promised it would be an intimate ceremony, "just us and Gucci's publicist in Los Angeles—a lady named Gloria Luchenbill."

Jet-lagged and in a suspended state of disbelief, my mother

steadied herself as the significance of his announcement began to sink in. Up until then, all he'd ever said was that Olwen would undoubtedly die before him and then they could be together. In his letters he'd often referred to my mother as *mia per sempre* (mine forever) and now it appeared that he was no longer prepared to wait for that day to come around. The legalities of the "marriage" would be questionable. The minister in charge of the service was probably as ignorant of the truth as the priest who'd christened me in London. By agreeing to Papà's proposal, however unrealistic it might be, she'd simply be accepting his commitment to her. Nothing more.

Delighted that this was his heart's desire, she consented. "Okay, Aldo," she told him with a smile. "If this is really what you want, then I'm happy to go along with it."

Gloria Luchenbill and her team had been briefed to ensure that proceedings were kept under wraps. If the other side of the family were to find out they'd be upset, to say the least. By chance, the ceremony took place the day after actress Natalie Wood drowned off the coast of Southern California, so the newspapers had no room for unsubstantiated gossip.

By the time I showed up at the house in Los Angeles he and Mamma had already uncorked the champagne. "Your mother and I are getting married!" he said, speaking the words I'd never expected to hear. As he explained the logistics, I felt numb. Olwen was still his wife and the whole thing felt absurd.

As a questioning teenager, I thought marriage at this stage in their life seemed utterly pointless and unnecessary. Nor would it change my life. Ever since the day my mother had told me that Papà had another family I'd come to understand that he and Mamma weren't married after all. Olwen was his legal wife and the mother of his sons. I accepted that the same way Mamma did and never longed for them to be husband and wife (other than if it made her less anxious). Nor would it make any difference if they were.

I lay in bed that night twisting and turning as I tried to come to terms with their news, a myriad of conflicting emotions flooding my brain. Whether it had to do with the illicit nature of their affair or because I'd hoped to spend a quiet Thanksgiving with them, I couldn't be sure, but it felt like yet another example of being asked to simply accept what was presented to me as a fait accompli. Yet again, I was on the outside looking in, feeling neglected and utterly perplexed. No matter how hard I tried or how much wiser I became as I grew older, I would never fully understand their relationship. All I really knew was that I was once more a party to their strange dynamic—the World According to Aldo and Bruna.

Nothing could burst their bubble, though, and as I fell asleep I resolved to put my own feelings to one side. I was genuinely happy for them after all and it had been a long time since I'd seen Mamma so upbeat. By daybreak I felt better, and when my mother and I went to Neiman Marcus to choose our wedding outfits, I got into the spirit of things. Mamma picked a pretty yellow chiffon dress with blue polka dots and I chose something from Chloé in dusky pink.

Out of all my concerns, however, I hadn't factored in what happened next. As I went to get out of bed the following morning, I discovered that I literally couldn't move. The muscles in my neck had seized, causing excruciating pain. I will never know exactly what the problem was—if I'd slept in an awkward position or suffered an emotional seizure of sorts. Either way, in my condition, even the short distance from my bedroom to the kitchen was too painful to contemplate, let alone the thought of sitting in a car for two and a half hours. The last thing I wanted was to spoil their day, so I suggested they carry on to the desert without me.

"No, Patricia, please!" Mamma entreated in a way I'd never

heard before. She applied cold compresses and tried to massage the spasm away but nothing worked, so she took me to the local hospital for a cortisone shot, which eased my agony. An hour later, I found myself propped up with pillows in the back of a limo en route to Palm Springs to witness the secret "wedding" of my parents. It was November 30, 1981, twenty-five years after they had first met.

A converted hacienda at the foot of the San Jacinto Mountains, the Ingleside Inn was the perfect spot. In its heyday it had been a favored haunt of Hollywood stars and it still had great charm. We gathered in my parents' light-filled suite overlooking the palm-fringed lawns and watched as the short ceremony got under way.

Papà looked so handsome in a navy blue suit with a pale yellow flower in his lapel. He was the happiest I had ever seen him and his joy was infectious. Mamma smiled timidly in her pretty frock and seemed remarkably calm. Their love for each other radiated in a way that took me by surprise. My memories of them together in recent years hadn't been nearly so joyful and it was hard not to forget the tumultuous times they'd had in the past. But in that sunny room, as they held hands and faced each other, the minister began to talk them through their vows, and his words resonated deeply with me. "To have and to hold from this day forward, for better or worse, for richer or poorer, in sickness and in health." Then my father vowed, "I will love and honor you all the days of my life."

Watching them pledge their troth, I couldn't help but rejoice. In the space of a few moments all my reservations melted away. The truth was that they had been de facto husband and wife for years, and none knew better than I how much each of them had borne for the sake of the other. Mamma had given up on the prospect of a free and open life. She'd been banished to London after falling pregnant and then couldn't be seen in public. Even in Berkshire, where she'd hoped for normality, things hadn't quite gone to plan.

My father had a far easier time of it and was able to dip in and out of our lives as he pleased, but he paid the price by fostering such anxiety and depression in my mother that she was never able to be the woman he'd hoped for. Two decades earlier he'd poured his heart out to her in the most touching love letters, declaring, *"I know our destiny is to be together . . . I love you hopelessly, you have conquered my heart and I belong to you."*

And now, finally, he truly did.

NINETEEN

*R*elationships can be tricky to navigate. Those we have with our parents can be the most complicated and often require compromises once we come to the realization that none of us live in a perfect world and that the people we love are flawed.

If I'd had more communication with my parents when I was younger, I might have understood them a bit better, but with little to compare our relationship to, I assumed that what we had was normal. I might have occasionally hoped for something more whenever I saw my friend Bee with her mother or read about happy families in books, but I never had any great expectations and simply accepted the way things were.

My father's relationship with his sons was never easy to interpret. So caught up was he in his whirlwind weekend in Palm Springs with his new "bride" that I don't think he considered the extent of the repercussions if they found out. When they did, his bubble of euphoria was burst.

"The rest of the family knows," Ruby Hamra, his New York

PR *supremo,* told him on the phone twenty-four hours after he and Mamma had toasted to new beginnings. "Word somehow got out. I'm so sorry." Their honeymoon was over before it had even started. In spite of every effort to maintain secrecy, my brothers had learned of the ceremony in the California desert via a loose-lipped member of staff at the Rodeo Drive store. The fact that they knew made my mother deeply uncomfortable. Just as with the poison-pen letters, until she discovered the source she worried who might have tipped them off.

Papà cared much more about the aftermath, although I don't think he had given much thought to what he might tell his sons. Fortunately, he had Ruby, who tried to derail the story by telling them they'd been given the wrong information. Aldo and Bruna, she insisted, had only gone to Palm Springs to celebrate their twenty-fifth anniversary together. "That's all there is to it," she assured them.

The good news was that it wouldn't be in anyone's interests to inform the press, so the story was unlikely to go public. The bad news was that my indignant brothers went straight to the registry office in search of their parents' marriage certificate to confirm that it was the only legitimate union. There they discovered what my father knew all along, that their mother's marital status was legally in question. Unless they reregistered their English marriage, under current Italian law their father could be free to do as he pleased.

Anxious to rectify the situation, someone rushed to England to obtain a copy of the certificate lodged more than fifty years earlier, according to my father. They then apparently escorted a frail seventy-three-year-old Olwen to the registrar in Rome to officially record the document. Her marriage to Aldo was formally recognized at last.

My father was furious that they'd interfered. "They had no

right! This was a private matter between their mother and me. They know I would have always taken care of her. This was none of their business!"

Mamma had a nightmarish sense of déjà vu. I was only a baby when Olwen's emissary knocked on her door asking her to leave Aldo alone. Since then everyone had come to a point of mutual respect and accepted the way things were. She'd hoped that the weekend at the Ingleside Inn would go unnoticed but with her marriage to Papà now out in the open, the sheen was off the occasion.

There was no need for her to worry. Although nothing had changed fundamentally, she could never have anticipated the transformation in my father, which began after his bout of pneumonia and was galvanized by taking his vows. She referred to this as *un miracolo*. Almost overnight, he became much more attentive and thoughtful, always answering her calls and wanting her to be around as well as seeking her advice. Even after all their years together, they really did feel like newlyweds.

She still felt for his real wife, though. She knew Olwen wasn't well and that the news of the marriage must have been as upsetting for her as it was for her sons. Mamma made sure my father checked in on her from time to time, especially on Sundays. "Don't neglect her," she'd remind him. When he presented Mamma with a gold bracelet one Christmas she suggested he give it to Olwen instead, knowing what it felt like to be the woman left alone at home. "Take her a gift. Spend the afternoon with her. Have some tea," she'd urge gently. He would dutifully march the thirty minutes to Villa Camilluccia from my mother's apartment and—after almost certainly pondering the complexities of women—he'd be kind to his first wife in order to keep his second wife happy.

Whenever he'd been to see her he'd hurry back to say, "Bruna, you can't imagine how Olwen has aged! She can hardly hear me and she barely understands a word I say. It won't be long now."

My mother always laughed. "Aldo, you are out of your mind. I'm telling you that woman is going to outlive you. You'll be gone before her, trust me."

In his quest to placate the rest of his family, my father took an unexpected step. It had been nearly a year since he had last spoken to Paolo so he invited him to Palm Beach to discuss a truce. A New York judge had recently dismissed the attempted trademark suit but Paolo was still demanding that his Gucci Plus line be allowed to exist. Papà was exasperated but before the year was out he planned to put an end to their feud. Under some pressure, he eventually agreed to most of Paolo's demands.

He then turned his attention to another relationship that was in trouble. His brother Rodolfo was still angling for a bigger slice of the pie and had hired an attorney to challenge the company's structure and distribution of dividends. Papà settled the dispute and sanctioned the restructuring, incorporating Gucci Parfums and allowing a flotation on the Italian exchange. The new company was renamed Guccio Gucci SpA (*Società per Azioni*)—the Italian denomination for publicly traded companies.

With this turn of events, Rodolfo suddenly gained a controlling 50 percent interest in the new entity and his son, Maurizio, was summoned back to Italy to help him oversee operations. My father was left with 40 percent and my brothers 10 percent between them. Papà then gifted a further 11 percent of his US shares to my brothers and gave them voting rights on the board.

At no point in this reorganization was my name ever mentioned, not that I would have expected it to be. Dating back to the time when my aunt Grimalda was forbidden from having a stake in the business, women weren't welcome in positions of authority.

Although my father had hired top female professionals over the years, that tradition lived on. Not that I had ambitions to work at Gucci anyway; I was too busy pursuing my dream to be an actor—a passion that had first been sparked in me when Bee and I used to put on little productions in Berkshire, and was further encouraged at Hurst Lodge and then at Aiglon with my involvement in productions like *The Boy Friend*. To that end, in 1981 I moved to New York and applied to Juilliard, the prestigious academy for dance, drama, and music.

It was a dream that would never come true. I felt I had the talent, but once I came face-to-face with the teachers and my fellow actors on the day of my audition, I realized I was out of my depth. I'd chosen a monologue from *Iphigenia in Aulis*—a play by Euripides—and during rehearsals I'd gone over my lines repeatedly, desperately trying to identify with Iphigenia, who begs her father not to sacrifice her as she reminds him of his "smiles and kisses" and time spent sitting on his knee.

I struggled to strike an emotional chord, so my acting coach urged me to draw on personal experience and especially my relationship with my own father. "Imagine it!" he told me. "Your father is standing over you with a knife. What would you say to him?" I read the Greek tragedy many times over and no matter how hard I tried, I simply couldn't envisage speaking to Papà the same way. We weren't like that as a family, or at least he wasn't that way with me. Due to the age difference, he was really more like a grandfather than a father to me, which meant he had difficulty identifying with my life. He also grew up in a generation where men simply didn't talk about love, loss, or dreams. It dawned on me then that I'd never heard him mention anything about his own mother or father, his childhood escapades, or stories about his sons when they were young.

I was at the whim of someone who rushed through his days,

engrossed in his work, and who rarely paused to discuss more mundane matters. Although he was always kind to me, my inter- actions with him had been fleeting and superficial at best. With my brothers it was a different story. Mamma always told me that he'd raised them in a near-tyrannical manner, permitting no chal- lenges to his command, and I wondered if that was why there was so much resentment and discord. There were so many unanswered questions.

Having always believed I had a good rapport with Papà, I began to question that preconception and for a while I felt as if I didn't know him at all. Or myself, for that matter. The discovery of this chasm in my emotional life was an epiphany for me, which had massive psychological connotations.

Even though I flunked my audition to get into Juilliard I was still determined to pursue my acting elsewhere despite the fact that my father had enlisted me to attend several more Gucci-related events on his behalf. I signed up for drama classes three times a week at the famed Herbert Berghof Studio but soon realized that—no matter how much I loved the theater—it wouldn't help. My classmates seemed to eat, sleep, and breathe acting, and in all honesty, I didn't. My head wasn't in it and I couldn't devote time to my craft with the steady, uninterrupted commitment it required.

Instead, I became adept at another role—as my father's emis- sary at a variety of high-profile parties. Older than my years, I found it easy to blend in with his business associates as well as movie stars such as Cary Grant or Gregory Peck, who were nothing less than endearing and immediately put me at ease. There was only one time when my youthfulness almost let me down. It was a black-tie gala at the Metropolitan Museum of Art in New York to launch *The Vatican Collections: The Papacy and Art*—a collec- tion of 237 sculptures, paintings, and tapestries on loan from the Vatican Museum, including an impressive Caravaggio oil called

The Deposition. I'd asked my school friend Enrico to be my escort and have to admit that we had too much champagne that night and were a little tipsy. Fortunately, we pulled ourselves together just in time to be introduced to Nancy Reagan, one of the most powerful women in the world. As tiny as she was, the First Lady exuded a commanding presence indeed.

Another person who left an impression on me was Prince Charles, whom I met at a Gucci-sponsored polo tournament in Windsor Great Park years later. He was playing in the tournament and when his team won I presented him with the cup. He flashed me a smile that almost made me blush. "Delighted to meet you," he said in that mellifluous voice of his, and then chatted with me in a manner that made me feel as if I were the center of his world for those few moments. It was all a bit surreal.

The more acting classes I missed in New York due to some company engagement, however, the more my ambitions melted away. I came to realize that my life in the theater would have to be sacrificed if I was to remain a part of the family business in the way my father envisaged. The two worlds were galaxies apart. Acting meant uncertainty and rejection, while my father was offering unlimited support and a clear path ahead, full of opportunity. I realized that everything had happened so fast and that I had, in effect, allowed him to take over. Although I'd have liked to pursue a degree, he'd never encouraged me to follow that path. To some extent, though, working alongside him made up for the decision never to further my education. For the first time in my life I had positive mentorship. "*Brava*, Patricia!" he'd say, and the prouder he was, the better I felt about myself.

The curtain may have fallen on my acting career but I had no regrets about being in New York with my friends, some of whom had moved from Europe—Maria lived in SoHo and Andrea and Enrico would come in from Boston. There was a distinctive uptown-downtown divide back then. I'd spend my days in my father's domain uptown but otherwise I was always downtown, which was mine. Lower Manhattan felt like a real village with all kinds of people on the streets. The gay scene was exploding and there was a freedom of expression that felt like a revolution. It was so radically different from anything any one of us had experienced before and we could all be whomever we wanted. I liked to dress up in Japanese fashions or eclectic outfits found in vintage stores paired with flamboyant costume jewelry and occasionally a wig if I was in the mood. "I dare you to wear these!" Enrico told me one day when he spotted a pair of nipple clamps in a sex shop. At a society party a few nights later I turned up in some wild outfit with the clamps clasped to the outside.

At a tedious debutante ball on the Upper East Side one night, I gathered a few people and made a suggestion. "Let's head downtown to Area or Danceteria on Twenty-First Street! I promise you will love it!" Off we went—the girls still in their gowns and the boys in black tie. Not that anyone was paying attention to what we were wearing in a place where the eclectic mix of attire might include leather-clad Madonna look-alikes with teased hair or people dressed like us. There was nothing quite like New York in the eighties.

Aside from the crazy nightlife, though, one of the best things about being there was being able to spend much more time with my father. We still shared the same restless energy, to the point that Mamma would say, "The two of you make my head spin!" Papà was indefatigable—even I found it hard to keep up with him. I would sit in his office and marvel at how he moved from one meeting to another, taking calls in between without missing a beat. If he had a spare moment we would go downstairs to the shop floor and do the rounds of the various departments, where he pointed out problems with displays to me along the way. It was fascinating to watch the way his mind worked and how he had an instinctive eye for what looked right as well as an innate need to mentor me and teach me all he knew. Being in his presence was all-consuming and every day was a learning experience.

The more he involved me in the business, the more I also came to realize that the name I had carried all my life meant an awful lot to people. Back in London nobody paid much attention but in Manhattan as soon as anyone discovered my link to Gucci they'd look at me differently, almost through me, which made me feel uncomfortable to the point that, if I could avoid it, I wouldn't tell people who I was. It wasn't that I was hiding my identity— after all, it was the only one I'd ever known—it was more that while my name undoubtedly opened doors, on occasion it was decidedly inconvenient.

There were a few advantages though. As the daughter of *il dottore,* I was asked to attend several more sponsored benefits, including a concert at Radio City Music Hall starring Frank Sinatra and Luciano Pavarotti. Another highlight was the biennial Carousel of Hope Ball organized by the Children's Diabetes Foundation where Marvin Davis, the industrialist and philanthropist, threw a "Florentine Fantasy"–themed party with a catwalk show featuring models in black leotards parading Gucci apparel and jewelry.

As my father was held up in Rome, I was chosen as the figurehead for the evening. Once the dinner was over I stepped up onstage to make a short speech. "On behalf of my father, Dr. Aldo Gucci, who unfortunately wasn't able to be here tonight, I am so happy to be here to support such a worthwhile cause. I hope that everyone is having a wonderful time and enjoys the show." Then, as part of the finale, I reappeared in a full-length white fox coat wearing a custom-made necklace with a huge aquamarine. Although it may seem hard to believe for one so young, I took it all in my stride. This felt no different to me than performing on a stage as an actress at school or in my classes. It wasn't me—it was just a role I was playing, and if I ever had any nerves they were never about representing the brand but about not embarrassing my father.

In those early days, Ruby Hamra—my mentor who coached me on what to say to the press and at public events—almost always accompanied me. "Let me know what you think of this," she'd say, showing me a speech she'd prepared for me to deliver. If I ever looked nervous, she'd tell me not to worry and claimed that with my English accent I could get away with almost anything.

I was still so young but getting used to the idea that public appearances were all in a day's work. I think Papà was quietly asking me, "Do you want to do this?" but not in a way that made me feel any pressure or expectation. He was testing the water, letting me go out and have some fun and seeing how I fared. Thankfully, I never lost my way or became starstruck. In fact, I found the A-listers as boring or as charming as the next man. But I did appreciate that these experiences were special and I was honored to be part of them.

My father must have thought I was doing a good job because new assignments started to accrue. Best of all, when I suggested some ideas for our windows on Fifth Avenue, he gave me free rein with a few guidelines on how to show the merchandise. I treated each window like a stage, using abstract works of art from up-and-coming artists I knew downtown and pairing them with various props and fabrics to make it all more eye-catching and fun. I mixed things up a bit—instead of having shoes match the handbags and the outfit, as had always been the Gucci way, I'd throw in something unpredictable like a brightly colored bag, a jaunty hat, or a vivid scarf.

The creative process came naturally to me and the results

were so well received that I eventually took charge of all shop windows in New York, Chicago, Palm Beach, Beverly Hills, and franchise stores across North America.

As always, I went along with whatever was required of me, delighted that Papà was prepared to take a risk and give me more responsibility. My new role meant that we now had some common ground, as I increasingly became a part of his everyday world in a way that had eluded me as a child. Not that we ever had any particularly deep conversations. We kept it lighthearted and he could still make me laugh so hard in restaurants that I almost choked. Especially whenever he singled out random people who caught his eye and sized them up.

"See that young lady over there with that old man? That's his secretary, not his wife."

Mamma always said there was no one he couldn't figure out. "He had everyone pigeonholed."

I found his ability to read other people's relationships fascinating, especially as he wasn't always the best at judging his own. Each time we parted, however, I realized with a sigh that although we were undoubtedly closer and more at ease in each other's company, nothing much had changed. After a peck on the cheek and a quick hug, I invariably came away feeling as if I hadn't really learned a thing about him or his life, and I sometimes wondered if I ever would.

TWENTY

*L*ove is a subject I feel more than qualified to talk about. I may have been deprived as a child but after all I've gone through in my life, I now feel I am something of an expert. It wasn't always like that, though. In my youth, when I played around with my first relationships, I was never very adept at picking suitable partners and often ended up in tears.

The unexpected benefit of this youthful heartache was that it brought my mother and me closer together. We still clashed but then gradually became allies as we sought out each other's opinion and advice. In time, I began to confide in her—especially about my love life, which was never a subject I could broach with Papà. Like most fathers with daughters, he was extremely protective and once interrupted someone who asked me when I might marry, "I won't allow it!" He added that he kept me "too busy" for a boyfriend. Little did he know.

Mamma knew though. She went through all the times I thought I was madly in love and all those occasions I realized that the man I'd fallen for wasn't right for me after all. Having been a front-row spectator to her relationship with my father, I had vowed to avoid Italians altogether. "They're all cheats," I declared. "They behave the same and they bore me. They're so predictable, especially when it comes to how they treat women."

I preferred Nordic or Anglo-Saxon types, all of them tall, handsome, and diverse. Although none of my liaisons came to anything, my mother lived vicariously through me and delighted in every detail of my romantic affairs.

By the time I turned nineteen, I was too busy to contemplate a serious relationship as my involvement with Gucci was ramped up a notch. Gloria Luchenbill sent my father a memo saying, "I think it's time we take advantage of Patricia's excellent and stylish image as a dazzling asset and representative to a lucrative teenage market." It went on to say that it would do the company "no harm at all" to be associated with the next generation and could help counter the "matronly" reputation we had acquired.

"What do you think, Patricia?" my father asked, showing me the note.

"What would it involve?"

"We'd create an advertising campaign around you, wearing the latest collection."

"Would I continue to have a say in the styling?" I asked.

"Of course," he replied reassuringly.

Everything happened in such rapid succession that I couldn't help but think he had planned it all along. I was suddenly brought out from behind the scenes to be a model and the public face of Gucci with five-page magazine spreads. As a teenage girl wearing our clothes, I already looked different from the previous older models. I turned up at the Gucci Galleria and was zipped into evening gowns, casual wear, and even swimwear while hairdressers teased my hair and attended to my makeup before the photographer clicked away.

Then my father did something else that surprised me. In a very casual way, he showed me a memorandum one day and when I inquired what it was, he said, "Oh, it is just the announcement that you are going to be on the board."

It seemed I was the last to know. "What does that mean?" I asked.

"It just means you have to show up to the odd meeting and then you'll have an inside track on how things are run around here." And so it was that, in a completely routine manner, I was appointed to the board of Gucci America. Not only had I been given a broader mandate in my day-to-day activities, I was now officially part of the executive committee. "I want to give you a more mature role," he told me, disguising the real reason behind my sudden promotion. Having a partisan vote on his side had its advantages; nevertheless I'm sure he genuinely thought I could bring something worthwhile to the table.

I wasn't yet twenty so I didn't give much thought to becoming the first woman in the family with a seat on the board. As I walked in dressed head to toe in Gucci and took my place at the oval mahogany table next to Giorgio, however, I could feel everyone's eyes burning into me. Keeping my composure, I simply nodded and smiled.

Everyone knew I was there chiefly to support my father but I relished the opportunity anyway. I was also fascinated by the dynamic between him and my brothers as he presided over the meetings. Roberto, his favorite, was seldom in the US, but on the rare occasions he showed up he could do no wrong. Giorgio was also an infrequent visitor but my father treated him quite differently, coming down hard on him every time he spoke. Paolo never attended a single board meeting the entire time I was in New York. He and my father were still at loggerheads and during this period he was mainly in Italy working on Gucci Plus. My cousin Maurizio was always there and remained in thrall to my father's every word.

Once the new marketing campaign took off, the press dubbed me "Gucci Girl" and the *New York Times* Style section named me "the most eligible girl in the world," describing me as the "Italian beauty with the English accent born into a male-dominated dynasty." Others tipped me to be Aldo Gucci's successor. The idea of being the heir apparent was preposterous, and if anyone asked me, my reply was, "I certainly hope not!" I was still learning and Gucci was hardly some little drugstore. I could only imagine what my brothers thought about that, but I didn't have to wait long to find out. Paolo, still jostling for position, claimed I wouldn't last a day without my father, although he did admit I had "more brains than the rest of them put together."

Meanwhile, I set off around the country to cut ribbons at various store openings. Dressed in camel-colored leather trousers or a suede skirt with a silk blouse—always with the obligatory Gucci accessories—my role was to show how our clothes could be adapted to a younger, more contemporary audience. "My generation wouldn't dream of buying anything with GG," I'd confide to Ruby Hamra en route to our next engagement. "Our image is too staid. I'd like to inject some energy and fun into the equation."

Papà must have had his reservations, but having seen how I handled the window displays, he knew I had a good eye and the wherewithal to succeed. "Just remember you're a Gucci," he told me. "You must be chic and elegant on every occasion." Aside from his recognition, what he gave me above all was a voice. I felt like I was "in-house" and could see a future in which I'd have the kind of creative freedom I yearned for. Maybe there could be a long-term role for me at the company after all, I thought.

Paolo, on the other hand, couldn't be so certain of his future at Gucci. After he returned to the fold he thought he'd be given more independence, especially when it came to his designs for Gucci Plus, but then he discovered that every drawing he submitted had to be approved. More often than not they were rejected. The board argued that he was out of step with the image of the company. He in turn saw this as a conspiracy led by Papà and my uncle Rodolfo and complained about how unfairly he'd been treated. Matters eventually came to a head in June 1982, when my father suspended him until a board review in Florence the following month.

I didn't attend that meeting, but I heard it was explosive. Instead of proceeding at its usual sedate pace, the session was repeatedly interrupted by Paolo, who made sure he aired his grievances. He then digressed from the agenda to quiz my father about alleged profits being siphoned to offshore holding companies, a fact he claimed to have recently discovered.

When proceedings descended into chaos, my father tried to regain order and asked the secretary to stop taking minutes. In the awkward silence that followed, there was an unusual clicking sound. "What's that noise?" Papà asked.

Everyone listened, then all heads swiveled toward Paolo. It was coming from a tape recorder hidden in his jacket. Knowing that he'd been exposed, he reached into his pocket and pulled out the offending device, which he placed defiantly on the boardroom table.

"He's been recording everything!" someone cried as there was a collective gasp at the gross breach of trust.

According to my father, the fracas that ensued began when Giorgio and Maurizio tried to seize the tape recorder from a near-hysterical Paolo. My father watched incredulously from the head of the table as his nephew and sons grappled with one another before Paolo grabbed his treacherous machine and fled the building screaming that he'd been physically assaulted. Sporting a few scratches on his face, he filed a $13.3 million lawsuit claiming breach of contract. He further accused his relatives of "battering and beating" him with fists and "various objects."

News of the punch-up broke with sensationalist headlines such as "Family Feud Rocks the House of Gucci," likening the squabbling to the troubles of the Borgias. My father's response was characteristically diplomatic. Shrugging, he said, "Paolo likes to exaggerate." Privately, he was beside himself with rage and told Mamma, "That boy shows no respect!"

Papà sacked Paolo as director, leaving him with nothing but his company shares. Knowing he wouldn't go quietly, we all wondered what he'd do next. We soon found out when he stirred things up once more by striking a deal to lend his name to a range of furniture. He even opened a Paolo Gucci store in New York— illegally. My mother and I weren't the only ones who worried about where this would all lead. She was especially upset to see my father dogged with problems at this stage in his life, which was meant to be the calmest.

There was further bad news to come, with the discovery that Uncle Rodolfo had developed prostate cancer. Radiation treatment confined him to a wheelchair and he retired to St. Moritz to recuperate. Within days, Maurizio stepped in and took control of the operation in Milan. When a self-aggrandizing profile on him appeared in a leading Italian magazine, my father was appalled that he'd cast himself as the future visionary of Gucci. My mother suspected who was behind the publicity and warned Papà prophetically, "Maurizio's wife will be the undoing of this company!"

As ever, the last thing I wanted was to create any problems. By the time I was approaching my twentieth birthday in early 1983, I was a full-time fashion coordinator and roving ambassador. I had my own office and was tasked with shadowing my father

My father's house in Beverly Hills, c. 1980

Our happy home in Palm Beach

Above: PAPÀ AND ME AT A PARTY
IN PALM BEACH, 1972

*Courtesy of Mort Kaye Studios,
Palm Beach*

Left: MY BROTHERS ROBERTO
AND GIORGIO WITH MY COUSIN
MAURIZIO POSING OUTSIDE THE
MILAN STORE

*Photo by Laurent MAOUS/Gamma-Rapho
via Getty Images*

ME AND MY MOTHER WITH PAPÀ AT THE
PALM BEACH PARTY WHERE HE SANG OUR
PRAISES

Courtesy of Lucien Capehart, Palm Beach

Above: ONE OF MY FAVORITE PHOTOS
OF PAPÀ

Right: MAMMA WITH LUCIANO
PAVAROTTI AT THE PALM BEACH
PARTY, 1980

Courtesy of Lucien Capehart, Palm Beach

My parents looking
gorgeous in 1980

Below: Wishing my mother
a happy birthday at my
New York apartment, 1983

Visiting Papà at Eglin
prison in 1986

ME BEING INTERVIEWED AT THE GUCCI
STORE ON BOND STREET, LONDON, 1988

Courtesy of Clive Limpkin/Associated Newspapers/
REX Shutterstock

Above: MODELING SWIMWEAR AT THE GUCCI
GALLERIA FOR *TOWN & COUNTRY* MAGAZINE, 1982

Courtesy of Klaus Lucka von Zelberschwecht

ME WITH RUBY
HAMRA AT THE
OPENING OF THE
LATEST STORE IN
NEW YORK, 1980

THE NEW FACE OF GUCCI: MY TURN IN THE
SPOTLIGHT FOR A SOCIETY MAGAZINE, 1983

Courtesy of Christophe von Hohenberg

WITH PAPÀ AT MY EIGHTEENTH-BIRTHDAY PARTY AT THE
SAVOY, LONDON—WHERE IT ALL BEGAN

on store visits, in meetings, and in interactions with staff, something I found invaluable.

"Attention to detail is paramount," he'd remind me, stopping in his tracks if he noticed that the glass countertops weren't cleaned to perfection, just as my grandfather had done. "Quality mustn't be compromised," he insisted as he checked for scratches or scuff marks on a bag. I memorized each of these maxims and took comfort from the fact that I had his experience and wisdom to draw on whenever I needed it.

I was an eager student, keen to continue to develop my role within the company even though I knew it would involve a lot of hard work and an itinerary to rival his. I didn't mind one bit. I was having fun and earning a salary for the first time in my life.

My father continued to jet around the world keeping tabs on our overseas operations while my mother carried on as usual, spending most of her time in Rome. I still didn't have much contact with her during this period, nor did she ever express any opinions about my involvement in the business, which was only a peripheral part of her world. When I found out that she'd be on her own in New York for her birthday that October, I decided to throw a party for her at my apartment across the hall from my father's. One of my favorite photographs of her was taken that night. In her mid-forties, she looked gorgeous in a pink angora sweater and black leather trousers. My friends plied her with champagne and made a huge fuss. Then someone dimmed the lights and I presented her with a flaming cake as everyone sang "Happy Birthday."

"*Buon compleanno*, Mamma!" I cried as she blew out her candles, and for once, she looked like she enjoyed being the center of attention as "*la festeggiata*"—the celebrated one. Although we still had our differences, we shared many more carefree moments together. It made me happy to see her so lighthearted. I only prayed it would last.

That spring my father and I flew to Milan, ostensibly to open a new store right across the street from the shop Uncle Rodolfo had run after the war. Maurizio stepped in to oversee the launch and it was strange for my father not to have his brother at his side. Normally, Papà would have taken a more active role but everyone knew why he was really there. Foffo was dying and he had come to say good-bye.

Until that day in Milan, I'd never really had a chance to know Maurizio. Apart from his low-key appearances in the boardroom, I'd seen him at a party in New York with Patrizia but we hardly spoke. So when I discovered that he had insisted on accompanying my father against his wishes to see Foffo for the last time, it revealed a disturbing side to his character that I hadn't previously been aware of. In fact, Maurizio supervised all such visits, to the point that my brother Roberto said later that it was as if he was "guarding a prisoner."

My father was shocked by Foffo's frailty. As Maurizio hovered proprietorially, they spoke only briefly until Rodolfo ordered his son to leave the room for a few minutes so that they could have a "private word." In the brief moments they were allowed, he beckoned Papà closer and made him promise that he'd keep a watchful eye on Maurizio and never allow his wife, Patrizia, near the company shares. My father reassured him and stayed with him awhile longer before kissing his forehead.

Rodolfo died in May 1983 and was buried in the family tomb at Soffiano outside Florence. He left my father—the oldest child—as Guccio's last surviving son. It was the end of an era and the start of a new chapter in the company's history, with the as yet unanswered question of who would inherit his 50 percent shareholding.

Immersed in my work, I was largely oblivious to the clashes between my father and the rest of the family. He rarely discussed such problems with me, and besides, by then I had fallen head over heels in love. Breaking my vow that I'd never fall for an Italian, I'd started dating a wine merchant from Vicenza in northern Italy. His name was Santino. We had met inauspiciously when I quite literally stumbled into his arms at a cocktail party in Newport, Rhode Island, that summer. It was hosted by the Aga Khan and sponsored by Cinzano in support of Italy's entry into the America's Cup with the yacht *Azzurra*. As I walked across the grass in a short black sequined Gucci cocktail dress, the heel of one of my stilettos got stuck in the soft ground and I lost my balance.

"Let me help you," Santino said, catching me as I toppled. When I looked up into his green eyes, I was hooked. Extremely handsome, he resembled a young Frank Sinatra. He was also spontaneous and naughty and I never knew what he was going to do next. Something about him thrilled me and we hit it off immediately. When I discovered he knew a friend of mine in New York I made sure he was invited to a catered black-tie party I was hosting at my apartment a few weeks later. He came and the following weekend he invited me for brunch with friends at his place in Greenwich Village so that we could watch the first-ever Gay Pride march. I rarely left his apartment after that, and for the first time in my life I had found a man who cherished me and did everything for me.

"I know what you're thinking, but this one is different!" I told my mother, who couldn't hide her skepticism. "He makes me feel special, unlike anyone else before." I didn't tell her that there was also something untamed about him that attracted me like no other man. I was completely smitten.

Not long afterward, when Santino suggested we jump on a plane and fly to Jamaica for a few days, I ran over to see my mother and tell her the news. "I have to go, Mamma! Will you cover for me?" No stranger to keeping secrets, she agreed to tell

Papà the bare minimum and off I went. It wasn't that I was afraid of my father but it was still early days and there was no point in telling him anything until he really needed to know.

In Jamaica, diving into the deep cold water of the Blue Hole, dancing 'til dawn at a reggae festival, or simply lying in a hammock under a palm tree, I don't think I had ever been happier. It all felt new and exciting, as everything in my life seemed to be coming together in perfect harmony. My father had given me more responsibility in the business, my mother was in good spirits, and I had someone who made me feel as if I were the only woman in the world.

What could possibly go wrong?

TWENTY-ONE

*A*lthough some might think my family was lucky in many ways, my father and I would disagree. He wasn't superstitious and he never believed in luck the way others do. Neither do I. We shared the view that people make their own fortune and through carefully considered decisions people are able to improve their lot in life.

My grandfather Guccio didn't go to London and work in the Savoy on a whim—he planned it. That wasn't down to luck. My father took a small Florentine business and turned it into a global phenomenon through his own vision and hard work, not because of serendipity. Mamma had set her sights on going to work and ended up at Gucci, although she almost certainly would have argued that it was written in the stars.

Later in my father's life he had every reason to start believing in bad luck, however, when a series of misfortunes sent his carefully constructed world spinning out of control. Between my grandmother's premonitions and my mother's psychic dreams, we should have been able to predict what was headed our way.

Mamma now says that the snake she encountered in Florida had far greater portent than she realized at the time even though she'd read it meant a calamity would befall the head of the household.

It first fell on a summer's morning in 1983 as my father sauntered into the lobby of his Fifth Avenue office. He was unexpectedly approached by a stranger who served him with legal documents. The man turned out to be a representative of the Internal Revenue Service and the papers he thrust into my father's hands were demands for his personal financial records plus those of Gucci America for the years 1979–81. This subpoena stemmed from one of Paolo's lawsuits for what he called "financial impropriety," with claims of tax-deductible payments being transferred to offshore accounts. Although the case was thrown out of court, the allegations were brought to the attention of the Criminal Investigation Division of the IRS.

Relations between Paolo and Papà had recently sunk to an all-time low. Having been ousted from the company and thwarted at every turn, my brother telephoned my father in Palm Beach begging for help, pleading poverty now that he had divorced his first wife and remarried, had two families to support and a new baby on the way. Mamma was there when my father took the call and she could tell from his body language that the conversation wasn't going so well. The subject of Gucci Plus came up again but my father flat-out refused to cooperate, unable to forgive the board incident or the fact that Paolo had brought a legal action against his own family.

Eventually, he exploded. Jumping to his feet he shouted, "No, Paolo! I cannot help you! You were invited back to the business and look at what you've done! How dare you? You have brought all this upon yourself!"

Then he slammed down the phone, cursing the day his son was born and calling him "*un idiota!*" before storming out of the room, leaving my mother speechless. What he didn't realize was how far Paolo was prepared to go to exact his revenge. "The idiot" was elevated to "*maledetto*," or "damned," once we discovered that he'd also agreed to cooperate with the IRS, who were now in possession of confidential documents that could only have come from my father's private papers.

Beneath Papà's simmering anger was something far deeper—a bitter disappointment that his own son could sell him out like this. The betrayal broke his heart and the effects were plain to see. When Mamma rang me to recount the episode, she was so distraught I thought she was heading for a breakdown.

"What's wrong?" I asked.

"It's your father. I can't bear to see him like this. He just sits and sits and doesn't say a word. It's all Paolo's doing. That man is despicable! I don't know what to do."

The latest news from New York only made things worse. Federal agents armed with warrants had stormed the Gucci offices and seized all company documents and bank statements. Financiers as far away as Hong Kong had been instructed to assist with the prosecution. This was a major international investigation and not something that was going to go away. As CEO, my father knew that he would have to take full responsibility, especially once the news was leaked to the press.

My mother and I were deeply worried but Papà tried to allay our fears, insisting it was all in the hands of his attorneys and accountants. They were the ones who'd set up the offshore payments to fund enterprises in the Far East, he said, and they'd now be called upon to sort out the mess. Determined to maintain an appearance of "business as usual," he returned to work.

I know that he felt terribly beleaguered during those few months. Rodolfo and Vasco were dead, Maurizio couldn't be trusted, and my father's accountant and the chief architect behind the money transfers had recently passed away. My brothers Roberto and Giorgio were so alarmed by recent events and the possible repercussions for them and their families that they bombarded my father with calls from Italy day and night.

The more the IRS excavated the company's affairs, the more disturbing the news became. The accountants claimed Papà had an income of just $100,000 a year but then the IRS discovered that his homes in Palm Beach and Beverly Hills had been paid for by the offshore entity. This led them to examine consultancy and other fees amounting to millions, where they claimed to have found further "irregularities."

My father's attorneys continued to work with the authorities, adopting a policy of openness and cooperation wherever possible. The company had conformed to standard business practices, he assured them, and there had never been any attempt to defraud the US government.

Mamma and I needed no convincing that everything he'd done was on the advice of his accountants and that he would never have knowingly taken such a risk. His legal team, in turn, assured him that even if there were some "inconsistencies," any owed taxes could simply be repaid along with a fine and that would be the end of it. They maintained that my father could still avoid a custodial sentence even though his was a high-profile case being handled by an ambitious young attorney named Rudolph Giuliani. All he had to do was assume full responsibility and remain in the US for the trial. "We'll cut you a deal," I heard them tell him. "You'll be fine."

He went along with whatever they suggested. He loved America and had no desire to flee to Italy like a common criminal, even if that was precisely what my mother implored him to do. "Let's go back to Rome, Aldo!"

"No, no, Bruna," he'd tell her with a smile. "That's out of the question."

Besides, he had too much left to achieve—not just in America but globally. Even if the thought of leaving ever crossed his mind, he knew that his decision to stay in the US and face the consequences was the right one.

One of my father's advisers felt differently, however, and took it upon himself to warn my mother one night over dinner that my father could well end up in prison. She became so upset that Papà had to cut the evening short and take her home. Once they were on their own, she went to pieces.

"Prison, Aldo? But you're almost eighty! They couldn't possibly lock you away, could they?"

He held her in his arms and promised that nothing like that would ever happen to him. "Don't worry. Everything is going to be just fine."

When Mamma told me, I felt sick to my stomach. "Prison?" I echoed. It was something I couldn't contemplate. My father was invincible: a man in charge of his own destiny who fixed things when they went wrong and held everything together. This couldn't be happening.

For the first time since he'd put me on his executive committee, I fully understood the benefit. I'd been placed there to agree with whichever motion was put forth and whatever decisions he made. This could be anything from approving the budget for a new store to setting sales objectives for the upcoming quarter. Even if I didn't always grasp the meaning or lost the thread in technical or financial discussions (numbers were never my forte), if ever my father needed allies it was now. As with the board resolutions he sought to pass, he knew he could count on my support but that didn't change the fact that he was under enormous pressure.

He may have kept up a façade with Mamma and me at home but in the boardroom I began to see a side to him I had only ever heard about. My brother Giorgio was the unwitting recipient of one of his worst tirades. I can't even remember what it was that tipped my father over the edge but he suddenly leapt to his feet and started yelling at Giorgio across the table. The man was a tempest and his rage shocked me. All my life he'd seemed so levelheaded and in control. To see him standing there with the veins bulging in his neck, his face purple as he let loose a torrent of abuse, was not a pretty sight. Inwardly, I willed him to stop.

Poor Giorgio looked like a rabbit in the headlights. I'd never seen anyone so humiliated in public, and sensing his embarrassment, I looked away. In that moment, I'm sure I was the last person he wanted in the room. I was embarrassed for him and ashamed of my father's unwarranted outburst. When his anger was finally spent, he sat back heavily in his chair, breathless. You could have heard a pin drop.

In that instant, I knew that his eruption had nothing to do with any perceived misdemeanor of Giorgio's but his utter frustration at the catastrophes that were dogging him. He knew he was in serious trouble.

My mother sensed it too, and terrified of what might happen, she began to fall apart. One day, I found her alone and sobbing in their New York apartment while he was visiting his financial advisers in Italy, something he was still allowed to do. The prospect of my father's going to prison had toppled her and she was fixated on the idea that he would never come out alive. I tried to reassure her but she couldn't be comforted, in a way that brought back unpleasant memories of her depression when I was a child. In the end, I had to ask Papà to come back from Italy at once. Between us, we made the decision that it would be better if she returned home and was kept well away from the unfolding drama.

As worried as I was about Mamma, I was also deeply concerned about my father—especially once she flew home. It
occurred to me that having to be strong for her had strengthened
his own resolve. All of my life I'd assumed that she was entirely
dependent on him. It wasn't until the early days of the fraud investigation that I realized their dependency was mutual.

Feeling the burden of responsibility, I did my best to be sup-
portive and distract Papà from his problems whenever I could. At
the time I was working on one of my most challenging projects—
the launch of our new ready-to-wear spring/summer range in front
of three hundred VIP guests and invited media at the Cotillion
Room of the Pierre hotel in New York. If it went well it would be
repeated in Chicago, Palm Beach, and Los Angeles. Being cast
as a director, choreographer, and producer was a welcome dis-
traction of my own. Inspired by a set design from our recent show
in Milan, which used a raised runway, I spent weeks selecting
the models and the music, styling the clothes and choreograph-
ing the various segments. For the show soundtrack, I compiled a
diverse playlist ranging from Brazilian and bossa nova music to
reggae and R&B. I was swamped with lists of to-dos and knew
that all eyes would be on me, which felt far more daunting than
walking into any boardroom. The finale would feature models
I'd chosen from hundreds of portfolios all emerging in skintight
black catsuits and our latest jewelry from the Oro Coccodrillo
collection.

To my great surprise, my father turned up early. When he saw
my face, he kissed my cheek and said, "What? Can't I wish my
own daughter good luck?" Then he went back to sit at his table to
watch the entire thing. I was so nervous that night and prayed that
everything would go to plan as models rushed past me and out into
the multicolored lights and the flashes of cameras.

As the show ended and the place erupted with applause, I

knew from my father's expression that I had given him a precious hour off from his woes, and for that alone it was worth it.

Seeing him standing shouting, *"Brava!"* and clapping along with everyone else, it no longer mattered to me that he hadn't shown up at school for Parents' Weekend or seen me in *The Boy Friend*.

"Patricia, I'm so proud of you!" he told me backstage later that night as he raised a glass of champagne in tribute. That was a moment of joy frozen in my heart. No matter what lay ahead of us, good or bad, I knew I would always have that.

TWENTY-TWO

I have heard it said that the worst part of betrayal is when it comes from those you thought were closest to you. That was certainly true in my father's case. All of us suffer betrayal of some form in our lives—starting with the formation and disintegration of childhood cliques. By the time we reach adulthood, however, any kind of treachery becomes that much more serious and can often have devastating consequences.

My mother had experienced betrayal from her onetime friend who sent those letters to Giorgio. Papà knew it only too well, but there was far worse to come. The next Gucci board meeting was set for September 1984 in Manhattan but my father was too busy to attend. The IRS had announced a grand jury hearing into his case so he was tied up with his attorneys. Even though the board meeting was being held in the same building, he sent his deputy Robert Berry in his stead. When Robert breathlessly burst into his office later that morning calling out his name, my father looked up in surprise and braced himself for more bad news. Was there some new development? Had Paolo come up with yet another plot?

The response he got was probably the last thing he expected. In a shock move, Maurizio—who'd inherited Rodolfo's holding—had lodged a motion to dissolve the board, dismiss my father, and create a new executive committee with him at its head. It was an outrageous coup planned with military efficiency. As Papà was to discover, Maurizio wasn't acting alone. Paolo had agreed to sell him his shares, thereby giving him full control of the company.

My father didn't even rise from his chair at the news. There was no point. The deed was done. A few floors below, his own nephew, whom he'd taken in as his own and taught everything, had forged a devilish alliance to topple him from his throne.

By the time I returned to New York a few days later Papà was about as broken as I had ever seen him. I found him sitting alone in his apartment at dusk, staring aimlessly into space. "Shall we get something to eat?" I suggested softly, but he didn't move.

"I'm not hungry," he replied. "You go ahead. I'll be fine."

My mother flew back to New York to be at his side while he continued to prepare his legal defense. She was better than she'd been in recent months but still deeply troubled. One day when she was at a low ebb, I decided to share some information that I hoped might make her happy.

"I'm pregnant." Speaking the words out loud made it much more real somehow. With the dark clouds hanging over us all, I'd been agonizing about the right time to reveal my recently discovered news. I loved Santino and I wanted this child more than anything, but I was painfully aware that my parents would think I was too young to have a baby.

"I knew it," my mother responded with something akin to resignation. "I had a dream about a little girl running around in a summer dress. You're going to have a girl."

Trusting her vision completely, I was pleased but had to

confess, "I'd always dreamed of having a boy." Then I told her the second part of my news. "Santino and I are getting married."

Her reaction wasn't quite what a daughter might have hoped for. She drew in a breath before saying, "Okay, but let's not tell your father right away. He has too much on his mind and he doesn't need another shock."

He had only recently been introduced to Santino and it seemed premature to make such an announcement. Although I'm sure he wouldn't have objected, the prospect wouldn't have thrilled him either. I only hoped that when the time came, he'd be happy for me.

After a pause Mamma asked, "Is it really necessary for you to get married?"

Coming from her, this surprised me. "I want my child to have the best possible start in life," I said, explaining what I thought to be all too obvious. "With a mummy and a daddy who are together as husband and wife, like a normal family—as you would have liked had things been different."

Seeing her dubious expression, I added, "Don't worry, Mamma, it'll be a small, intimate affair—just us, Santino's family, and a few of our friends."

Heeding my mother's advice, Santino agreed that we should wait until Christmastime to tell my father, when we'd all be together in Palm Beach. He'd be more relaxed there and it would be easier to broach the subject without too many distractions, we thought. I picked my moment a few days after we arrived. Settling next to him, I fanned my fingers across my tummy and said, "There's something you should know, Papà—I'm going to have a baby."

He stared at me, his face expressionless. Eventually, he said flatly, "I'm happy for you."

Speaking quickly, as if to catch his train of thought before he had a chance to say anything else, I hurried to explain. "We didn't plan this and I know it's not what you would have wanted right now but Santino and I are in love and we're getting married—in Jamaica."

He turned away from me and closed his eyes, adding another item to the list of quandaries he had to ponder. Eventually he spoke. "We'll have to make some arrangements to protect your interests. I'm not taking any chances." Softening, he turned back and said, "Organize a nice wedding—anything you want."

When I told him what we had planned he just nodded and smiled. This wasn't what he had in mind for me but I was prepared for that.

Like any man who has to ask a father for his daughter's hand in marriage, Santino was anxious. In the end he blurted out the question on Christmas Day while my father was carving the turkey. With a twelve-inch knife in one hand and a fork in the other, Papà glared at his future son-in-law for a moment before putting down his tools and shaking Santino's hand in consent.

We were to be married three weeks later on January 19, 1985. Friends and family, twenty-five in all, were invited to take part in a ceremony to be held in a quaint sixteenth-century church built by Catholic missionaries in St. Ann's Bay, on the north side of Jamaica. Santino's parents would be there along with his two brothers, but only one member of my father's family. The sole representative would be Roberto's thirdborn son, Uberto, who happened to be passing through New York and decided to come at the last minute.

My friend Maria and her boyfriend were coming, along with Andrea—my maid of honor—and several of my friends from New York. The dress code for the men was strictly white but Santino's father and brothers decided to ignore our request, showing up in black suits. After the service, guests would be taken to the ocean-front villa we had rented for our time in Jamaica for a reception on the beach.

A couple of weeks earlier while my fiancé and I were in Montego Bay taking care of all the arrangements, Papà's attorney flew in from New York with a prenuptial agreement for Santino to sign. He did so willingly.

The morning of the wedding was chaotic, with a lot of last-minute problems, which fell upon me to sort out, as my mother had not been involved in any of the planning. When everything was calm, I put on my outfit—*shalwar kameez* trousers and a long cream silk shirt, which hid my growing bump. It was a gift from the African-American designer Willi Smith—my landlord and neighbor downtown in Tribeca.

Once I was ready, Andrea accompanied me to the church, where my father waited to walk me down the aisle. Although neither of us would have had it any other way, it still meant the world to me that he had taken time off from his crazy schedule and the pressures of the pending legal case to put me first.

He looked so distinguished in his blue shirt and cream linen suit waiting for me near the path that led to the chapel. "*Sei bellissima!*" he pronounced with a smile, his arm bent for mine. "This is your day, Patricia. Nothing will spoil it."

My nerves began to kick in as we walked up the aisle toward my waiting groom, also dressed in white. Like every bride, I wondered if I was doing the right thing. I felt my father's arm tighten around mine as we approached the priest, who stood smiling at us in his cassock.

Mamma stood impassively in the front row, still showing signs of her reservations about my decision. "I'm not sure he's the one for you, Patricia," she had said. We came from different worlds, something my parents were only too quick to point out. She knew that kind of incompatibility, coupled with having a baby at such a young age, would come to haunt us. She also appreciated I was strong, however, and she hoped for the best.

Breathing in deeply one last time, I stepped up alongside Santino and faced the priest, his hands folded together as he waited for everyone to settle. I went to slip my arm from my father's but he refused to let go and pulled me even closer.

"Very funny, Papà," I whispered. Still, he clung on, staring straight ahead with a strange expression. After an awkward pause, I tugged my arm free, only for him to grab my wrist in view of everyone. Turning to me, his eyes filling with tears, he loosened his grip before giving my hand one last squeeze. I thought he was going to say something but in the end he didn't have to say a word.

Pulling himself together, he attempted a smile and then went to join my mother. Blinking back the tears, I fought the urge to embrace him and tell him that I understood. The fact that he loved me had always been an unspoken certainty and yet, in that moment, he wanted me to know it. In that rickety old church he gave me the greatest gift a father can give a child—his unconditional, unspoken love. And, with his actions, my most precious memory of him.

Later that afternoon we all gathered on the lawn of our villa, where we served a traditional Jamaican spit-roast goat on the beach while a calypso band played Harry Belafonte tunes, which got everyone into the island spirit. Santino's father got my mother tipsy and I have never seen anything quite so hysterical, nor has she ever laughed so much since. The whole day was scintillating and perfect, as I had always imagined it would be.

For three days and nights we were a regular, happy family. Nobody would have known that Papà was in the midst of a crisis. From the moment he arrived, all his stress seemed to melt away. Although there were clearly things on his mind, he took off his jacket and tried his best to enjoy himself, determined not to let anything spoil our few days together, and for that I will be eternally grateful.

When we returned to America there was little to be happy about, however. Maurizio, the self-proclaimed "peacemaker" who claimed he would "repair" the damage, had maneuvered himself into the position of chairman of Guccio Gucci SpA as well. He made my father "honorary chairman" of the Italian arm, but the title was meaningless. In Papà's view, Maurizio then tore the soul right out of the business. He transplanted the Gucci headquarters from Florence to swanky new offices in Milan, a short drive from his home. Then he began to squander millions, marking the beginning of an obscene spending spree.

Having bought a jet and with a profligate reputation, he was dubbed "the free-spending rampant heir" by the press and continued to drive the company further into the ground. With little regard for loyalty or experience, he fired many of our longest-serving staff, including Ruby Hamra. He then pared down the franchise operation and "streamlined" the organization, which would report record profits of $63 million that year, demolishing a huge part of what my father had spent decades building up.

Papà stood by helplessly as he watched this systematic dismemberment of the business—his business. Maurizio, who he said was suffering from "disastrous megalomania," then reneged on the deal he'd struck with Paolo; in exchange for Paolo's shares, he had agreed to give him the autonomy to create his own designs. Fresh legal battles ensued. My father was distraught. He had promised Rodolfo on his deathbed that he would watch over his only son and not let Patrizia near the family millions. Now, as the company's PR machine proclaimed her the virtual "Queen of Gucci," he felt he'd let Foffo down.

The one thing my uncle Rodolfo would have welcomed,

however, was the unexpected crumbling of Maurizio's marriage. Abandoning Patrizia—mother to their two daughters—he locked her out of one of their homes and publicly humiliated her. Few had any sympathy but all suspected she wouldn't go quietly.

I was far too busy with complications of my own to worry about what was going on in Italy. My marriage was beginning to show signs of strain, and by the time my daughter Alexandra was born on July 2, 1985, after a difficult labor in Mount Sinai Hospital in New York, I suspected things weren't right between us. Andrea and her sister came to see me, and my mother was there but had to rush back to Rome to be with my father, who was trying to sort out his decimated affairs. She stayed just long enough to see her granddaughter, commenting on how beautiful she was.

Being in Santino's presence was difficult for her. "This man is no good for you," she would say, sensing he would not be there when I really needed him. Unsurprisingly, he left a couple of weeks after she did, saying he had business to attend to in Sardinia.

I had been in the hospital ten days and it took me weeks to recover from an infection as a result of my Caesarian. I was so weak I could barely stand up, let alone hold Alexandra in my arms. I only wished my mother were there to take care of me. Thankfully Andrea came to the rescue when Santino left and with the help of a trusty book by child care expert Dr. Spock, she and I figured out the basics.

When Papà eventually returned to the city, five weeks after his granddaughter's birth, he jumped in a cab and made his way to my loft downtown in Tribeca—a district that seemed to him like the end of the world. As he picked his way through garbage bins and past sweat factories, he wondered what on earth a daughter of his was doing living there. When he held Alexandra in his arms, however, all that was forgiven. Even though he was a grandfather ten times over, this was different. My mother said she'd never seen him so enamored as Alexandra brought out a tenderness in him that he hadn't even shown with me.

Santino and I went through good and bad days but we enjoyed being new parents, and seeing our baby girl's early interactions with the world. And although I loved being a mother, I knew that I would eventually be returning to work and, more important, be at my father's side.

He would never admit it but I think he increasingly felt that he was fighting a losing battle. The more he grappled for power, the more elusive his objectives became. Relinquishing control was the only way to survive. My mother had come to this realization years earlier and he'd seen how it had brought her a sense of peace. He began to listen with greater interest whenever she spoke of the release she found in her beliefs.

Having grown up in a devout Catholic environment, she never questioned the existence of God, and yet she had never really come to terms with her faith.

"I was faithful without being religious," she told my father. "I believed but not with any passion. Then my guru told me that *everything* was God and I suddenly grasped all that he said. That resonated with me."

Deciding it was finally time to meet this guru of hers, my father flew to London so they could visit him together. To his surprise, he was completely won over by the soulful Indian sage. "You must pray and pray, then trust in the outcome," Sari Nandi advised. Before their encounter my father had always gone to church on Sundays and been religious in his own quiet, understated way. But from that day on, he prayed regularly, often stopping off at St. Patrick's Cathedral on Fifth Avenue, a short walk from his apartment.

His prayers seemed to have been answered when he discovered something that looked as if it might change everything. Uncle Rodolfo's assistant Roberta had contacted my father from Milan to tell him that two days after Foffo died, Maurizio had ordered her to forge his signature on some Gucci share certificates. When she refused, he had someone else do it. Once "signed," these false documents released him from millions of dollars of inheritance taxes.

Papà took the information to a Florentine magistrate, who immediately sequestered the shareholding, pending further inquiries. My father then launched a civil action claiming his nephew had taken control of the company "by illicit means." Maurizio flatly denied the allegations but before he knew it he was ousted from Guccio Gucci SpA, paving the way for Papà to resume normal service as chairman.

With a series of twists and turns that were slavishly reported in the press, he was thwarted at the last minute when Maurizio had the decisive board meeting postponed. In his nephew's last act of betrayal, my father returned from Italy to find his New York office had been stripped in his absence and a letter of dismissal waiting. There were almost twenty members of his family working for the company worldwide by then but for the first time in more than sixty years, he was no longer one of them. Maurizio, as the US chairman, issued a press release confirming that Gucci had "terminated Aldo Gucci's role in the company" and that he would no longer have any position whatsoever.

Distraught, my father immediately rang Mamma. "They've taken everything—everything, Bruna!" he wailed. Unable to console him, she urged him to keep the faith, as Sari Nandi had told him. "We must pray, Aldo," she insisted. "We can do nothing else."

TWENTY-THREE

*O*ur name is very often what defines us. Who we are and, importantly, who others think we are have an immediate effect on how we interact with them. Since my days at Hurst Lodge I have understood that my surname carries a certain prestige and have learned to live with the double takes every time I hand over my credit card or book an appointment. Whenever I'm asked to spell it out, I take a breath and slowly enunciate it letter by letter, "G-U-C-C-I."

When I met people in London and New York, I introduced myself simply as "Patricia." It was easier that way. Later I used my married name, preferring to remain anonymous. Things have come full circle now because my daughters, against my best advice, have all decided to incorporate the name with their fathers' surnames, running the risk of being perceived as something other than who they really are.

For my father, his name meant everything. Long before he and my grandfather reinvented the company history, he was proud of what they'd achieved and how they'd turned the family's fate around through hard work, vision, and determination. They went from destitute hatmakers in rural Tuscany to a luxury goods powerhouse with an unrivaled brand identity. These were heirlooms Papà fully intended to hand down through the generations to his sons, his nephew, and—ultimately, I suppose—to me and my children.

At eighty years old, he could never have imagined that his name would one day be sullied or—worse—that it would be his own flesh and blood who would bring about its disgrace. The change of circumstance was a huge adjustment for him and I knew how unsettled it left him. With no office to go to for the first time in decades and no clear direction for him in the business, he had no choice but to set up a temporary New York base in an apartment adjacent to his and try to maintain his dignity. Mamma was mostly in Italy, flying into New York for a month at a time and then retreating back to her sanctuary. His secretary came in every day to help him with his calls and his endless correspondence with lawyers, accountants, colleagues, and his family back in Italy.

When he suggested that Santino and I move from Tribeca back to my old apartment opposite his, I immediately agreed. Our new "home" was dated and somewhat depressing after our bright, white, airy loft, so my father gladly let me update it to suit a young family.

It felt good to be close to him again, especially at such a dreadful time. He was, by then, greatly diminished, and there was a ragged look about him that broke my heart. Fortunately, I was kept so busy I didn't have time to dwell. Still on the board and a director of the company in charge of displays, I had my work cut out for me, which included voting on motions put to the board regarding the direction of the company. Giorgio and Roberto were also on the board but remained in Italy, from where they could report back to Papà. I had very little contact with them, and my father was the only one who dealt with their concerns. Whichever side of the Atlantic we were on, we were all forbidden from divulging any information to my father, although, of course, we did. I, especially, became his eyes and ears for anything to do with reports, minutes, and letters that passed to and fro. I knew Maurizio and his cohorts could dismiss me if my indiscretions came to light but it was a risk I was prepared to take.

Once my father's first court appearance was set for January 1986, it was agreed with his legal advisers that—even though he insisted he'd been kept in the dark regarding the company's accounting practices—he would plead guilty, pay back the money owed, and hope for a fine. As the date approached, his preparations for the hearing intensified. I lost count of the number of meetings we attended with his defense lawyers, who continued to assure us that they'd be able to negotiate his freedom.

To protect the family assets, my father decided to distribute his shares in the Italian operation between Giorgio and Roberto, giving Paolo nothing. This left him with just 16.7 percent of the US operation, which in hindsight was the most disastrous decision of his life. He was desperate to protect the family legacy and never for one moment did he consider that they couldn't be relied upon.

With so much going on in my father's life, I was left with little time to think of much else. Six months had elapsed since Alexandra's birth and she still hadn't been christened. As observant Catholics, Santino's parents warned that if anything happened to her, she would end up in purgatory. So when they invited us to spend Christmas with them in Italy that year, we arranged her baptism for December 30 in their hometown in northern Italy.

My father was unable to come. He had to prepare for his upcoming trial and opted instead to spend a quiet Christmas in Rome. Besides, he needed time alone with Mamma. In recent months his dependence on her had grown and it pained him greatly that she'd been so far away. Although they spoke on the phone every day—long calls that lasted well into the night—he missed her desperately.

Together once more in the city where they'd fallen in love, my parents tried not to dwell on the possibility that he could go to prison—an unthinkable outcome, especially for Mamma. She had long since accepted that he would likely predecease her—that was an inevitability she couldn't hide from. When he'd caught pneumonia in Florida, she thought his time had come but took comfort from the fact that she was by his side. In prison, there would be no such solace, and being separated by such sickening circumstances would, she believed, surely bring about his demise. There were moments when she thought it might also bring about hers.

Christmas had come and gone and their festivities had been bittersweet. Neither of them slept much; they woke up in the middle of the night with the cold realization that these might be their last days together. On the eve of Papà's return to the States, he was more solemn than ever. He'd spent the morning packing and making last-minute preparations when, an hour before he was due to leave, he asked her to sit with him, as he had something important to say.

Handing her a large envelope, he told her, "I need you to look after this, Bruna. You're the only person I can trust. If anything happens to me, you must give this to Roberto and Giorgio." Opening the package, he showed her leather-bound books of shares along with a bundle of *lire*. As per the long-standing tradition at Gucci, the baton was being passed down the male line. My brothers had worked a lifetime in the business and were arguably entitled. I wasn't even considered, not that I expected to be. This was simply the way things were—a classic example of my father's conservative mindset and the generation he came from.

My mother knew she held our future in her hands and was

moved by his unparalleled show of trust. "Any other woman would have fled to South America and lived a hundred lives!" she told me afterward. She was, however, terrified of the responsibility and hurried to the bank with the shares hidden under a woolen cape, eager to secure them in a safety-deposit box.

A few days later Alexandra was baptized at the Chiesa di San Martino in Schio, one hundred kilometers from Venice. It was a chilly, foggy day and we shivered in the church. Mamma came but was very sad. It was an emotionally charged day—my dear friend Maria, whom I'd asked to take on the role of godmother, had been killed in a car accident a few months earlier and a friend of Santino's stepped in to take her place. Enrico became the godfather, and our baby girl was formally given her name.

When he returned to New York, my father went to court on his own, as per his wishes. He had already insisted that my mother remain home, as it was "a mere formality," he said. He'd enter his plea and the case would be adjourned until a full hearing for sentencing later in the year. There was no need for either of us to attend. In truth, he didn't want anyone to see him so shamed and my mother didn't think she could bear it.

Knowing what he was going through without either of us by his side, however, I felt so helpless and couldn't help but rail at the unfairness of it all. Not only had he been forced to take the blame for a scheme he had no part in, everyone else had reaped the benefits, especially Rodolfo and—via his inheritance—Maurizio. Yet because my father was the head of the company and the only green card holder, he became the fall guy. Not that he would have had it any other way. A man of high principle, he believed that with authority comes responsibility and, in any event, ignorance is no defense in the eyes of the law.

Standing at the front of the courtroom, a few feet from the press gallery packed with reporters eager to portray him as a crook, my father admitted two counts of tax evasion and one count of conspiracy to impede and distract the IRS. Each count carried a maximum sentence of five years, although his lawyers promised he'd walk out a free man, albeit considerably poorer. Lawyers from the IRS claimed that a total of $18 million had been diverted since 1972, much of which went to "unnamed co-conspirators." They insisted my father owed them nearly $8 million in back taxes. In a brief statement, Papà told the judge, "I was not involved," reiterating his position that he was unaware of the way in which the offshore payments had been carried out.

After a ten-minute hearing, the judge ordered him to set about paying the owed taxes and watched as he wrote a check for $1 million there and then before the case was adjourned.

By the time I returned to Manhattan, he was clearly relieved that the experience was over. In all his years in business he had never faced such public humiliation and it didn't sit well with him. As he said, he had incriminated himself "for the welfare of everyone."

His next few weeks were so focused on the ongoing legal battle and the decision to adjourn sentencing until September 1986 that when he turned up unexpectedly for my twenty-third birthday in March, I was delighted. Santino had organized a surprise party at an Argentinian restaurant in the Meatpacking District, an area considered a virtual no-man's-land in those days. For that one night, surrounded by my friends and some of the more colorful characters from New York's nightlife, including Dianne Brill, the five-foot-nine self-acclaimed "queen of the downtown scene," I saw a sparkle return to his eyes that I hadn't seen in ages. Known as "Bubbles" and with blond hair teased skyward, Dianne warmed to my father immediately and he couldn't help but ogle her famed bosom from across the table. With Mamma still in Rome, Papà had brought Lina Rossellini instead, who seemed overwhelmed by it all, wondering what was going to happen next as my friends went into full party mode.

Not long afterward, my father did something astounding. Although he was still entitled to attend the next board meeting in Florence, everyone was on tenterhooks wondering if he'd really show up and face Maurizio, who had never relinquished control. When he did, they could have cut the atmosphere with a knife. In spite of all that Maurizio had put him through, my father embraced his nephew as if nothing had happened, kissing him on both cheeks.

Sitting at the table he'd once presided over, he referred to the new chairman as "young man" and suggested with an avuncular smile that they put their disagreements aside and work together. Maurizio refused to play his game. Even though he was still under police scrutiny, he made it clear that he fully intended to move forward with his reorganization plans. The only saving grace was that my two brothers remained as vice presidents.

As ever, the media maintained a keen interest in the company's affairs. After the meeting, my father told a waiting journalist that he was still an optimist, returning to New York with hopes that "an accord [would] be imminent." Back in Manhattan, he certainly appeared more hopeful, and for a while, we resumed our normal routines—going to our favorite restaurants or having dinner at home in my apartment. Santino was a great cook and anything he prepared was better than eating out. Papà played with his "Alexina," the love of our lives, who'd started to utter a few words, including one for her grandfather—"Babbo," the affectionate name for a Tuscan patriarch. He loved that moniker, as his sons had always called him "Daddy."

Prompted by my mother, Papà set in motion the legal registration of me as his daughter in Italy so that there could be no further obstacles to my inheriting the minimum, plus whatever he chose to leave me. My mother made it clear that unless he did so, I wouldn't be formally acknowledged. "You'll have an Italian passport," she explained.

"But I love my British passport!" I replied. "I'm proud of it!"

Losing her patience, she was adamant that I'd be allowed to have both. "Just do as I say, it's in your best interests," she concluded.

I didn't argue.

My status became official that May. At the age of twenty-three, I could finally be considered an Italian citizen and was now officially Aldo Gucci's daughter, with equal entitlement to my father's estate as my brothers. Not that this was foremost on my mind, or his for that matter, as he must have wondered what he'd have left when all was said and done. He still had to find the several million he owed in taxes and that wasn't the kind of cash he had in his bank account. The first asset to be sold was a property and some land he owned in Palm Beach, and then—much to his distress—he was forced to auction off the works of art in the Gucci Galleria, one by one. Of all the painful moments he faced, I think this was one of the worst, as he had no choice but to dismantle this beautiful reflection of the business and all he had created.

Although he maintained a veneer of composure as his sentencing hearing loomed, he lost weight and seemed paler, older somehow. His conversations with my mother became deeper and more emotional. She, too, became increasingly morose, and—while I struggled with motherhood and the ongoing trouble with my marriage—I spent much of my time on the phone to Rome trying to cheer her up so that he wouldn't hear the anguish in her voice.

"Pray and trust in the outcome," Sari Nandi had told them both. Heeding his words, my father frequently walked to St. Patrick's to kneel and reflect on what had become of him. The great name of Gucci seemed lost to him now. What did he have to show for his lifetime's work?

I, too, was left floundering. Although I didn't want to join the business to begin with, my father had won me over and given me a fulfilling and rewarding role that I had grown to love. I hadn't planned a career in retail but I had started to believe there was a place for me at Gucci. "What will the future hold for me now?" I asked myself.

I had never been particularly religious but that long hot summer in New York, as the date of my father's potential incarceration neared, I have to admit that I, too, turned to God.

TWENTY-FOUR

We rarely know our own strength until we are truly tested. That's when we discover hidden reserves that we didn't even know we had. Throughout my life, I have had to draw upon those reserves in times of hardship.

Without doubt, one such moment was the day I climbed the steps of the imposing New York State Supreme Court building in Foley Square clutching the arm of my eighty-one-year-old father as he faced the possibility of imprisonment. It felt like scaling a mountain and I could barely catch my breath. Papà never expected me to go to court with him that day, nor did he ask, but Mamma was in Rome and I refused to leave him alone to his fate.

Built in granite in the style of a Roman temple, the courthouse has a Corinthian colonnade and wide stone steps that sweep up to a triangular pediment bearing the inscription *The True Administration of Justice Is the Firmest Pillar of Good Government*. Just as Papà hadn't wanted to let go of my hand on my wedding day, so I didn't want to release my grip on him as we entered the courtroom and took our places—my father and his attorneys toward the front, Santino and I a few rows behind.

As the sole defendant in a multimillion-dollar fraud trial in Manhattan's highest court, he must have cast his thoughts back to those days in 1953 when he'd stared up at the Statue of Liberty before disembarking in New York Harbor with dreams of conquering America. He'd walked up and down Fifth Avenue, where he set his sights on the first US store, imagining his name in big bold letters in the heart of the city. A few years later, when jet lag and the excitement of it all kept him up at night, he'd write one of his many love letters to his "Brunina" back in Rome. He told her, "*I wanted you to know how beautiful everything is here . . . New York really is the high life . . . How wonderful it is to live like this!*"

Those dreams were now in shreds as he sat in court, his hands tightly interlocked in his lap. Betrayed, ousted, and shamed, he looked smaller than usual—shrunken in his seat and staring straight ahead as the press and public filed in behind us. This was it—the moment we'd all been waiting for. The months of talking and pleading were over. Aside from Santino and me, there were no other family members present or any of his former colleagues or staff. The only show of solidarity came in the form of a series of character references, reminding the judge of the many charities my father had supported. Maurizio stayed away. Papà's sons Roberto and Giorgio opted to remain in Italy and Paolo, a key informant, was notably absent.

As I fought to stay strong, the proceedings got under way with a presentence conference in the judge's robing room. It was agonizing not to be privy to what was going on behind the heavy oak door but a stenographer would later provide an official record of everything said. My father's attorney Milton Gould, who was only four years younger than my father, began by reminding the judge that Papà had not only cooperated fully and paid back much of what he owed but that he could easily have fled to Italy to avoid prosecution. Instead he had chosen "deliberately, intelligently and understandingly" to face up to the charges and his responsibilities. "What do we do with an eighty-one-year-old man who has given such a dramatic demonstration of repentance?" he asked.

The judge showed little sympathy from the outset. "I understand Mr. Gucci is eighty-one years old, but he was seventy-one when this whole scheme began. . . . And it is certainly the most massive tax fraud I have had anything to do with." He did, however, agree with Gould that it was also one of the most "amateurish" fraud cases either of them had ever encountered.

"We are not dealing with a man sophisticated in the ways of finance in the United States," Gould concurred. There was no proof, he said, that my father was the designer or even "active in the mechanics" of the fraud—he simply enjoyed the benefits, as did the rest of the family.

When Papà was asked if he wanted to say anything, his attorney began to speak for him but he interrupted. He could tell that the judge was losing confidence in him and believed that if he addressed him directly—from his heart—he could appeal to his sense of compassion and justice. Reading the transcript later, I realized how nervous he must have been because his normally impeccable English failed him. He spoke of how much Gucci meant to him, his family, his friends, and his collaborators—"Two thousand people, whirling, working around. My work has been my joy." He admitted he was going against legal advice in speaking but added, "In circumstances so grave, so important, so heavy as this, I cannot refrain." He apologized for any financial impropriety and accepted that he would have to face the consequences but he went on to explain that in thirty-two years he had probably only signed two checks. He said he rarely went to the bank and "never knew too much."

Then he started to choke up. "It is no use to try and defend myself for what I've done by saying 'I didn't know.' No. No. I am not a child. I'm a man of conscience and I plead guilty. I only pray Almighty God," he continued, "to give me the strength to overcome this day. I am so sorry. Please, I am angry to myself."

When Gould interjected to tell him he didn't have to do this he sat back down, vanquished. His lawyer then told the judge that they were witnessing "the most dramatic phase of what is the disintegration of a human being." He added that there was great dissension in the family. "The man has actually been locked out of the edifice he erected. He made this business. He made the name Gucci a worldwide enterprise and he is now excluded from it, and he is in terrible shape." As Papà wiped away his tears, his attorney likened his situation to that of Shakespeare's King Lear, whose controversial dispersal of his realm between his children ends with his dying from a broken heart. "The people [Aldo Gucci] elevated to positions of power and wealth are the people who not only benefited from this scheme but they have destroyed him," he concluded.

The judge adjourned proceedings before they all filed back silently into the courtroom. The minute I saw my father's face, I knew that something momentous must have happened. His expression was unfamiliar and my heart sank. Then the clerk announced, "All rise," and the judge swept in, wearing his gown. When I noticed how set his jaw seemed, I thought I might be sick.

Papà rose to his feet along with his legal team. He was so close I could almost touch him but instead my eyes bored into the back of his head, desperately trying to transmit my undying love and support. Every muscle in my body tensed as the prosecutor opened with a summation of the case and the formal request that the defendant receive a prison sentence. Then Gould made his closing remarks, but instead of listening in silence, the judge repeatedly interrupted to counter many of his points.

My skin began to prickle with heat and I felt bile rising in my stomach. My mouth was so dry I could hardly swallow. This whole case was a travesty and yet I sensed that others wouldn't see it that way.

When Gould sat back down with what seemed to me like a sigh, the judge asked my father if he had anything to add. Knowing that every word he said would be reported back down the long chain of betrayal, he cleared his throat, stood once more, and, in a voice I barely recognized, said how "deeply sorry" he was. Then he began to stumble over his words in a way that wounded me.

"This is the last period of my life and we close very poorly, very negatively . . . ," he began falteringly. He pleaded for leniency and appealed to the judge's "indulgency." Dabbing at his eyes with a handkerchief, he claimed he had been the victim of "reprisals . . . by a son who has repaid me very badly." Thinking of Paolo, he pulled himself together and declared, "I don't know how to hate, Your Honor. I forgive him. I forgive anybody who wanted me to be here today, and others who have had the satisfaction of revenge that only God will judge. . . . Thank you."

I resisted the urge to leap to my feet and say something too. I wanted to cry, "This is not right! You cannot send this man to jail. Please—it will kill him!" Instead, I was frozen to the spot, rendered speechless as the judge spoke for several agonizing minutes before directing his gaze at my father.

"You are committed to the custody of the attorney general for one year and one day."

Time in that courtroom stood still for me then.

"One year and one day."

My eyes spilled tears but still I couldn't move. Everything my father had ever achieved was going to be obliterated by this moment. For the rest of his life, he would be identified as Aldo Gucci, the man indicted for tax evasion.

Papà swayed on his feet slightly. Still unsteady, he bobbed his head in thanks when the judge agreed to defer the sentence for a month to give him—and us—time to prepare. He was instructed to surrender his passport so that he couldn't flee back to Italy. There was commotion all around me as journalists rushed out to file their copy and further publicize my father's shame. His lawyers murmured to each other as they filed away their papers. My attention remained fixed on my father, standing there alone. I feared his legs would give way at any moment—as mine might have done.

As I watched him be taken to a side room to complete some formalities, I struggled to comprehend the "justice" in jailing such an elderly man. How could it be that his immense contribution over the years would not be taken into consideration? The truth was, he was too high-profile for that. The government needed to be seen as making an example of him, as reiterated by the future mayor of New York Rudolph Giuliani, who told waiting reporters on the steps that the sentence should serve as a lesson to others. To our great surprise, Gould told the press that he didn't think the sentence "harsh or unjust." Well, I bloody well did.

By the time I was reunited with Papà in an anteroom, he had composed himself enough to face me. He was so embarrassed by his black fingertips, which had been pressed into an inkpad, that he clenched his hands into fists. There was further indignity to come because he had yet to face the press, who were waiting for him outside, their cameras and microphones ready. He shepherded me through the baying to our waiting car. In the glare of the flashing bulbs, my father no longer looked like a defeated, besmirched man on the worst day of his life but once again like the indefatigable Dr. Gucci, who'd face this latest setback like any other. I had never been more proud.

When we eventually reached the car and the driver pulled away from the courthouse, he pressed his body back into his leather seat and undid the button on his jacket. All he wanted, he muttered, was to go home, see Mamma, and fly to Palm Beach.

We'd already agreed that she would come out immediately after the trial so that we could go to Florida together. We'd hoped to be celebrating the end of the nightmare there. Instead, we'd be counting down the days to when Papà would be taken to the Eglin prison outside Pensacola, Florida, in October—one month's time.

It felt good to be in the sun. Santino flew in and out and we all tried to make the best of our time together. Mamma prepared lunch for us on the veranda; we rested and went for long swims, trying our best to take our mind off things. I loved watching Papà with his "Alexina" ever by his side, even if there was a constant aching in my heart knowing that the hourglass had been flipped.

When the dreaded morning came, we had to draw on every ounce of strength we had just to get through it. My mother and I were well accustomed to seeing my father in a suit, carrying an overnight bag and setting off to work. However, the morning of October 15 was no ordinary business day. We tried hard to be stoic but the knowledge of where he was headed broke us and we both wept.

Dry-eyed, my father kissed us good-bye.

"Okay, Papà, I'll come visit as soon as they let me," I promised.

He slid into the rear seat of his waiting car without even looking back. I don't think he could allow himself to. He'd insisted that he go alone and nothing could persuade him otherwise. I would have gladly defied his wishes to spend every last moment with him, but prison rules stated that no family members could accompany a new inmate beginning his sentence.

Mamma and I stood in the driveway and watched as the car sped away and created a gravel wake. No matter how we tried to support each other, nothing we said could allay the deep-seated fears we shared about whether he might survive the coming year. We were tormented by thoughts of him in a prison uniform and having to sleep on a bunk next to God knows what kind of criminal, separated from everything he knew.

Federal Prison Camp Eglin was categorized as a minimum-security prison for white-collar offenders in what is known as the Florida panhandle. Situated on Auxiliary Field 6 at Eglin Air Force Base near Fort Walton Beach, it was dubbed "Club Fed" or a "country club" by the press, but it was still a jail and they weren't the ones locked in with strangers each night away from all they'd ever known.

On arrival, my father had his fingerprints taken once more and was issued with prison number 13124-054-E, his new identity. He was assigned a bunk in a thirty-two-bed dormitory in section D. His clothes were traded for a starched blue shirt, pants, and a sweater paired with white socks and sneakers. He wasn't allowed to keep his belt, his wristwatch, or any personal belongings apart from his horn-rimmed spectacles.

Shown by guards to a block housing seven hundred inmates, he was issued a pillow and blanket, a towel, and his uniform. He had his own bed and a small cubicle but no privacy beyond that. A prison officer apprised him of the daily routines, which included lights on at five thirty a.m., lights out at ten thirty p.m., and roll calls five times a day. Thirty minutes were allowed for breakfast and an hour for lunch, with dinner at four thirty p.m. Every prisoner was expected to work approximately forty hours a week for "performance pay" of a few cents per hour, which they could then spend on telephone calls, newspapers, candy, or fresh fruit. Papà was assigned to the tailoring department, tasked with mending and ironing numbers onto clothing—a suitable job for someone with his background, the warden must have thought.

Each inmate was allowed two fifteen-minute telephone calls a day while fellow prisoners lined up behind him. There was no privacy and the pressing feeling of somebody else waiting as they snatched a few precious minutes with loved ones.

My father's first collect call was to Mamma in Palm Beach, whose voice he longed to hear. He stood in line with the rest of the inmates and waited his turn, the start of a daily ritual that would sustain them both throughout his incarceration. As soon as he said, "Hello, Bruna . . . ," and then stopped, she could tell he was not himself. It was only the second time she had ever heard him cry. The first had been when she'd tried to break away from him early on in their courtship and he'd shocked her by dropping to his knees promising to make her his queen.

Then, as now, she quickly put a stop to his tears. "Aldo!" she interrupted when he started to complain that the guards had taken everything. "Aldo, listen to me!" she insisted. His whimpering faded and she heard a sudden sharp intake of breath.

"I will always be here for you, but on one condition," she told him. "You have to stay strong." Her response was met with stony silence but she knew he was listening. "If I ever hear you like this, you will never see me again. Do you understand?"

Their minutes were almost up but there were just enough left for my father to gather his thoughts and tell her, "Yes, Bruna. I understand. *Te lo prometto* [I promise]."

When the line went dead, she prayed she'd done enough to help him get through that first long night. As she sat at his desk overlooking the garden, weeping her own bitter tears, she had no idea that her tough love would set the tone for the rest of his time inside. "Bruna is my Rock of Gibraltar," he'd boast. "I get all my strength from her."

I was shocked when she told me what she'd said to Papà that night. For the first time I came to realize how tenacious her survival instincts really were and how resilient she could be. I made a point of telling her so. "All your life you've believed that people dismissed you as the mercurial mistress. Now they'll know you are a woman of courage, unwavering and determined. This is the woman Papà knows and loves. This is your legacy."

More powerful than anything I could say, though, were the words of Ruby Hamra, who met her for lunch soon afterward. They had become friends over the years and before Ruby left New York for good, Mamma took her for blini at the Russian Tea Room. "Bruna, I don't know if we are going to see each other again but I want to tell you something—you are the strongest woman I have ever met," said the PR powerhouse as my mother listened in amazement. "Nobody handles Aldo the way you do. He's like the devil with everybody but as soon as you're around, he changes. I don't know what you did to him, but it worked."

My mother was taken aback but for the first time it dawned on her that maybe she was tougher than she'd imagined. "He grew up in a very strict family," she told Ruby, defending the man she loved. "He was taught to show who was in charge. He could never relax until he was away from all that. I suppose I was the one person with whom he could really be himself."

Stripped of his name and his pride, he had no choice but to do just that—be himself. And, with so few trappings of his former life left to him, he came to realize that there was only one person he wanted to spend the rest of his life with—his beloved Brunicchi with the hidden core of steel who loved him simply for who he was.

TWENTY-FIVE

I can remember how much my mother and I longed for the next visit from my father when I was a little girl. We began to look forward to his company in the same way as we looked forward to summer. And like a welcome change of season, he'd blow in on a warm wind and change the color of our world.

Now the tables were turned. It was Papà whose life was monochrome, and it was he who was looking forward to our visits in just the same way. Frustratingly, that was forbidden for the first few weeks—a rule designed to let prisoners settle in. With nothing to do but wait, Mamma and I returned to New York, where she became his lifeline, accepting his fifteen-minute calls at approximately six p.m. every night—depending on when he could get to the phone—as he talked her through his day and she fussed over his welfare.

"Are you eating enough? Are you sleeping, Aldo? Are people being kind?" He, in turn, was only interested in one thing—when she might visit him. She'd promised to come soon but they both knew that was unlikely in the immediate future. He realized how hard it would be for her and didn't want to pressure her into doing something that would upset her. Neither of them could give up on the other and each knew they couldn't fall apart, but both needed time to grow accustomed to their change of circumstances.

Visitors were allowed at Eglin on Sundays between the hours of eight a.m. and three p.m. At the first opportunity, Santino and I flew to the Gulf Coast without any idea of what to expect. I was relieved that the place, with its sun-drenched landscape and oak trees dripping with Spanish moss, was nothing like the images I had conjured up of prisons I'd seen in the movies. Instead of guard towers and barbed-wire fences, there was a rudimentary checkpoint with nothing more than a yellow boundary line painted on the ground.

Each Sunday, the prisoners were assembled in an open picnic area with concrete tables, bench seats, and umbrellas for shade. Scores of families were already there when we arrived, each congregated around a prisoner in a blue uniform. They'd bought snacks and soft drinks from prison vending machines and the atmosphere was more like that of an outing in the park than a correctional facility. Nervously, my eyes darted left and right through the unfamiliar crowd, looking for Papà. Then I spotted him, standing in the distance. I waved and hurried across to him. Once I reached him, I fell into his arms as I fought back my tears. Overwhelming as it was to see him again, it felt strange to be with him in those surroundings and see him in the most unlikely clothes imaginable.

"White sneakers?" I cried, staring down at his feet, my mouth agape.

He followed my gaze and asked, "Do they suit me?" I was glad to see he hadn't lost his sense of humor.

"No, Papà," I replied, half laughing, half crying. "You look ridiculous!"

Settling down next to him and taking his hand, I stared into his face and asked how he was faring. Knowing how protective he was of Mamma, I expected that he'd glossed over things when he was on the phone to her. "I'm fine," he assured me, trying to allay my fears. "Take a look around, everybody in here is harmless." The men in blue, of every color, size, and creed, certainly didn't look like criminals as they laughed and chatted with their loved ones. Most were doing time for drug offenses or fraud. "It's really not too bad," my father insisted. "I'll be okay."

Even so, I knew that it would be hard for my mother to see him there. When he asked about her I told him she was coping well but we both knew she wouldn't be coming any time soon. Over the course of the next few hours, we chatted as normal and once we got business matters out of the way, I lightened things up by telling him about Alexandra. Then we all had a snack together before he took us to the chapel, eager to show us where he attended daily Mass. He was reading a lot and becoming increasingly conscious of his faith. Prayer had become a lifesaver for him and helped to while away the endless hours where time stood still and days felt like weeks. The restless man who'd rushed from one city to the next was suddenly forced to acclimatize to a whole new schedule, to slow down and contemplate his life.

Having found God on a big level, he was memorizing passages from the Bible and other books that had been recommended by Sari Nandi. In one of his first notes from prison to my mother he wrote, *"I live in a world created by God and filled with divine blessings and power."* He also started sending maxims that encouraged her to *"live life fully, feel love deeply, . . . see beauty brightly and hear Christ only."* As if she could live life fully without him by her side.

He told us there was a library where he could borrow books and a classroom where—on account of his Italian passport—he was obligated to sit through English lessons with mostly Spanish-speaking classmates. He was given homework to improve his reading skills and taught elocution from a fourth-grade textbook. It was like being back at school. One pronunciation exercise he showed us with a wry smile explained that taxes (pronounced *tack-says*) was the correct plural of tax (pronounced *tacks*). In spite of the fact that he was fluent in several languages, he did all that was asked of him uncomplainingly and tried to help others where he could.

Several of the prisoners came up to tell us, "Your dad's the man. We love this guy!" They'd dubbed him "Bubba Gucci"—using the endearing Southern nickname for an older sibling or a "good ol' boy." One of them told me, "There's not a day goes by when he doesn't pick up his photos of you and stare at them." I didn't even know Papà had any photographs of us with him until that moment and was deeply touched.

I was also reassured that—with the respect of so many of his fellow inmates—no harm would come to him there. When our time was up we hugged and kissed and said good-bye. It had been an emotional day. Making me promise to look after Mamma, he squeezed my hand and then it was time to go. "She'll come soon," I assured him.

The only member of my father's family that visited him in prison was Roberto's son Cosimo. Although I found it despicable that no one else ever came to see him from Italy, my father never mentioned it—almost as if that part of his family had ceased to exist. To my mother's delight, he started to write letters again—after a thirty-year gap. In one *"smattering of lines"* dedicated to her, he said, *"I love you darling as ever, ever before!"* He told her that his thoughts were always with her as he imagined her at home, organizing her day, and then he sent her *"a warm embrace and eternal love,"* evoking memories of one of his letters from the 1950s in which he'd written from afar: *"I was checking my watch throughout the day, imagining where you were and what you might be doing . . . how were you dressed today, my darling?"* The very thought of her being without him made his heart *"tighten with pain."*

I tried to visit Papà as often as I could, flying into Pensacola from New York for the weekend every two or three weeks and checking into a local motel. On Sunday mornings I'd show up at the gate and go through the motions with the security staff, who searched my bag and scanned me with a metal detector. Nothing whatsoever was allowed in, so bringing any personal effects or gifts was out of the question. The trepidation I felt when going through the protocol for the first time soon slipped away and I sailed through each checkpoint after that without too much fanfare.

Each time he spotted me across the yard his face would light up and I'd hurry over to fill him in on all the news. Most of the time, he did a good job of pretending to be upbeat and only ever complained about the food and the lack of freedom to communicate. "I miss your mother's cooking and I can't tell you how frustrating it is to have to stand in line and then only be able to speak for a short while." Knowing how happy it would make him, I took Alexandra on one visit as a surprise and the effect was miraculous. At just eighteen months, she was already so gorgeous that she quite literally drew a crowd. As Papà hugged and kissed her, his eyes glinting with joy, many of his friends came over to say hello as he proudly presented her to everyone.

"You have a beautiful family, Bubba!" one prisoner exclaimed. Another assured me, "We're all watching out for him. He's an inspiration." A third added, "Unlike him over there . . . !" indicating with a jerk of his thumb an inmate sitting with his family in a corner. I discovered later that the man he had pointed to was the fifty-eight-year-old American fashion designer Albert Nipon, who was at the end of a three-year sentence for tax evasion. By all accounts, Nipon wasn't as popular as my father, chiefly because he remained aloof. My father tried to explain that everyone coped differently and it was all down to one's personal ethos. He strove to be charitable and "share good freely," as he put it, which included respecting the guards as much as the convicts. It was a philosophy that seemed to work.

Five weeks into his sentence, I was horrified to arrive one Sunday to find him in a neck brace with several stitches in his head. "It's not as serious as it looks," he told me sheepishly. "I skidded on the wet floor of the laundry room and knocked myself out. I've got a few bruises but I'll be fine." I was worried that might not be true at first but his fellow inmates convinced me it was and I was so relieved. On further questioning, I discovered that the prison doctor had sent him to the hospital for an MRI scan and some other tests but there was no lasting damage. Nevertheless, it reminded everyone that Papà was of a certain age and needed to be looked after.

He brushed aside my concerns about his injury and asked me not to trouble Mamma with it. Then he focused on the one thing he was finding it most difficult to live without—his watch. All his life he had been enslaved to it. His days ran like clockwork as he hurried from one meeting to the next. Time had been his master, and without it he felt bereft.

"People smuggle things in here all the time—usually cigarettes or drugs," he said with a shrug. "It shouldn't be so hard to get me a watch, right?" We both knew he wouldn't be allowed to wear it but just knowing he had it and could check the time—especially during the long, hot nights—would be a small but important victory.

Santino immediately volunteered to take the risk. Slipping one of my father's watches on his wrist for the next visit, he waited until we were all in the chapel for Mass before removing it and passing it to an inmate laid flat inside a Bible, as instructed. That was how my father got his Gucci timepiece back and a little piece of his dignity along with it.

Without my father to fuss over and left to her own devices, my mother busied herself in Rome, Berkshire, and Palm Beach, and she did so with a sense of purpose. However occupied she kept herself, though, most of her life she'd been accustomed to taking care of Papà at least once a month and now that routine had gone. "In truth, I was a better mother to him than I was to you," she once told me. "No matter where I was or what I was doing, from the moment he walked back into my world he became my sole focus. Everything else became inconsequential. That was my weakness."

My father, too, felt lost without Mamma, but at least he had business to attend to. Just because he was in prison didn't mean he wasn't still connected with the company—at least in his own mind. I became his mole on the inside, checking in with his lawyers, accountants, and other allies and reporting back on the latest developments. His first collect call of the day was around ten a.m. EST and was always to me, typically accompanied by a long to-do list and various people to contact. When I could, I'd connect him on a three-way conference bridge so he could continue to orchestrate what was happening on the outside.

Plagued with insomnia again, he'd stay up all night drafting dozens of letters to be sent to the board in my name and his, questioning what he called the "catastrophic mismanagement" of the Gucci executive committee in turning a "thoroughbred into a carriage horse." As he dictated each one to be typed up and dispatched, I was sure that most would be ignored but knew that sending them made him feel connected, and that alone was a worthwhile exercise.

In his first letter to Maurizio since his imprisonment (copies of which were sent to the rest of the family), he said he had kept his silence long enough. *"Over the last eighteen months your revolutionary policies and antagonistic leadership have proven to be totally destructive. You have dilapidated the economic foundations of a company that was built with much effort over the course of forty years of hard work."* He went on to say that he had *"total disapproval and disdain"* for Maurizio's foolish and immature conduct and condemned him for his *"superficiality . . . lack of sensibility and . . . ingratitude"* for those like Papà who had spent a lifetime building a *"cultural and economic patrimony"* long before he was born. He concluded, *"I pray that God will forgive you for what you have done."*

He was itching to get out and take up the battle in person, but that didn't seem likely any time soon. Ever since he'd crossed the threshold of Eglin in October, we'd been pushing his legal team to ask for a reduced sentence, but that motion was denied. After his fall, we campaigned for Papà to be released on probation but didn't make any headway with that either. As days turned into weeks and then months, my father began to realize that he'd been all but abandoned by those who'd promised to help him and that there were only a handful of people left he could rely upon.

He had other worries, too. Although he'd paid off all his personal tax liabilities, the IRS was pursuing him for $20 million in corporate tax. Then the authorities in New York jumped in, claiming that he owed state taxes as well. As if that weren't enough, there was the ongoing Italian police investigation into the forging of Rodolfo's signature, which he knew could be crucial to deposing Maurizio.

With his favorite time of the year fast approaching, the idea of not being able to spend Christmas with us also saddened him deeply. His tone became flat on the phone and his wit began to desert him. We all sensed it.

"Maybe it's time for me to go and see him," Mamma suddenly announced. She'd been steeling herself all along but she knew the time had come. Leaving Alexandra with a nanny, Santino, Mamma, and I flew to Pensacola and drove the hour east to Eglin. The closer we got the more nervous she became. Her oversized sunglasses were fixed firmly to her face so that no one could see her eyes, and by the time we'd entered the prison compound and were walking toward where I knew he'd be waiting in the yard, she could hardly speak.

Holding back a little, I let her go to him first, and their affection for each other was touching to witness. They embraced warmly, and then she peered up through her shades to scrutinize the face she knew and loved so well. They both knew that he could never have hidden his true feelings from her. Once they'd had their moment together, Santino and I joined them at one of the picnic tables and the four of us spent the afternoon together, chatting about anything whatsoever other than how we were really feeling. Although she took part in the conversation, Mamma remained rigid with tension in that alien environment and never once took off her sunglasses. Whether that was because she didn't want us to see her bleary eyes or because she was ashamed and wanted to hide her embarrassment, I couldn't be sure.

Impressively though, she didn't shirk from her responsibilities and after a sleepless night in our motel she returned with me the next day for a special Christmas Day Mass arranged by the prison chaplain. As the four of us sat in a row on the unforgiving wooden seats in that chapel, we couldn't help but think back to all the family Christmases we'd spent in Florida and New York, and how different our lives were now. Papà had always cherished this time of year and loved going out to select a tree for the living room. There were rarely any gifts—they were reserved for the traditional Italian Epiphany celebration on January 6—but it wasn't about the presents, it was about being together as a family, breaking bread, eating fine food, and enjoying the spirit of the season. As he sat proudly at the head of our table each year he'd raise a glass to his Bruna and to me, his only daughter, and—no matter how little we might have seen of him—everything suddenly felt perfect.

Christmas 1986 certainly didn't feature among our most anticipated get-togethers. What we didn't expect, however, was the palpable sense of community spirit between the hundred or so inmates, their families, and their friends. The atmosphere held us spellbound, due in no small part to the reason we were all there in the first place. Total strangers shook hands with one another. Common criminals mingled with children and wives and all were welcomed. The chapel was packed with worshippers, all sorrowful about the enforced separation from their loved ones and eager to share this special moment together. By the time it came to the carols and an emotionally charged homily on the importance of family, Mamma and I weren't the only ones in tears.

Bizarrely, it was probably the most meaningful Christmas we have ever experienced as a family and I wouldn't have missed it for the world.

TWENTY-SIX

*L*ike my father, I prefer to think that we are in charge of our own destiny and that not everything is set in stone. I am drawn to the author Anaïs Nin, who speaks of finding ways to improve our circumstances and have a better life. She writes, "The knowledge that we are responsible for our actions and attitudes does not need to be discouraging, because it also means that we are free to change this destiny."

My father's destiny—and consequently my mother's and mine—had veered dramatically off the path we'd all expected it to take. Instead of presiding over Gucci in the final years of his life before proudly electing a member of the family to take over, he was shamed and locked up. Eager to regain control and take charge of his life once more, he refused to be diminished by his experience and began the New Year in fighting spirit. It was all too apparent to everyone that as long as he had breath in his body, he was never going to give up.

Sitting at a desk in the prison library one morning, he drafted a letter to the entire Gucci family in which he set out his case for saving the company. It was a bold and brave move. Addressing us all as his *"Dear Ones,"* he reminded everyone that he had been the *"driving force of the Gucci Empire"* for over three decades. He gave credit to his children (even Paolo) and claimed that we all bore the *"family hallmark."* Maurizio's actions were, he said, a *"source of considerable pain"* but he hoped to come up with *"remedies and solutions"* from the *"ashes of this moral and economic devastation"* to restore the *"values and traditions that ha[d] given such enviable prestige and glory to the Gucci name."* In effect, he was letting it be known that he no longer sought control of the company and was prepared to leave it to the next generation. We were the future now.

Two months later, after what felt like an agonizing tussle with the authorities to secure a date for his release on parole, we hired a new lawyer to look into the case. It was largely thanks to him that in late March 1987, Papà was freed to serve the remainder of his sentence at a halfway house in West Palm Beach. Run by the Salvation Army, the property catered to more than a hundred inmates, who could do what they liked during the daytime but were required to return each night for a ten p.m. curfew. This transition was offered to everyone released from Eglin, and in my father's case, it gave him the chance to spend his days with Mamma. Although he still had to spend every night with prisoners, it somehow felt to us all that the worst was over.

The day "Bubba Gucci" left Eglin was, by all accounts, a memorable occasion. Those convicts who'd come to love and respect "the old man" were especially sad to see him go. For many, he had become a mentor and given them a sense of purpose and direction in their lives. Scores of his friends lined up to give him a send-off, cheering and patting him on the back. I only wish I'd been there to see that. Rather wonderfully, we received some letters from fellow prisoners after his release, which were a testament to him. One in particular, from a man I knew only as George, spoke of the day Papà left. It still moves me to tears.

He wrote,

> *Well, today was the big day for your father!*
> *When he first came in, I told him this day would*
> *come and that if he could just relax and enjoy*
> *himself, everything would be all right. I think he*
> *did an excellent job . . . maintaining his unique*
> *sense of humor and making friends in a very*
> *uncomfortable environment. You should always be*
> *proud of the way he handled himself in here. . . .*
> *He impressed a lot of people with his kindness . . .*
> *and he never did let them [the officers] whip him*
> *and we all admired him for that. I'll never forget*
> *those times we sneaked out and ran down the*
> *back way to get into the dining hall—he'd be*
> *right there with you. I told him we could get into*
> *trouble. He just smiled and said, "Let's go!!" Well,*
> *I just wanted to say "Goodbye"—tell him I said*
> *"Good luck." I enjoyed knowing all of you and*
> *will never forget having had the opportunity to*
> *know Aldo Gucci! Take care of him—George.*

Although Papà's time in jail had been both traumatic and life-changing and had turned him into a ghost of his former self, he was elated at the prospect of being able to spend his days with Mamma. She was equally overjoyed to have him back and quickly fell into her mothering role, although she soon had to accept that he would spend most of his time on the phone to New York and Italy. In May 1987, he was going to be eighty-two years old. She was turning fifty. In their almost thirty years together, they'd been through more than most and their journey had been far from smooth. As a lifelong spectator to their rapport, I had often wondered what it was that sustained it, constrained as they were by circumstance and their own complicated backgrounds.

Strangely though, since his release from prison the dynamic of the relationship had shifted and he'd become more vulnerable and dependent on my mother. Even though he was still on a mission with the company, he was openly more affectionate, seeking her out when she wasn't within sight, eager to find her and lay a hand on her shoulder—like a touchstone. He clearly needed her more than ever and she knew she had to be strong for him. This role reversal saddened me and I was worried that things might never be the same.

Their peaceful sojourn in Florida only came to an end when his probation period was up in the fall of 1987 and his passport was returned. After such a stressful year, Mamma was relieved they could move about freely and resume their normal life. My father looked forward to getting back into the swing of things—he would first go to New York, and then on to Florence to see his sons and meet with his legal team with the objective of putting the company back on track. My mother would use their time in Italy to catch up with things in Rome and take a break.

Then something surprising happened, which my father learned about while still in Palm Beach. Armed officers from the Guardia di Finanza (the Italian IRS) attempted to arrest Maurizio in Milan, but a loyal employee tipped him off in time, allowing him to flee across the border into Switzerland. Unexpectedly, the warrant had nothing to do with Rodolfo's shares but with Paolo. My brother had sought his revenge for what he saw as Maurizio's double dealing by informing the tax authorities of his purchase of the sixty-year-old *Creole*, the largest wooden sailing yacht ever built, which he'd paid for with an illegal transfer of funds. As a fugitive,

Maurizio was now in an extremely tenuous position, so Papà and my other brothers quickly applied to the New York Supreme Court to dissolve Gucci America, claiming gross mismanagement.

The legal bickering that ensued back and forth across the Atlantic led to a magistrate in Florence calling a halt. In the shareholders' interests, he appointed an economics professor as acting chairman of the Italian arm of the company, sparking newspaper headlines such as "Can an Outsider Fill Aldo Gucci's Loafers?" My father was distraught that control had passed to a total stranger—something he'd never expected to witness in his lifetime. His last remaining hope was to convince the US courts to dissolve Gucci America. The outcome looked promising until Paolo stirred things up again.

"Your son has sold his shares to an anonymous third party," my father was told by his advisers.

"What?" Papà replied incredulously. "Who?"

"We don't know yet." As we would soon discover, Maurizio had been in private negotiations with the Bahrain-registered Investcorp, which had acquired Tiffany in 1984. He had then tricked Paolo into handing him the majority stake. The code name for the buyout was "Project Saddle"—a nod to Gucci's equestrian theme. Fearing the worst, my father's attorneys challenged the sale, but the judge was unsympathetic and told them, "It's very simple . . . you've been stabbed in the back."

It was over. My other two brothers were persuaded into selling their shares as well, meaning that it was only a matter of time before the company fell into foreign hands with Maurizio at the helm, unimpeded by family meddling.

By March 1988, the deed was done. Without any prior consultation or even mentioning anything to Papà, Giorgio and Roberto had signed away the shares they'd been given in perpetuity to preserve continuity in the family business. My father never intended them to be sold for profit, nor did he expect his sons to deny their own children the opportunity to take up their places in the company he'd created for them all. My brothers insisted that the offer from Investcorp was too generous to resist and they'd been advised that they might lose their value otherwise. They had their own families to think of, they added, and they couldn't fight Maurizio any longer.

Papà was shattered. Winding up in prison may have been the worst thing that had befallen him but he could never have imagined that his sons would turn their backs on him in this way. What else could destiny possibly have in store for him?

"I'm done with all of them," he told Mamma. "*È finita*" (It's over). Poignantly, he added, "If it wasn't for you and Patricia, I think I would have shot myself."

Devastated, he flew to Italy with my mother and a heavy heart. Not long after they'd arrived back in Rome, one of the first things she did was to hurry to her bank and retrieve the shares and money he'd entrusted to her before his sentencing. Glad to be rid of the responsibility, she handed the package back to him with a sigh of relief.

"I knew it!" he exclaimed, his eyes glinting with gratitude. "You're the only person in the world I can really trust."

Gucci may no longer have been a company my father recognized but he still had a precious 16.7 percent stake, and that at least made him feel like he owned a piece of the empire he'd built. It wasn't over yet. Since his days as a delivery boy riding his bicycle on the bumpy streets of Florence, he'd been committed to the success of the family business. For over seventy years, he had been utterly devoted to the company. He knew nothing else, and—for him—there was no Plan B.

Even though my mother had been waiting patiently in the wings and we'd have both loved for him to be more involved in our lives over the years, we knew that his continued involvement with the business is what kept him going. I'd seen firsthand how he never gave up without a fight and I couldn't help but wonder what his next move might be.

When he heard that an old friend wanted to see him, he was pleased. Severin Wunderman was the Belgian-born Holocaust survivor and watchmaker whose fortune Papà had helped make back in the 1970s. Wunderman was now on the Gucci board and my father hoped he might be able to influence his nephew to allow him to stay on as a shareholder at the very least.

Papà had asked me to join them and when I opened the door to let Wunderman in he seemed friendly enough, but within a few minutes of his arrival, my father realized that this was more than just a social call. No sooner had we settled around the coffee table than he interrupted my father's discourse about his visions for the company. "Come on, Aldo, it's time to let go!" he said with a smile that stretched his sallow skin over the bones of his face. "You've accomplished great things! Now spend some money and enjoy your life!"

My father's expression froze and I sensed the immediate shift in his temperament. He stared at Wunderman, who carried on trying to use whatever leverage he could to persuade Papà to sell the last of his shares. Knowing how much my father had done for him over the years, I felt my flesh crawl. Wunderman seemed to completely overlook the fact that my father had already been so badly treated by members of his own family.

I watched the shutters come down on my father's face and knew that the meeting was over. As soon as Wunderman left, he fell back into his armchair, physically deflated. Inadvertently, his visitor had achieved exactly what he had been sent to do, as it was now painfully obvious that my father didn't have a single ally left anywhere. When he pulled himself together, the words he spoke were spat in anger. "Sell, he says! It is I who has been sold out! They've all turned their backs on me! Even Severin!" In that moment he wanted nothing more to do with Gucci. He would sell after all, he announced. "You and Bruna are my priority now."

As if to ratify his decision, he was informed by the US authorities that because of his criminal conviction his residence permit would be revoked. Without it, he would no longer be allowed to remain indefinitely. In choosing to make his home in the States and pay federal taxes, he'd inadvertently opened himself up to future prosecution while his family escaped scot-free. He joked that he'd return his green card gift-wrapped in Gucci paper with a red bow but in the end it was stuffed inside a bundle of other documents and mailed to the authorities.

With his American dream shattered, it was time to wrap up his affairs and return home to Italy for good.

I, too, had fallen out of love with the United States and decided to move back "home" to Berkshire so I could be closer to my parents once they settled in Rome. Santino and I enrolled Alexandra in my old school Hurst Lodge and it was a joy to be back in the English countryside and watch my daughter playing in the garden where I'd spent so much time as a young girl.

Papà visited us often, delighting in the precious moments with his beloved granddaughter, who would be "a great beauty," he foretold. One of my happiest memories of this sorrowful period in his life is of Alexandra sitting with him at the grand piano while she bashed at the keys and they sang together disharmoniously. There he was, blessing our house again with his color and vitality. It felt good to be back there together.

Eager to ensure I was looked after, my father managed to secure me a position at Gucci UK as creative director for London, Hong Kong, and Tokyo. The arrangement would keep me connected to the business until such time as I wanted out or he sold his shares. Left to my own devices, I had little contact with anyone in Milan or New York. I retained my place on the board but couldn't bring myself to attend meetings if it meant sitting across the table from my cousin Maurizio.

The curtain fell in April 1989. After protracted and painful negotiations, my father's time with Gucci was drawing to a close—as was mine. I flew to Geneva with him for a meeting with Investcorp, where, in my capacity as a company director and Aldo Gucci's daughter, I would be asked to sign a number of documents as part of the settlement—or, as I called it, hush money.

The night before our fateful meeting we had dinner at the Beau Rivage, the lakeside hotel with a view of the city's historic Jet d'Eau fountain, a landmark symbolizing strength, ambition, and vitality. Several legal advisers accompanied us but it was by no means a sociable event. Needless to say, Papà didn't take much interest in the food on the table. Even though he was going to leave Switzerland a wealthy man, he couldn't help but reflect on how his life's work was about to be cut away from him at the single stroke of a pen.

The following morning, we walked the short distance to the office, where we were ushered into a boardroom full of expectant faces and took our places around a large black table. On it sat a single telephone and two small parcels wrapped in Tiffany blue. My father's mood was somber and his gaze steely as he addressed the phalanx of Investcorp representatives, warning them that their new power-hungry young chairman would ruin the business they were buying. It was a symbolic if futile gesture on his part but his last task at Gucci. This was his moment and he wasn't going to let it pass without saying something.

"Heed my words, gentlemen, this company will not be the force it was for as long as my nephew is in charge."

They thanked him courteously and then waited as he stared at the sheaf of papers setting out the terms of the sale. These included an order preventing us from discussing company affairs or divulging any information for ten years, and banned us both from using our names on any product or venture.

As his fountain pen hovered over the dotted line, I felt a rush of blood to my head. It was a similar feeling to the one I'd had in the New York courtroom. Once again, he was forced toward a destiny other than the one he would have chosen.

Accepting that there was no alternative, he lowered his pen. I heard the nib scratch the paper as half a dozen pairs of eyes bored into him. Signing his name with a flourish, he then handed over his share certificates and—in the process—his last connection with the company. In the awkward minutes that followed, the document was checked and rechecked by lawyers and then, while the ink dried, we had to wait in silence for what seemed like an eternity until the telephone on the desk rang, shattering the hush. Only when someone on the other end of the line confirmed that the funds had been wired to his bank were we free to depart.

To mark possibly the worst moment of my father's life, our hosts then handed us the two farewell gifts. My father received a heavily engraved silver Tiffany box that would hold no more than two cigars. I was given a small silver milk jug. God knows what they were meant to symbolize. After a lifetime of dedication unsurpassed by anyone in that airless room, these gaudy little trinkets no doubt chosen by a clueless secretary were so implausible that they were practically insulting. It would have been better to receive nothing at all.

On the theme of destiny, the author Anaïs Nin once said that none of us are "in bondage to our past" if we have the courage to examine how the past shaped us. The past was what Gucci had been all about, and for my father it had also been about the future—not just his but mine and that of his family. What future did he have now? he must have wondered as we left that building.

All his life he had felt he had the power to change his destiny, but toward the end, circumstances forced him into situations beyond his control. As a witness to what he experienced, I, too, learned a valuable lesson—that none of us know what's around the corner.

TWENTY-SEVEN

There are consequences for every choice we make in life, some of them unforeseen. When my father decided to gift his sons his shares in Gucci he'd never have suspected that they'd sell them one day, or that the nephew he brought back from exile would prove to be so duplicitous.

I'd never considered the ramifications either, and now I pondered what to do next. Having been paid off by Investcorp not to talk about what I knew, write a book, or get involved in any commercial ventures in the name of Gucci for the next ten years, I was at a loose end. Needless to say, I no longer worked for the company and faced the difficult prospect of helping my father pick up the pieces after the spectacular loss of everything that was so dear to him.

Soon after our trip to Geneva, he flew to Palm Beach alone. There was no need for my mother or me to accompany him, he'd said. We both had things to take care of at home, and besides, he was only going to supervise the sale of the house. We knew how difficult that would be for him. After returning from his farewell dinner at Club Colette one night, he walked into the house to hear the telephone ringing. It was my mother in Rome and she was hysterical.

"Aldo! Are you all right? I had a dream—a terrible dream!"

Accustomed to her random nightmares and realizing it was the early hours of the morning for her, he tried to calm her down. This time, though, she wouldn't be placated. She said in her dream she'd had a clear vision of him lying facedown on the rug in the bathroom. Papà assured her he was fine and then went to bed. The following morning, however, he called her back to admit that something was indeed wrong and that he was having difficulty urinating.

After extracting a promise that he'd return to New York and see his doctor immediately, she called me in London. "Please, Patricia, fly to New York today and make sure he keeps that appointment. I'm worried he won't and I'm convinced there's something wrong." I was on the next Concorde flight out. Within hours of my arrival later that day, Papà was sent to the hospital for urgent tests on his prostate, which had become grossly enlarged. After I called Mamma to give her the news, she too jumped on a plane.

By the time she arrived, my father had been diagnosed with terminal cancer. It had started in his prostate, just like it had for his brother Rodolfo. Although he was in otherwise excellent health for his age, the doctors said the disease had already spread and had metastasized to his bones. Chemotherapy might slow things down, but there was no cure.

"No cure."

I heard the words but to begin with they fell on deaf ears as we tried to absorb this latest blow. Papà appeared to be in complete denial. He didn't care to know the medical details and instructed the doctors to deal only with my mother and me. Under further questioning, however, he admitted that he'd experienced discomfort for months but—coming as it had in the middle of negotiating his severance from the company—he had chosen to ignore it. These, then, were the consequences.

Wringing her hands, my mother kept repeating, "I knew it, I knew it!" Her worst nightmare had come true.

"I don't want anyone else to know," my father announced.

"But, Aldo, what about your family?" she asked.

"No!" he snapped. "They don't deserve to be told." Turning to us both with a grave expression, he made us swear that we wouldn't mention anything so we gave him our word.

In spite of his diagnosis, over the next few days he remained remarkably upbeat, talking about what we'd all do together once he was released from the hospital. As soon as he was allowed home, he and Mamma flew to Palm Beach for a few weeks to be alone in the place that was so dear to them both. My father had built the house from scratch just for us; no one outside our little family had ever stayed there and nothing had ever tarnished the magical quality that seemed to act as a salve on any woe. They were never able to recapture that special alchemy anywhere else.

This, their last visit before it was sold, would have been a sorrowful trip, especially for Papà. To stroll around his tropical garden and tend to his precious lawn must have broken his heart anew. Although I longed to spend every minute I could with him from now on, I'm glad I didn't witness that final farewell.

Almost as soon as they flew back to New York, I was able to share some news with them of a different nature. "I'm expecting," I told them, hoping that it might bring some respite. "The baby's due in February." They were delighted to have something to look forward to and, I think, glad to see that things between Santino and me seemed to be more bearable.

By coincidence, my father and I attended the same ultrasound clinic—he for his prostate examinations and I for my pregnancy. One day we emerged simultaneously from our respective appointments and locked arms in the reception area. "Papà, it's a girl!" I declared.

My father laughed. "Thank goodness!" he cried. "If it was a boy I wouldn't have wanted to know." The prospect of another granddaughter certainly seemed to boost his morale, at least for a while. That is, until the time came for him to leave America for good.

Having prolonged his stay for as long as he possibly could, he and my mother boarded a Concorde to fly out of John F. Kennedy airport for the last time. After thirteen years of shuffling back and forth to London en route to Rome, he had become one of the supersonic jet airliner's most familiar faces. For all its glamour, champagne, and caviar, what he loved the most about the Concorde was its speed—as though it was a reflection of him. He was saying good-bye to that, too. Shortly after takeoff, he took my mother's hand and, turning to her, asked quietly, "Is it okay if I cry now?"

Unable to answer, she nodded and squeezed his hand as he stared out of the window at the disappearing cityscape and allowed his tears to fall.

In spite of his condition and the course of chemotherapy he'd started, the summer of 1989 was both memorable and without precedent. Gathering our little family, Santino, Alexandra, and I, along with Mamma and Papà, went to the seaside town of Porto Ercole, an hour and a half by car north of Rome, where my parents kept a small apartment. My father had suggested we charter a boat for the week we were there and sail along the Argentario coastline, famous for the shimmering olive trees from which it gets its name.

Heading across the clear open water on an old wooden schooner, we'd drop anchor in a secluded bay and settle down for a plate of *spaghetti alle vongole* followed by *branzino* (sea bass) with boiled potatoes and parsley. Lying under a canopy in his swimming trunks, enjoying the salty air and the warmth of the sun on his ravaged body, Papà read and occasionally swam before taking a nap. I had never seen him so at peace, no doubt wondering why every summer couldn't have been like this. Facing the last few months of his life, he realized that it isn't money or success that matters, but the company of those we love. I can't watch the video footage of those wonderful few days without a feeling of great sadness.

Back in Rome, he continued his treatment and insisted that Mamma look after him rather than the nurse at his disposal. He had such complete faith in her that she'd joke, "If I told him to eat dirt mixed with olive oil, I think he would!" His Brunicchi took care of everything—from his diet to how many hours of sleep he had each day. For a while, her program paid off and he bore his treatment remarkably well.

As the year drew to a close and while he was still well enough to travel, we decided to have a traditional Christmas at home in Berkshire, a place he'd always loved. I was also eager for them to see the life I'd breathed into our house. With music playing in the background and Alexandra sitting in front of the TV watching cartoons, the house no longer felt like the mausoleum it once was.

By the time her *babbo* and *nonna* arrived the week before Christmas, Alexandra was beside herself with excitement. She ran to my father's arms the minute he walked through the door, as he bent down and patted her on the head just as he used to with me. Then he began the game they always played together. *"C'ho una cosina!"* (I've got a little something!) he teased, before flamboyantly taking some candy or a toy from his pocket and dangling it just out of reach, laughing all the while. Their little ritual is one of Alexandra's fondest memories of him.

Papà seemed very happy. As my mother always said, "Your father has three passions—food, gardens, and women. I would say that out of all of them, he loved his gardening the most." In Berkshire he had all three, so while she prepared dinner he would wander around the grounds like in the old days, admiring the roses and the maritime pines he'd planted years earlier. My former playground was now dotted with strategically positioned life-size bronze sculptures by Emilio Greco, one of his favorite artists. He used to say the sinuous forms reminded him of my mother and he always took great pride in polishing every curve, much to every-one's amusement.

Mealtimes in that house were hilarious as my father enlisted me, Santino, and Alexandra as his accomplices so that he might eat some of the things Mamma wouldn't allow him to indulge in anymore. She knew exactly what he was doing, of course, and played to the gallery—shaking her head or wagging her finger whenever she caught him pinching some cheese or the fatty skin from a roast chicken. We'd giggle as he pretended to look chastised and the minute my mother turned her back, Alexandra would call for a repeat performance. "Again, Babbo!" she would cry over and over.

Everyone was in the Christmas spirit but then fate intervened. Mamma received word that burglars had tried to break into her apartment in her absence, so she rushed to Rome to make sure it was secure, promising to be back in a few days. Even though the intruders never got in, they'd done a lot of damage to the door and she felt uncomfortable about leaving the place unattended. Papà couldn't bear to be separated from her so he, too, decided to fly back and we ended up spending Christmas on our own.

Mamma always said that everything happens for a reason, and when my father's health suddenly deteriorated a couple of days after he flew into Rome, she believed something was written in the stars. He was admitted to the Villa Flaminia clinic, where further tests revealed that the cancer had now spread to his liver and pancreas. The hourglass had been turned once more.

Unable to make any sense from her weeping down the phone, I called the doctors myself to ask the question she was afraid to ask—"How long?"

"One to two months. Three if he is lucky."

The response drew my hand protectively to my belly. I was just seven weeks from my due date and already booked into London's Portland Hospital to give birth to my daughter in mid-February. The airlines typically refused to let heavily pregnant women fly, and never did beyond thirty-six weeks, so I had to act quickly. Canceling my plans to give birth in England, I flew to Rome on January 14 with Santino, Alexandra, and her nanny to be near my father and spend whatever time we had left together.

I arrived to find Mamma in her own little world, as though she had some preordained knowledge of the situation that she hadn't shared with me. I waited as she made some last-minute preparations to her hair and makeup before we left to visit Papà that first morning. As always, her appearance was paramount but neither lipstick nor blusher could disguise how drained she looked.

On my way to the hospital that first morning I expected the worst but was relieved to see him livelier than ever, sitting up in bed reading the newspaper through his horn-rimmed spectacles. A telephone was on a table at his side. He looked as if he could have gotten up and walked out any minute. Making light of his predicament and commenting on how advanced I was in my pregnancy, his first words to me were, "Patricia! Shouldn't you be the one resting?" My mother didn't see the funny side, shaking her head as she pulled up his bedcovers and adjusted his pillows.

It may have been cold and miserable outside but he appeared to be back to his sunny old self. That first day, the only one

where—deceptively—he appeared to be well, he was very ani-
mated. He still refused to have us let anyone know he was sick,
so no visitors came, just the way he wanted it. The only people to
have any knowledge of his condition were right there in his room.

"How much longer?" he'd ask me, alluding to the impending
arrival of his new granddaughter.

"I'm having her here in this very clinic," I told him, happy
with the sense of continuity. "I'm seeing the gynecologist in an
hour to make the necessary arrangements."

"*Brava,*" he said. "I'm glad you were able to sort everything
out at such short notice." I forced a smile as we spoke about
the next generation and the joy she would bring to all our lives.
Mamma tried not to talk about anything too sentimental, masking
her feelings by continually fussing over Papà, making sure he'd
taken all his pills, her hands in constant motion. Then she'd take
her seat on a sofa by his bed while I settled into the chair on the
other side.

"I'll be out of here in no time," Papà told us, sounding overly
optimistic in his striped pajamas. "There are still so many places
I haven't taken you," he said, looking affectionately in Mamma's
direction. "Places you always wanted to go to. We can still make
that trip to Greece—"

"*Smettila* [Stop it], Aldo! Don't say such silly things," Mamma
would interrupt. "You have to concentrate on your health now."

Then he'd start again. "I should have spent more time with
you, I . . . ," then he'd nod off, just like he had when we watched
westerns together on Sunday afternoons in Berkshire. It felt
strange to be close to him as he slept, so accustomed was I to his
frenetic activity. I simply couldn't imagine him any other way.

My mother and I worked out a rota in order to keep vigil.
As he seemed so well and we weren't expecting the situation to

degenerate any time soon, I told her she needn't worry about being at his bedside all the time and that she could take care of whatever she had to do during the day.

If I wasn't with him, I'd invariably be at my prenatal appointments or with Alexandra, who was being looked after by the nanny back in the apartment. The carefree, golden-skinned child who bound us together always blew her *babbo* a kiss that I had to catch in my hand for him each time I left for the hospital. "He'll be home soon," I told her. And so we lived, going through the motions, still refusing to believe that his days were numbered.

On the second afternoon I arrived at the clinic with a bunch of flowers to cheer him up. He hated being confined to his room, deprived as it was of color and light, so when I found him out of bed and sitting in a wheelchair I wasn't so surprised.

"Ah, Patricia!" he cried. "One of the nurses tells me the sun is shining. I want to get out and see it for myself." We both knew his doctors wouldn't approve but he assured me with a wink that they'd never know. So I wheeled him down the corridor toward a long stained-glass window and positioned him so that he could sit in the shafts of light and feel the heat of the sun on his face. I found a chair and settled quietly next to him, not wishing to disrupt this treasured moment.

"Could you fetch my briefcase?" he asked me after a short while without opening his eyes. I did as he requested and watched as he flicked the catches, reached inside, and handed me a manila envelope containing a single sheet of paper. "Read this," he instructed softly.

My eyes scanned the opening lines and then I stopped. Drawing in a breath, I stared down at his last will and testament and started to protest. "Papà . . . I can't!"

"Carry on," he insisted, his eyes closed once more. Gesturing to it with a sense of urgency, he was suddenly the consummate businessman sorting out his affairs. He had something that needed to be done and I was the only one who could attend to it.

I did as I was told and read the document in silence before sliding it back into the envelope. We then sat together for several minutes, neither of us saying a word as I struggled not to cry and reflected on the seismic consequences of what I had just read. Not that I cared about that in the slightest. All I cared about was him. Up until that moment, my entire focus had been on his surviving—beating the odds and walking out to fight another day. That was the only way I'd managed to get through so many dreadful recent events. Any other outcome was unthinkable and when I pulled myself together, I told him as much, adding, "This is too painful for me right now. . . ."

"I know, I know," he said soothingly, "but you do understand what this means?"

"Yes, Papà," I replied. "I understand."

In truth, I wasn't sure I did.

TWENTY-EIGHT

There are times in our lives when we're expected to face difficult moments or confront those we'd prefer to avoid. Of all the things anyone ever asked me to do, my father's next request to me was by far the most unpleasant. It only came about because my mother also decided to take the more difficult path and force us to address something we'd all been avoiding until then.

"Aldo, I've been thinking," she told my father the same day he showed me his will. "It's time to tell your sons." Seeing his fierce expression, she added, "You have to."

To our surprise, he nodded. "*Va bene*, Bruna. Okay."

Turning to me then, he said quietly, "Will you arrange it? I'll give you the numbers to call. Tell them to come."

"Tomorrow," my mother said, pressing him.

My relationship with my brothers had never been close and after everything they had done to Papà, I had no desire to see them again. Nevertheless, I did as I was told and made arrangements to meet them at the Cavalieri Hilton first thing the following morning. Arriving ahead of time, I settled myself down at a table and ordered some tea. They showed up moments later, clearly curious as to why they'd been summoned.

After a courteous but stiff greeting, I blurted out the news. "I'm afraid your father—*our* father—doesn't have long to live. It's cancer," I said, steeling myself to retain my composure as I uttered the words I still couldn't contemplate. "He was diagnosed last year. . . . He says you may see him if you wish."

None of them expected that. Even though Papà was in his eighties, he'd hardly had a day's illness in his life and I think we all thought of him as immortal. There was a moment of shocked silence as they all stared at me and then Roberto spoke out. "Why have you and your mother kept this from us for so long? We're his sons! Why didn't you say anything?" Further accusations followed as I—eight months pregnant and equally as upset—faced open hostility from them all.

"It was your father's decision not to tell you. It was nothing to do with me," I told them flatly once they'd finished venting. "Now he is ready for you to know. You can see him tomorrow afternoon. He's at the Villa Flaminia. Three o'clock."

I rose to my feet as steadily as I could and rushed out of the hotel lobby. I never even touched my tea.

If I hadn't looked forward to meeting them, then my father's dread of his final encounter with those he regarded as traitors must have been tenfold. And yet he seemed strangely focused. There was a new sense of purpose about him that had been building up to this conclusive day. As Mamma and I helped him get ready we sensed his determination to let his sons see the price he had paid for what they had done. For many years he'd used tonic to smooth down his silver hair, which also made it appear darker. The day before the meeting, in what felt like a hugely significant move, he asked my mother to rinse out the lotion in the sink. The effect was extraordinary—his hair turned white in an instant.

After changing out of his pajamas into a navy blue pinstripe suit that hung loosely on his frame, he lowered himself into the leatherette armchair and settled into position. Brushing an imaginary speck from his trousers, he straightened his posture, signaling he was ready to receive his three sons. Sitting bolt upright yet strangely shrunken, he looked every one of his eighty-four years.

As the bells of a nearby church tolled three o'clock, we heard footsteps approaching along the long stone corridor. Taking a few deep breaths, I perched on the edge of my father's bed while my mother took her seat in the farthest corner and donned her sunglasses, wishing she were anywhere but there. She'd only stayed in the room because my father had begged her to.

The door opened and like self-conscious schoolchildren appearing before the headmaster, my brothers shuffled in one by one. On seeing Papà, they couldn't disguise how appalled they were by his appearance. After cordially greeting Mamma and me with the customary kiss, they stepped up for what they knew was their last embrace. To their surprise, their father remained utterly impassive.

"How are you feeling?" Giorgio asked in a conciliatory tone, trying his best to reduce the palpable tension in the air. "Had we only known sooner, Daddy . . . I can't believe this is happening." Still, my father acknowledged his comments with nothing more than a nod.

Paolo was noticeably taken aback at the sight of his father, muttering something about how sorry he was, while Roberto—the most vocal of them all—complained once more that they should have been informed earlier. Almost as an afterthought, he added, "I hope you are not suffering."

Papà's few responses were curt, aside from one telling comment: "My time in hospital—*like in prison*—has given me plenty of time to think things over." Then he said nothing more. His indifference toward them was chilling as Giorgio nervously asked if there was anything they could do. Still my father refused to engage. I thought at first that he was waiting for an apology from them or an explanation—anything that might have gone some way to justifying their behavior and how it had led to the sale of the company. Instead, they offered him nothing but platitudes.

After watching in silence from her corner, Mamma couldn't bear to be in the room a moment longer and hurried out after excusing herself. My three brothers glanced nervously at one another and then at me before turning back to Papà, still sitting like stone. One by one, they gradually began to appreciate why they had been summoned. This was Judgment Day.

Papà had no intention of saying any poignant last words. There was to be no forgiveness or absolution whatsoever for their souls. His near-silence said it all. He was dying and he had invited them so they could see that the only people who truly mattered to him were those who'd remained at his side all along.

There was nothing else for them to do but go, his contempt seared into their eyes.

They kissed him good-bye and filed out of the room, quietly closing the door behind them. It was only then that his posture caved in, and he slumped forward. There was nothing else left for him to do.

Still upset by the encounter, my mother went home to rest, so I stayed with Papà for the remainder of that day. He was pensive, bordering on melancholic. It felt to me as if a door had closed and he no longer wanted to engage with the outside world. I asked if he needed anything. He shook his head almost imperceptibly. Glancing back one last time as I was about to leave, I had a sudden premonition.

"Are you going to be okay, Papà?" I asked anxiously.

He looked up, as if he'd only just realized I was still in the room. "I'll be fine," he replied, attempting a smile. "Go home, Patricia. Rest. It's been a long day."

At some point during the night, the nuns discovered him collapsed on the floor next to his bed. He had suffered a brain hemorrhage and was barely conscious. At around five a.m., they called my mother and we hurried to the clinic. Bursting in, we found him motionless and staring at the ceiling as if he were waiting to see Mamma for one last time.

"Aldo!" she gasped, and the blue eyes he'd fought to keep open for so long held her gaze for a fraction to say *addio*. Then they closed. She was so glad she'd gotten there in time. He had once told her he wasn't afraid of dying but leaving her behind was a far more daunting prospect. She knew he'd held on for her.

For the next few hours he lay in a semi-coma as my mother and I gripped his hands from our sentinel positions on either side. It was clear from his ragged breathing that his body had finally surrendered to the disease that had returned to claim him. Dutifully, and at my mother's behest, I called Giorgio and asked him to inform everyone of this latest turn of events, thinking that they should know.

What Mamma and I never expected was that they would return so soon—this time descending on the clinic en masse with their families and congregating in the reception area just outside my father's room. My brothers eventually filed back in sheepishly to gather around the foot of the bed. All that could be heard were Papà's rasping breaths. Praying for a miracle, I squeezed his fingers tight—just as he had with me on my wedding day—knowing now how it felt to have to let go of somebody you loved.

By lunchtime on January 19, his wheezing became labored, and as we leaned in closer, my mother felt the tiniest pressure of his fingers around hers. His heart was still strong and she could tell he was fighting to remain with his beloved Brunicchi. She knew it was time to do something she had been avoiding doing for so long. Brushing away her tears, she stood up, leaned over, and pressed her mouth against his ear.

"Aldo, *amore mio*, can you hear me?" she said, her voice suddenly surprisingly forceful. "Go, Aldo. Let go, Aldo. God is with you. Go in peace."

There was an almost immediate change in his breathing and though still painful to listen to, it seemed to take on a deeper, more measured quality.

Desperately trying to stay strong for them both but sensing he could slip away at any moment, my whole body began to shake. A nun who'd been caring for Papà placed her hand on my shoulder to inform me that the last phase of my father's life was about to get ugly. "You have a life to protect, my dear," she added softly. "I think it's time for you to say good-bye."

Stricken, I looked across at my mother, who nodded. It was clear that she would remain until the end. My limbs heavy, I rose to my feet, and placing a protective hand over his unborn grandchild, I bent down, kissed his cheek, and whispered, "I love you, Papà."

I don't recall leaving the room or hurrying past the rest of the family I barely knew, but I do remember some of them looking at me in the corridor with open resentment. Seeking oxygen, I hurried downstairs and out of the building as quickly as was safe. Sucking in a welcome blast of air, I burst out crying, knowing that I would never see my father alive again.

Ever since I was a little girl, I'd been perfectly content in the knowledge that even if he couldn't physically be with me, Papà loved me and would always be back. That was enough. All that was about to change and I didn't feel grown-up enough to handle it.

Feeling my baby shift inside me, I closed my eyes, took some more deep breaths, and tried to regain control of myself to save her from my grief. She was the blameless next generation and I prayed that something of my father would live on through her.

Just as he had, I took some comfort from the synchronicity of what was about to happen. As his life ebbed away, so a new one was about to begin. I couldn't help but think that the man who'd planned everything so meticulously his whole life had somehow orchestrated this too. From the cradle to the grave and back again.

His mother, Aida, had once been as pregnant with him as I was now, and her hopes for her baby's future must have been as bright as any young mother's. She had loved her son Aldo in her own way, just as my father had loved me. The family line was continuing, and I was carrying the next generation and, with it, their dreams.

Papà died later that evening with the love of his life, Bruna Palombo, at his side.

Much later, long after he was lost to us forever, my mother recounted the story of a dream he'd told her about the night before he fell out of bed. It was one of the last things they ever spoke about. "I saw my mother," he confessed.

"What was she doing?" Mamma asked, fascinated by the meaning of his vision.

Papà smiled. "She was standing at the top of the stairs," he replied. "I think she was waiting for me. . . ."

EPILOGUE

*I*nner peace, that all-pervading sense of contentment and harmony, is an elusive dream and one that has been largely absent from much of my life. And yet it is something we all long for.

There was hardly any peace to be found in the days immediately after my father's passing. Not for me, and none whatsoever for my mother, whose worst torment was only just beginning. Papà's funeral on January 21, 1990, brought us little comfort, and our deliberate separation from the rest of his family in the church that day epitomized the unhappy rift.

There was no respite even once the service was over, as we joined a three-hour motorcade that took him on his final journey to the family crypt where my grandparents Aida and Guccio had lain side by side for almost fifty years. Grimalda and Rodolfo were entombed there too, while Vasco had been buried elsewhere. My father had outlived them all. The only notable absentee on that interminable drive to Soffiano outside Florence was Olwen in her wheelchair—the trip would have been too arduous.

I had managed to remain composed all morning but once we arrived at the cemetery gates and made our way through the headstones behind Papà's coffin, I cried like never before. Never again would he breeze into our lives as he always did, with a ready smile and a kind word. Never again would I feel that energy and vitality—the zest for life that was so uniquely his. He may not have been the greatest father in the world, but he was the only one I had. And in the last five years he had peeled back the layers to show me the real Aldo Gucci, the man my mother and I adored, unconditionally. I was grateful, at least, for that.

Following the rest of the family, who remained several paces ahead, we crammed together at the entrance to the marble mausoleum, surrounded by those I struggled to consider my own. Mamma stood next to me, catatonic. Only once everyone else had shuffled away were we able to move in closer to have a silent moment alone. On a table in a corner I noticed a crucifix above the altar and four candles, plus several faded, framed photographs placed there by relatives over the years. My grandparents were there, along with my aunt and uncle. Most of the great Gucci dynasty was now reduced to dry, crumbling bones.

A few months later I felt compelled to make a pilgrimage back to the cemetery on my own. Reaching into my handbag, I retrieved a photograph and placed it next to the others, completing the tableau of this once-proud family. It was a picture of my father taken at my wedding in Jamaica. He was dressed all in white, his arm outstretched as he pointed toward the ocean and the setting sun. "I miss you, Papà," I whispered, and kissed the frame, before saying a quiet prayer and heading back to Rome.

On February 19, 1990, exactly one month to the day after he died and just two doors down from the very room in which he had given up his fight, my daughter Victoria had come into this world.

With uncanny symmetry, the nurse who tended to my baby and me was the same nun who had closed my father's eyes.

Victoria was born at a traumatic time of my life and it showed. Gangly and highly strung with a delicate nature, she demanded more care and attention than Alexandra had as a newborn and I spared a thought for Mamma, who hadn't always found it easy to be the perfect mother. I now had two children to look after, a marriage still in crisis, and countless loose ends to tie up, not to mention my mother, whose grief had developed into full-blown hysteria. I genuinely feared for her sanity. Without the man who had become father, friend, husband, and son all rolled into one, she had nobody to guide her or ease her inner torment. Her guru, Sari Nandi, had recently died, so she felt utterly bereft, looking to the heavens and calling out my father's name until she cried herself to sleep.

Her only comfort was the fact that Papà still came to her in her dreams.

I consoled her as best I could, but there were more practical matters to attend to. The *notaio* in charge of my father's will had summoned me and my brothers to his office in the center of Rome. The document he read to us was dated April 12, 1988—four weeks after Roberto and Giorgio had cashed in their Gucci shares. I was the only one who knew its contents. He began by reading out a list of things my father had left to Olwen, his grandchildren, and to various members of staff. Then he got down to the part everybody was most interested in. Declaring himself to be of sound mind, my father disinherited Paolo completely and appointed me as his "sole and universal heir," even though such a proclamation was more symbolic than absolute in the eyes of the law.

The change of atmosphere in the room was palpable. Squirming in my seat and staring straight ahead, I wished I were anywhere else but there as I felt half a dozen angry eyes boring into me. My brothers could have been under no illusion that they had been deliberately snubbed. It was an unexpected outcome for everyone. As the only female descendant, no one was more surprised than I when my father handed me his will at the hospital. His decision was final, he said. Besides, his sons had already received their patrimony in the form of shares gifted while he was still alive, plus a lifetime of endowments. He had nothing more to give, apart from the minimum under Italian law—but he did have a few more things to say.

In a farewell read out in a monotone voice by the *notaio*, he condemned Paolo's "meanness and humiliation" but then added magnanimously that he forgave all those who had "offended" him. His last wish, he said, was for his family to find "harmony, tolerance and affection with one another, in [his] memory."

Harmony: defined in a relationship as one "characterized by a lack of conflict or disagreement." Papà wanted the impossible. He wanted peace.

My brothers, who had first met me as a little girl and who knew that I'd never sought to capitalize on my position or take any part in their power struggles, were clearly incensed. The three men from whom I would become largely estranged forever left that office without so much as a word.

Tellingly, my father's predictions about the company were to come true. Investcorp would have done well to heed his advice. Within a couple of years Maurizio was ousted after accumulating such massive debts that he pushed it to the brink of bankruptcy. His departure allowed others with vision to slowly return Gucci to its former glory, starting with moving its headquarters back to Florence—its rightful home. In 2011, the latest owners opened the Gucci Museum in Florence, in which my grandfather's entrepreneurial spirit and my father's achievements were finally honored.

My brother Giorgio would be the only Gucci of his generation left when Papà was publicly acknowledged as the visionary that he was. In 1995 Maurizio was shot at point-blank range four times by two gunmen hired by his vengeful ex-wife, Patrizia. Dubbed "the Black Widow" by the press, she served a sixteen-year sentence for his murder. Paolo died after being sent to prison for missed alimony payments and Roberto died five years later of cancer. Not even Olwen, who survived my father by several years just as my mother had predicted, would witness the splendid Florentine commemoration of her husband's legacy. Nor was she interred alongside him in the Soffiano cemetery. Instead she was buried on her son Giorgio's property on the Argentario coast, where Paolo would also ultimately be buried. Roberto would be laid to rest in the Gucci crypt, where two empty spaces remain to this day.

For a year or possibly more after Papà's death, my mother's inner torment continued unabated. It was a time that I prefer to forget and one that she chooses not to remember. Eventually she found her bearings, but more than twenty-five years after he left us, she has never found anyone else to match up to the man who once pursued her so ardently. Only recently has she even been able to talk about her years with him.

"What a story we had, Patrizina!" she'd tell me, her brown eyes bright. "You don't know the half of it! For a long time I didn't realize how important I was to him." Using a Roman expression, she threw up her hands and cried, "*Me n'ha fatte tante!*" (He put me through the wringer!), adding, "I know he wasn't a saint but neither was I, and still he loved me. There will never be anyone like Aldo."

She still keeps my father's precious Madonna and child on her nightstand and has a few framed photographs of him scattered around her apartment. Although she has her friends, she's not naturally sociable and prefers to be left to her own devices and look after her affairs. Accustomed to isolation, she enjoys her own company and boasts about the number of days she can spend alone in one stretch. Possibly for the first time in her life, she is serene and has recently declared that having me made all her suffering worthwhile. I certainly appreciate her more than ever before and I speak to her on the telephone almost every day. It took over forty years but we are finally at peace with one another.

Mamma has fully embraced her role as a grandmother with enthusiasm and all my girls love their "Nonna B." She is also showing us the sense of humor that my father so loved, describing people and situations in her own particular way, using Roman expressions that never fail to make us laugh.

By her own admission, she has settled into her true potential, albeit late. "Your father always insisted that I was clever in my own way. When he knew he was dying he repeated that to me many times, telling me, 'Brunicchi, you're going to be okay!' I didn't believe him."

For at least two decades after his death, Papà continued to visit her in her dreams, something that gave her great solace. Then one day, she had a dream so vivid that she will never forget it. My father was dressed in his suit and fedora—just the way she remembered him when he used to rush through the store on Via Condotti. She was standing before him, struggling in vain to open a locked suitcase.

"I don't have the keys, Aldo!" she complained as she fiddled with the lock. He calmly assured her that he'd given them to her. "No, you didn't!" she cried in frustration, but he continued to smile knowingly as he waited to see what she would do. When she looked down she saw that the keys had been in her hand all along. Laughing, she looked up at him but he had vanished.

The moment she awoke the next morning, she felt as if a great weight had been lifted. He would appear to her only once more, waving good-bye as he melted away into the distance—his eyes the last thing she could see. He never came to her in her dreams again. From that day forward, she became the strong woman he always knew she could be.

It was that same woman who found the strength to share his letters with me in the summer of 2009, and thus set me on a path to discover the real story behind the headlines. Not that it was easy to coax more information out of her—it never had been. I remember one incident as a child when I was rooting through my mother's cupboards and stumbled across a photo album of my earlier years. When I opened it with excitement, I found that dozens of pictures had been ripped out, leaving yet more blank spaces in my life.

"Why did you do that, Mamma?" I asked, confused.

"I didn't like the memories," she replied flatly. "I didn't want to remember." Then she slammed shut the door to her memories once again, too scared to feel because she'd learned in the past that emotions could drag her back to a dark place.

Trying to piece all this together, bit by bit, I continued to gather information and chronicle as many details as I could. Whenever I went to visit her I hoped that there might be something more—something unexpected. Then, on another visit to Rome, there was.

When I arrived at her apartment, Mamma was waiting at the edge of her terrace, eager to buzz me in. Nothing much had changed since my father's day and every detail was just as I remembered it. She had opened the shutters that would otherwise stay firmly closed to keep the living room cool and protect the furniture from the sun. In spite of her advancing years, even in the bright light she looked as beautiful as ever, with just enough makeup to enhance that still-flawless skin.

Knowing how private she'd always been, I tentatively brought up the subject of my book, longing for her to read certain passages. "I'd really like you to see what I've come up with, Mamma," I told her with a softness born out of our much-improved relationship and a new love in my life.

She smiled. "Maybe, Patricia. One day. But first, I have something to show you."

Then, just as she had a few years earlier, she rose from her chair, wandered into her bedroom, and emerged with yet another letter. This was the one she hadn't been ready to let go of at the time.

Sitting at the dining room table, her reading glasses perched on the bridge of her nose, she showed me the single page with its almost unrecognizable handwriting. Clearing her throat, she said, "This was your father's last letter. It is dated January 18, 1990. It was the finest and the dearest he ever wrote. . . ."

Seeing her falter and realizing that she wasn't going to be able to read the words he must have written on his deathbed, I took it from her hands. Bracing myself, I sat upright in my chair and began reading it aloud:

> *To express my feelings, I feel the duty to recognize,*
> *and offer my dedication, to the woman who has*
> *been a faithful life companion for more than thirty*
> *years. The feeling of love and affection I have*
> *for Bruna is immeasurable. For what you did for*
> *me, thank you Bruna, for your spiritual strength*
> *that helped me in all my endeavors. You are an*
> *exemplary woman who is modest, and you deserve*
> *the respect and admiration of everybody who has*
> *ever had the privilege of meeting you. Twenty-six*
> *years ago, you gave me a daughter, our Patricia.*
> *What a divine gift. She could not be more*

beautiful because she inherited your best qualities.
I can never express enough of the gratitude and
joy that you deserve. To my sons, I demand that
you observe the moral obligations inspired by a life
fully lived in my admiration for Bruna. Giorgio,
Paolo and Roberto, I want them to respect Bruna's
qualities. This letter

That was where it ended. My father's handwriting had simply stopped. A line of blue ink trailed to the bottom of the page and then off the edge.

I looked up at my mother, her eyes glistening.

I was speechless.

My mother quickly brushed away a tear. "The nuns think that may have been the moment he had his brain hemorrhage," she said. "They gave this to me afterward, with the rest of his belongings. I'd like you to keep this now too."

Staring incredulously at my father's frail script, my eyes lingered on the words, which leapt off the page. This was his true last will and testament. This was when he knew that he would die and the moment, I think, when he found his peace. In the last few years of his life, he had seen everything he ever created destroyed. All his purpose was lost. His life became meaningless and I don't think it was the kind of existence he could have survived for long. In the end, though, he recognized that all that was truly important was Mamma—and I.

Papà wanted my life to be full of gratitude and joy. And, with his help, I realized that it was. He asked for harmony, tolerance, and affection in his memory, and we had finally achieved that. My relationship with my mother was transformed and I loved her to bits. My father was right. She was an "exemplary woman." Long ago, I was once asked for a happy memory of my mother, and I couldn't honestly think of one. I know now that my happiest memory of her is probably yet to come.

"*Dono divino*" was how my father described me. And what a divine gift he had given me with this—a loving message from the grave almost twenty-five years after his death. Half crying, half laughing, I knew then that I had come full circle, as had she. Our journey together wasn't over by any means, but it had taken us on a new path.

And as usual, my father—the inimitable Aldo Gucci—had the last word.

ACKNOWLEDGMENTS

I would like to express my gratitude to the people who saw me through this book. To my agent, Alan Nevins, for bringing the project together, and to my editor, Suzanne O'Neill, for her support and input throughout.

To my cowriter, Wendy Holden, for capturing my voice and synthesizing a complex story spanning one hundred years. To my dear friends Enrico, Andrea, and Bee, who provided their own perspective on the rapport with my parents and long-forgotten anecdotes that make me smile.

To Gregory Lee, who has brought so much love and peace into my life and who has been at my side from the outset of this literary adventure, endlessly helping me edit, proofread, and translate.

To my daughters, Alexandra, Victoria, and Isabella, for waiting patiently until the end to finally read about their heritage and tolerating me when I was at my wit's end with yet another deadline.

And, most important, to my mother, without whose contribution—at times reluctant—and deeply personal insight into the three decades she spent with my father none of this would have been possible.

Last and not least, I salute all those who have been entwined with me, my family, and Gucci over the years and whose names I have omitted.

I hope I've made my *Papà* proud.